THE NATURE OF

RELIGIOUS EXPERIENCE

H.C. Macintosh

THE NATURE OF RELIGIOUS EXPERIENCE

ESSAYS IN HONOR OF
Douglas Clyde Macintosh

By

Eugene Garrett Bewkes
Julius Seelye Bixler
Robert Lowry Calhoun
Vergilius Ferm
Hugh Hartshorne
Cornelius Krusé
Helmut Richard Niebuhr
Reinhold Niebuhr
Filmer S. C. Northrop
Daniel Sommer Robinson
George F. Thomas

Essay Index Reprint Series

BOOKS FOR LIBRARIES PRESS
FREEPORT, NEW YORK

INTERNATIONAL STANDARD BOOK NUMBER:
0-8369-2286-7

LIBRARY OF CONGRESS CATALOG CARD NUMBER:
78-152202

PRINTED IN THE UNITED STATES OF AMERICA

THE SAMUEL B. SNEATH
MEMORIAL PUBLICATION FUND

———

*The publication of this volume has been aided by The
Samuel B. Sneath Memorial Publication Fund. This
Foundation was established on October 19, 1922, by a
gift to the Divinity School of Yale University from Mrs.
Laura S. Sneath, of Tiffin, Ohio, in memory of her hus-
band, Samuel B. Sneath. He was born December 19,
1828, in Tiffin, where he resided until his death on January 7, 1915. As merchant, manufacturer, banker, and
organizer of public utilities, he made, throughout a long
and public-spirited life, a substantial contribution to the
development of his native state.*

CONTENTS

FOREWORD

A LITTLE over twenty-five years ago Professor Douglas Clyde Macintosh, a Canadian of Scottish descent, came to the United States to take a position on the faculty of Yale University. As he crossed the border the immigration official asked him if he had a job. Professor Macintosh replied in the affirmative. "In that case," said the official, "I can't let you in, for it would violate the contract labor laws of this country." After some parleying Professor Macintosh happened to make the statement that he was planning to teach theology in Yale University. "Oh," said the inspector, with a show of surprise, "why didn't you tell me so in the first place? I thought you said that you were going to work!"

The incident made more of an impression on Professor Macintosh than on the official, for later, when he was ready to take out naturalization papers, the Government could find no record of his having crossed the border. Professor Macintosh then assumed the position of the plain man and insisted that he was actually here, since his senses and those of his friends testified to the fact, while the Government took the part of the philosopher and claimed that his presence must be appearance only and not reality. Finally he again entered the country, started to take out papers, was disturbed by the wording of the oath of allegiance, refused to promise to bear arms in an unjust war, and eventually, as the newspaper-reading public knows, was denied American citizenship by a five to four decision of the Supreme Court.

Some of Professor Macintosh's former pupils have felt

that parts of this story should receive more emphasis than has been given them. The general public knows that Professor Macintosh was denied American citizenship because he maintained that his ultimate loyalty was to the will of God. A much smaller group, limited to students of philosophy, know Professor Macintosh as an author. His monumental work on *The Problem of Knowledge* is regarded as a classic. His book on *Theology as an Empirical Science* is recognized as original and provocative. His book on *The Reasonableness of Christianity* won the Bross prize in 1925, and his Calcutta lectures on *The Pilgrimage of Faith* have had an appreciative audience, while his other books and articles have been well received. But a still smaller group has known him primarily as a great teacher, who did indeed come to America to work on their behalf, and who has treated them as he treated the government, forcing them to take the part of philosophers and to try their skill against his in the discipline of dialectic.

Prompted by their vivid impression of him as a teacher, a few of his former students have attempted to regain the atmosphere of his classroom by renewing the discussions of former days in the light of subsequent reflection on the problems he had set. This volume, embodying such an attempt, is different from the usual *Festschrift*. It is not a collection of essays on separate themes. Nor is it an effort to bring unity into the conflicting views of different writers by a mere common expression of homage to the master. It is rather an attempt to show how the problems set by one teacher have aroused a critical response in the minds of his students, and have stimulated them to find new ways of treating the fundamental issues concerned. Thus while all have addressed themselves to the central question of Professor Macintosh's interest—the problem of religious knowledge—the writers have developed their own ways of viewing the problem and have not hesitated to express freely their differences from him as well as from one another. They have done this in the hope that his own criticism of their work is not merely a memory to be cherished but an active relationship to be renewed.

The problem of religious knowledge is indeed not a topic to be discussed without controversy. When one recalls the endless debates over the problem of knowledge in general one is not surprised to find in the problem of religious knowledge a seemingly infinite source of disagreement. Religious knowledge contains two variables and not merely one, two fluctuating terms which must be defined and set in their proper relations to each other. Each new scientific discovery and each new philosophical analysis has its bearing upon the vague and inarticulate religious intuitions to which the human spirit desperately clings for all their lack of precision and proof. He who would deal with this problem must thus be prepared to be both rigoristic and tolerantly appreciative, clear in his formulation of intellectual issues yet sensitively aware of the promptings of the heart. Since this is the case it is perhaps a mistake to expect too great a degree of unity when the philosophy of religion is under discussion. Agreement we must have where the data lend themselves completely to intellectual analysis. But we miss the point of the religious life if we neglect that area where individual insight rejects standardization, and where faith points to objectives which knowledge has not yet reached. Because of this view that the problem of religious knowledge is one on which to take sides the contributors to this volume have not waited for Professor Macintosh's retirement, but are presenting it to him on his sixtieth birthday, when he is at the peak of his powers. They hope that it may call forth comments as critically useful as those which they have known in the past. Meanwhile they are not unaware that such antitheses as they have presented have been occasioned by the fruitfulness of the thesis which they learned from him.

Professor Macintosh's treatment of the problem of reli-

gious knowledge has been fruitful in our time because of
his success in aligning the problem itself with the most
powerful of the intellectual currents of the day. The scientific method is now acknowledged to be the method by
which knowledge must come. Professor Macintosh has applied it to religion. The special questions attending its
application lead to an examination of our ability to perceive
both with the eye of the body and that of the spirit, of our
right to form hypotheses on the basis of what we perceive,
and of the possible success that we may expect when we try
to establish these hypotheses as true. With each of these
questions Professor Macintosh has dealt, and in each case
he has refused to allow obstructions to break up the fundamental unity of the stream of life. In this sense he is truly
an "empiricist." His final test has always been that of experience in its widest sense. But his empiricism meets the claims
of common human convictions as adequately as those of
subtle philosophical analysis. In his theory of knowledge
Professor Macintosh defends the view of the plain man that
the object he knows is independent of himself, no matter
what changes his knowledge may make in it. Similarly in
his theory of religious knowledge he defends the conviction
of the common believer that God is actually present to the
worshipper and not an idea in his mind. The empiricism and
realism of Professor Macintosh's argument are thus, on the
one hand, a justification of "common sense" and of the
fundamental intuitions of humanity as a whole, while on
the other they make an acute and original contribution to
the present philosophical situation. This relevance of Professor Macintosh's work to the modern problem, along with
his great learning and his gift for incisive statement, is what
his former pupils chiefly remember. When to their respect
for his wisdom and their admiration for his integrity is
added their love for him as a friend, it is not hard to understand why they have wished to do him honor, and have

believed it worth while to express their wish in this volume, however inadequate the expression itself might be.

The first essay here offered gives a brief statement of Professor Macintosh's position and places it in the setting of Scottish realism instead of against the more commonly drawn background of Hegelian and Ritschlian thought. The next group of five essays raises several questions which must appear in any discussion of religious knowledge. The first attacks the all-important problem of the nature of religious experience and the possible uniqueness of its content. The next inquires about the nature of religious intuitions and the possibility of their verification. Following this comes a criticism of the attempt to adapt scientific empiricism to religious purposes and a plea for a further exploration of the field of value experience. The point of view of this essay is criticized in the one immediately following in which it is argued that dependence upon value experiences in religion leads to subjectivity and illusion. The fifth essay in the group returns to the problem of intuitions and values by asking what truth may be found in myths. The next four essays broaden the field of inquiry to include questions of metaphysics and psychology which bear directly upon the central theme. The first of these examines the place of values in a realistic epistemology. The second asks whether modern empiricism is losing its grip on the idea of a distinct and separate knower. The third essay shows how inescapable in any such inquiry as the present is the problem of the one and the many. The fourth indicates that problems of religious as of other knowledge must be studied in the light of what psychology reveals of our growing awareness of the environing world. The volume concludes on a practical note with an essay on the kind of liberalism which an empirical religion like that of Professor Macintosh might be expected to support.

The contributors wish to express their obligation to Dean Luther A. Weigle of Yale Divinity School for his encouragement and support and to Mr. Raymond P. Morris, Librarian of the School, for the preparation of the bibliography of Professor Macintosh's writings which is appended.

J. S. Bixler
R. L. Calhoun
H. R. Niebuhr

THE NATURE OF

RELIGIOUS EXPERIENCE

I

COMMON SENSE REALISM

By

Eugene Garrett Bewkes

Professor of Philosophy, Colgate University

WHY are modern philosophers so afraid of the term "common sense"? Theologians in particular should not look askance at it. Aware as we are that "common sense" has been pilloried by rationalists and empiricists alike, either as lacking in definiteness or else as hopelessly mired in naïve sense experience, the fact of its actual influence yet remains. The whole modern movement of realism is an effort to keep our philosophical feet on the ground. Certainly the pragmatic movement was such. And within the folds of idealism there is much common sense realism in T. H. Green, Edward Caird, Pringle-Pattison, and recently in Norman Kemp Smith and A. E. Taylor. The fact that we find it in both philosophical camps is a reminder that there is a Golden Mean between extreme rationalism and extreme empiricism. This should have particular significance to the theologian. Extreme unbalanced rationalism leads to dialectical absolutes which make finite experience illusory and unreal. On the other hand, extreme empiricism gives us an unorganized parade of sensations, all claiming equal rank. But religion at its best is not served by either extreme. Christian religious experience, in its realistic claim that God is directly knowable, is in line with the belief of the common man that he knows the world in which he lives. The effort to criticize, evaluate, and justify the common sense element in both the secular and the religious claim has formed a major part of the work of Professor D. C. Macintosh. The result is the position which he himself calls common sense or critical realism. In order to refer appreciatively to several of the main features of this position, it is desirable to set it against a brief historical background of common sense realism in Scottish thought.

Before Hume, philosophers concerned themselves less with the question of the possibility of knowledge than with that of how it might best be obtained. After Hume came Reid, Kant, Hegel and the resulting division of interest between the subject as knower and the object as known. Idealism emphasizes the knowing mind, while realism places its emphasis on a substantial object known. Recent years have seen a trend toward realism. We find not only a group of philosophers who call themselves realists, but idealists in metaphysics who profess to be realists in regard to the knowledge situation. This modern emphasis on realism should have made itself felt much earlier, because the ground work for it was laid down a considerable time ago by Thomas Reid. A sketch of Reid's work should help us to understand the historical background of Professor Macintosh's thought.

Reid's philosophy is genuinely important in the history of realism. He was a profound philosophic mind, as Charles Peirce has said. Obviously we could hardly expect Reid to be fully appreciated in the heyday of British idealism, but in later years such men as Pringle-Pattison and W. R. Sorley have paid high tribute to him. A. E. Taylor, despite his idealistic background, tells us that he really did not get acquainted with Reid until quite late, and as a consequence acknowledges a marked influence on his more recent thinking.[1] A careful study of Reid must leave us with the impression that, had more attention been paid to him, modern realism would have come into its own much sooner, and philosophy as a whole would have been much enriched.

We should notice, in passing, Stewart, Brown and Hamilton, who are usually bracketed with Reid as the Scottish Common Sense Realists, but we can hardly group them into a school. It is possible only to say that four vigorous Scottish philosophers followed each other in succession. Reid should have been the founder of a continuing school, but Stewart did not develop the position. He made apologetic modifications where further analysis was necessary. Brown was completely off the track, as no one can forget who has read Hamilton's scathing criticism of him. Brown attacked Reid as not a realist at all, while he himself claimed to be such. Hamilton rightly remarks that though there are errors in Reid, Brown had not the good fortune to fall upon a single one. Hamilton admired Reid greatly and was in sympathy with what he wanted to do, but, stimulated by Kant, he had started on a philosophic line of his own. We must regard Reid, then, as the significant representative of Scottish realism. Reid struck out in a direction which would have attracted more attention had it not been eclipsed by the work of Kant and the German idealists. Reid and Kant both took off from Hume, but they went different ways, as we shall note, and both ways were important.

As we cannot assume that Reid's position is as well known as that of Kant, a few connecting references are necessary. What is generally known is the commonplace fact that Hume's reasonings drew consequences from the works of his empirical and rationalistic predecessors, such as to drive philosophy into an apparently inextricable skepticism. Hume believed he had shown that philosophy was shut within psychological walls of relationless units of impression,

[1] Taylor, A. E., *Contemporary British Philosophy*, Second Series, p. 272.

and that, therefore, we could have no confidence in the
actual validity of organizing principles of knowledge. The
mind drags in such principles, to be sure, but there is no
warrant for thinking them derived from or applicable to
an independently real world. Reid, some years earlier than
Kant, saw that Hume had reasoned correctly from the philosophical assumptions inherent in the preceding philosophies. Philosophy had thus come to the end of the road.
It was a question, either of accepting Hume, or discovering
new leads altogether. It seems not to have occurred to Reid
or Kant that philosophy would have to remain where it
was. The skeptical consequences were accepted as evidence
of a fundamental unsoundness somewhere. Since both men
admitted that this was not to be found in the logic of the
argument, it was felt that it must lie in the basic premises
or presuppositions of the preceding philosophies.

Reid's examination of the earlier writings is a splendid
piece of critical evaluation. He singled out the underlying
assumption present in these former systems, and describes
it in the Dedication and the Introduction to *The Inquiry
into the Human Mind*. "The hypothesis I mean is, that
nothing is perceived but what is in the mind which perceives it; that we do not really perceive things that are
external, but only certain images and pictures of them im-
printed upon the mind, which are called impressions and
ideas. . . ." With this should be coupled the other famous passage about "Ideas" which "seem to have something
in their nature unfriendly to other existences. . . . They
have by degrees . . . undermined the existence of everything but themselves." Reid shows that all philosophy from
Descartes to Hume is warped by this Doctrine of Ideas,
which we now call "the Doctrine of Representative Perception." His judgment in this regard is confirmed by a
statement of Kemp Smith, who asserts that "the Doctrine
of Representative Perception" has been an overwhelming
influence in philosophy since Descartes, and is continued in

Kant and his successors.[2] Reid set himself against the doctrine that the mind knows only ideas, recognizing that if you begin with this assumption, you never can get knowledge of objects except by indirection or by inference. In this situation we are driven toward an increasing mistrust of the senses, with attendant consequences of agnosticism.

Observe now how clear are the two philosophic roads that open before us, one to be travelled by Kant, and one by Reid. If you are, with Reid, going to question the validity of dualistic or representative perception and frankly operate from the realistic standpoint, it is incumbent that the process of perception and sensation be thoroughly examined. Kant, on the other hand, turned in the direction of the mind, seeking those organizing principles or categories of knowledge that we use, such as time, space, cause, substance, accounting for them as of necessity prior to experience, and as the mind's contribution to experience. Now both of these philosophic roads needed to be travelled, and ultimately their reports must be reconciled with each other. It turns out, of course, that when you do examine sensation and perception as Reid does, you very soon discover the need for categories or organizing principles. Kant's contribution is just the thing that Reid reached for and needed to complete his contribution from the side of perception. Even so, Reid enumerated some of the primary principles or categories such as those named above, but he did not give us their analytical deduction. Reid's realism, however, might have been used and followed up to offset the Kantian agnosticism in regard to that which lies behind perceived objects. And not only that. Had the realistic emphasis been developed further by one of Reid's followers, the organizing principles or categories might have been grounded in the external order of nature, and not in a genetically unaccountable subject, as with Kant. Then the Kantian and real-

[2] Smith, Norman Kemp, *Prolegomena to An Idealist Theory of Knowledge*, p. 16.

istic contributions could have been brought together. This is practically what has been done from the idealist side by Norman Kemp Smith, and from the realist side by D. C. Macintosh.

The essentials of Reid's common sense realism can be quickly stated. In his analysis of sensation, Reid agreed with his predecessors that our sensations, that is the bare sensations as such, are not like the qualities of the objects that occasioned them.

As to heat and cold, it will easily be allowed that they are only secondary qualities, of the same order with smell, taste, and sound. And, therefore, what hath been already said of smell, is easily applicable to them; i.e. that the words heat and cold have each of them two significations; they sometimes signify certain sensations of the mind, which can have no existence when they are not felt, nor can they exist anywhere but in the mind or sentient being; but more frequently they signify a quality in bodies, which, by the laws of nature, occasions the sensations of heat and cold in us; a quality, which, though connected by custom so closely with the sensation, that we cannot without difficulty separate them; yet hath not the least resemblance to it, and may continue to exist when there is no sensation at all.

The sensations heat and cold are perfectly known; for they neither are or can be anything else than what we feel them to be; but the qualities in bodies which we call heat and cold, are unknown. . . . "It is the business of philosophers to investigate, by proper experiments and induction, what heat and cold are in bodies. And whether they make heat a particular element diffused through nature . . . or whether they make it a certain vibration of the parts of the heated body; whether they determine that heat and cold are contrary qualities, as the sensations undoubtedly are contrary . . . these questions are within the province of natural philosophy. . . . But whatever be the nature of that quality in bodies which we call heat, we certainly know this, that it cannot in the least resemble the sensation of heat. . . .[3] At the same time, it is a fact that such sensations are invariably connected with the conception and belief of external existences.[4]

What has been said of one sensation is true of all, namely, that sensations do not resemble qualities of bodies. The dualism implied by this statement, however, is only partial and does not exclude realistic direct acquaintance. Reid drew a very important distinction between sensation and perception,[5] pointing the way which any realism has got to follow in some form. The distinction in modern parlance is that between data of sense and intuition. Reid discerned that the consciousness which is aware of sensation is at the same time intuitively aware of much else beside the sensation. Sensation is the feeling we have when perceiving objects. Sensations are, therefore, subjective as feelings, but sensation is only a part of the total awareness. The process of awareness of objects is much more complex, including the "original judgment" or "suggestion" of objective reference concerning the thing perceived, plus implicit judgments also of cause, time and space. Intuitive awareness by the subject of his own identity is also part of the apperceptive whole. Reid is really trying to express the thought that the objects of our sense experience make their appearance to us in terms of a variety of qualities which are more or less relative to the sensing organism, and that by reason of this conditionedness are therefore secondary. But there are primary aspects, including certain relations which objects have, and these are not essentially conditioned by the senses, but are perceived directly. There is much in Reid's manner of statement that is open to criticism, but he wishes to recognize the primary direct awareness of objects which experience attests, while

[3] Reid, *Inquiry*, Chapter V, Section I.
[4] *Ibid.*, Ch. V. Sec. III.
[5] *Inquiry into the Human Mind*, Ch. II, Sec. VII; Ch. V, Sec. V and VII; Ch. VI, Sec. VIII; *Essays on Intellectual Powers of Man*, Essay II, Ch. XVI, XVII, and XIX.

at the same time he allowed for obvious secondary features. We shall see presently how this insistence on intuition is defended in modern philosophy. Meanwhile we would defend Reid against the charge of dogmatism in regard to his position on direct acquaintance. To be sure, if one insists that we know only ideas, the charge may hold, for then we are forced to admit that either objects are represented by ideas, or objects are ideas. But to insist that we know only ideas is itself a dogmatic assertion and an unwarranted restriction of the term knowledge and a misreading of the function of ideas. Reid knew his history of philosophy well, and he understood the problem of primary and secondary qualities. He believed that there would be little to add to what had already been said since their revival by Descartes and their burial by Berkeley and Hume, were we limited to a representative theory. But we are not thus limited. In a world of real space and real time, the distinctions which Reid has drawn actually follow. We shall have to omit Reid's insights on space and time, noting simply that he makes a realistic case, and then proceeds to support further his distinction between primary and secondary qualities on the basis of a functional or biological interpretation of perception.

Reid regards the senses as the agencies of our contact or adjustment with the world of nature, and as making it possible for us to get along in it. According to him, it is an argument for realism that there is such an immense variety of sensations possible to the senses. Through it we are enabled to make the many distinctions so important for practical living as well as for science.[6] The difference in the appearances of the same objects at different times is to Reid only a further argument for a critical realism, as well as evidencing a wise provision of nature, enabling us to perceive an object under a variety of conditions. He points out that,

[6] Reid, *Inquiry*, Ch. IV; *cf. Essays on Intellectual Powers*, Essay II, Ch. XX.

especially in the case of the secondary qualities, nature has provided a variety of aids by means of which we may be made aware of objects. From the point of view of our relation to external nature, the important thing is for us to be aware of objects, and the secondary qualities are of special significance in this awareness and identification. They clothe or dress up, so to speak, the primary character of the object. There may be many qualities or attributes of body, not at first discernible, which we may become aware of either by more careful scrutiny or by experience or by means of instruments. Even so, this fact is no ground for asserting that the percept and object are dualistically separate. There is here what we might call a pragmatic realism. On this view, appearances are the dress in which an object is presented, and objects have a variety of appearances. If we could only know an object in the dress of one color, we might have been annihilated long since. Appearances are not avenues of deceit, but avenues of direct knowledge of objects.[7]

Furthermore, even in the case of apparent and real size, there is no ground for dualism. In answering Hume in regard to the difference between the real (measured) size of a table, and the apparent size, Reid has a sound argument based on optics and the function of seeing. As a device of nature, the organ of seeing is admirably adapted to its purpose of direct acquaintance. Reid argues that, in order to see at all, this variation between actual size and apparent size is necessary. It must occur if a body or organism in space and time is to perceive other bodies in a space-time world. In fact, it is geometrically demonstrable, as Reid shows, that given position and distance of a measured object, its apparent size and figure can be defined. Further, he recognizes that as the field of vision widens and deepens, the apparent sizes enable us to understand the field. In other words, Reid shows that the apparent sizes are relational rather than de-

[7] *Essays on Intellectual Powers*, Essay II, Ch. XXII (On Sense Fallacies).

ceptive, for in relation to the field they must be what they are.[8] These various devices for knowing objects are multiplied into difficulties in the way of knowledge by philosophers. A critical use of common sense is, in Reid's view, the only satisfactory approach, and the only one likely to provide consistency with the many-sidedness of the facts of experience. It is a sound instinct which recognizes that we must begin with simple realism and move to such modifications as the facts and only the facts require.

Modern common sense realism has followed much the same course in general theory of knowledge, though with much greater refinement of statement and even more ground of justification. In the writings of Professor D. C. Macintosh there are affinities with Reid which are quite striking. Such coincidence is due entirely to parallels of circumstance and motive, and not at all to conscious following, Macintosh, like Reid, was first an adherent of idealism. And, also like Reid, he found that current philosophies seemed to falsify the actual experience of men. The problem of knowledge thus appeared to be the paramount problem of philosophy. Neither the intellectualism of Bradley, nor the anti-intellectualism of Bergson, nor the new realism of Alexander, nor American neo-realism, nor pragmatism seemed to Macintosh to do adequate justice to the actual facts of the knowledge process. Thus, like Reid, he found it necessary to establish his position by a thoroughgoing examination and critical analysis of the epistemological field. This he did in his first major work, *The Problem of Knowledge.* In this work he laid down his realistic position of critical monism in epistemology, which he also calls critical common sense. With Reid, he felt that it was necessary to give much attention to the question of our knowledge of the external world, in the confidence that if we can defend our knowledge from dualism and scepticism, we have established confidence in the essential testimony of our moral and religious experi-

[8] *Essays on Intellectual Powers,* Essay II, Ch. XIV.

ence. Interesting it is, too, that both men were influenced by scientific method and procedure as a check-rein on rationalism and speculation. Both men are not afraid of common sense. They both mean by it, not an uncritical exaltation of opinion, but rather a sane intellectual balance that knows how to escape the extremes which come from riding too hard some philosophic steed, good only for a limited distance. Of neither of these men can it be said that the adoption of common sense is an escape from rigorous intellectual discipline. And, still further, there is a parallel in the fact that both men were profoundly concerned with religion. Certainly no realism is complete that dares to ignore religion. To do so would be a denial of realistic integrity, for realism means to give due weight to all elements in human experience.

In addition to these general parallels, there are certain particular characteristics held in common regarding our knowledge of the external world. And this despite the far greater refinement of the modern statement. For example, Macintosh gives considerable weight to the functional character of our sense organs. This biological argument has much more force now than formerly. It is a pragmatic argument which has stood the test of time. There is also a similar contrast between sense qualities which exist only when they are experienced, and primary qualities which exist independently. And this in turn involves a similar distinction between sense experience and direct perception. We find, too, a recognition of the space-time character of perception which is relational, but not on that account deceptive. The following passages give us the core of Macintosh's critical monistic realism:

We may not be able to say anything about colors or sounds except in relation to eyes and ears and perceiving minds; but the necessary relativity and conditionedness of sense-qualities does not necessarily extend to mass and energy, quantitatively and causally considered. If, in spite of the fact that objective relativism seems to apply to some characteristics of the object, it does not necessarily apply to them all, then in spite of the fact that we cannot experience physical things except as clothed with sense-qualities, it is conceivable that through our sense-experience we may get immediate experience of some qualities and relations of physical things which do not depend for their existence upon their being experienced by us. . . . As a matter of fact, in my immediate awareness of the pain in my finger, I am likewise directly aware of my finger. When I immediately intuit or perceive the redness of the rose, I immediately intuit or perceive the rose which is red. Thus we are perceptually aware of independently existing things in real space-time. We perceive directly the independently existing physical thing, clothed with the colors which it has when perceived by us, but in the space-time in which it exists whether it is perceived by us or not. We get things in a perspective which varies with changes in the spatial relations between them and our organs of sense, but we get them as they exist in real, objective space. This is not knowledge in the form of deductive inference, of course, but knowledge as a practical achievement. . . . Moreover, in spite of the fact that part of what is immediately perceived is not independently real and part of what is independently real is not immediately perceived, enough of the immediately experienced is independently real, according to our theory, and enough of the independently real immediately experienced, for the view to be classed as a form of epistemological realism and monism . . . Seeking to remain, in order to understand the possibility of knowledge, as realistic and monistic as it may be while becoming as critical as it ought to be, it finds that it can hold on to the essentials of a direct realism as regards the existent thing and its primary qualities by admitting an objective relativism in relation to its secondary qualities.[9]

[9] Macintosh, D. C., *Religious Realism* (a symposium) Ch. XI; *Experimental Realism in Religion*, p. 365 ff; cf. "The Next Step in the Epistemological Dialectic," *Journal of Philosophy*, April 25, 1929; also *The Problem of Knowledge*, p. 310 ff; also, *The Reasonableness of Christianity*, Ch. XI.

If we should add to that the position of Macintosh in regard to the meaning of judgments, in which he is concerned with the practical truth of judgments as against the idealistic view, we feel how great is the kinship between Reid and Macintosh in essential outlook. To be sure, Macintosh, by endeavoring to strike a balance between epistemological dualism and epistemological idealism, encounters the same criticism which was levelled at Reid, namely, the charge that dualism has not been overcome, and therefore, at best a kind of semi-dualism has been produced. Perhaps this is not so serious as might first appear. It would be as natural to call it semi-monism. It may just be the function of common sense to affirm the fact that the knowledge of objects is not adequately stateable in terms either of idealism or dualism. Common sense as a critical pragmatic realism can admit that in our knowledge of objects the sense organs are not passively selective of qualities existing as experienced, but that the sense organs are in part generative of the sensa. And yet at the same time the contention can be made that we have direct knowledge of objects in their appearances by intuitive perception. One trouble with much of the discussion on this subject is that we get the ontological problem mixed in with the epistemological problem. We do, as a matter of fact, have knowledge of objects. What those objects may be in the "last analysis," or for physics and chemistry, whether a substance of one kind or many kinds, is really another problem. But we do know objects, though we are not therefore required to maintain that the objects must be in reality in all respects what they are experienced as.

A very interesting contribution and confirmation along these lines of thought comes from Norman Kemp Smith.[10] He does not call himself a common sense realist, but, approaching the knowledge problem against a background of idealism, he arrives at a realistic position which is essentially

[10] Smith, Norman Kemp, *Prolegomena to an Idealist Theory of Knowledge.*

like that of D. C. Macintosh. He also emphasizes the intuitive factors in perception, which was the thing that Reid was striving for in establishing his realism. Further, when Kemp Smith addresses himself to the problems of sensation and perception, he is doing so with full appreciation of the part which the mind plays, as we should expect from such a distinguished expositor of Kant. In other words, we see the realism for which Reid strove, and the organizing principles which Kant deduced, brought together in a realistic synthesis.

Kemp Smith divides the problem of perception into a consideration of the sensum and intuition. The data of the senses as such are sensa—to distinguish them from the process of sensing. These sensa, or objects of sense, are the secondary qualities. But what Kemp Smith shows is that sense data always come to us within a larger or more extensive matrix, both of time and space intuitively apprehended, without which the experience would not have either organization or meaning. The "intuitive apprehension of time and space involves the apprehension of meanings, and as factors indispensable to the possibility of such meanings, certain categorical relations."[11] We saw earlier that Reid recognized the need for categories, or, as he called them, "original judgments," but their function was not fully analyzed. Reid needed them for his doctrine of perception or intuition, for, as Kemp Smith has remarked, "Intuition is impossible without categorical thinking; nothing can be intuited save by the aid of meanings conceptually entertained." On this view, "sensa can never by themselves constitute a complete presentational field," but are supplemented by categorical thinking which makes intuition and realism possible. These ideal forms of thought enter into what is utterly immediate, namely, "The discrimination of the given shapes and sizes, and the given times and motions."

But now, "If the sensa and extension be really, in their

[11] *Ibid.*

intrinsic nature, independent of one another, how come they
to be thus in our experience, inseparably connected? . . . It
must also be explained how intuition can be distinct from
sensing, and yet at the same time be a direct, face-to-face
apprehension of the independently real." The following
quotation is the answer to that question:

Our conscious experience is thus a function of two distinct factors, each of which must have its own specific set of
conditions, and in accordance therewith its own appropriate
value. Through the constant factors a public world is revealed; through the sensa, in terms of which alone this public world can actually be experienced, it is apprehended in
a perspective suited to the individual's practical needs.
. . . Another way of stating this position is the following:
What we apprehend is, in all cases, a complex situation.
Within this complex situation we discriminate the contents
of what it is usual to call our sensations. But as these contents are discriminated within the situation, they cannot be
the materials out of which the situation as a whole is constructed. A whole cannot be constructed out of a selection
of its own constituent parts. Indeed, the sense-contents can,
it would seem, come into existence at all only under the
conditions which the situation itself supplies. If there be no
vibrating body and no air, no ear with its inner labyrinthine
structure and no brain connected therewith, there will be
no sounds. If the light of the sun, consisting in wave vibrations, does not act on the retina and through it on the oc-
cipital lobes, no colors will emerge. The sensa are events
determined by, and happening within, the space-time situation; and to make them possible, the total situation is required. All that we therefore are justified in saying is that
we come to apprehend the situation in terms of certain of
the events which occur within it.

If we seek some other body of sense-material out of which
the situation as a whole may be constructed, then with Kant
we must postulate a manifold more comprehensive than, and
different from, the data of the special senses. But this surely
is a needless and perverse procedure. Kant, it would seem,

himself only does so owing to the subjectivist manner in which his phenomenalism, very different though it may be from the subjectivism of Berkeley and his like, is still propounded. If we adopt an out-and-out realist position, no such postulate need be made. Independent reality will then be regarded as directly apprehended, that is, as making entry, not by proxy, but in its own person, into the "field of consciousness."[12]

It has seemed to us an interesting observation that the spirit of Scottish common sense has not left itself without a witness in these two present-day philosophers, both of whom may be counted among the Scots. There is an added significance here also, for when, epistemologically speaking, realism and idealism lie down together, then the facts as they really are have presumably been discerned.

Reid did not make direct application of his realism to religion, but he saw that the establishment of realism was of great importance for religion. He knew well enough that philosophical scepticism in reference to our knowledge of the external world would soon run the gamut of all our experiences, undermining their testimony and validity. Theologians were quick to discern the value of Reid's work. They safeguarded themselves, sometimes too complacently, behind his labors. Reid was set up as a defense and a refuge for uncritical theological minds. These men overlooked the scientific attitude in Reid which is one of the important sources of his common sense. Nevertheless, in Great Britain, France, and the United States, Reid exercised a tremendous influence, as has been pointed out by several writers.[13] He was a bulwark against scepticism for a considerable period.

The task remained, however, of extending realism into the field of religion. Not until well along in the nineteenth cen-

---

[12] Smith, Norman Kemp, *Prolegomena to an Idealist Theory of Knowledge*, 186 ff.

[13] McCosh, James, *The Scottish Philosophy*; Riley, I. Woodbridge, *American Philosophy—The Early Schools*; Rogers, A. K., *English and American Philosophy Since 1800.*

tury was this done. Again it was a Scotsman, John M'Leod Campbell, who is increasingly being recognized as "the greatest of all Scottish theologians,"[14] and by many as the pre-eminent British theologian of the past century. Campbell's work is independent of Schleiermacher and Ritschl, and comes in between them in time. He did not know Ritschl, and, as to Schleiermacher, he believed there was a lack of intimate personal religion. Campbell was a student of Hamilton. During his years of graduate study at Edinburgh he became thoroughly acquainted with the Scottish philosophers.

Campbell's interest in re-stating theology in terms of religious experience got him into trouble very early in his career, for, after a heresy trial, he was deposed from the Established Church of Scotland in 1830. He came to be an important figure as an independent theologian and made a genuine contribution on the problem of religious knowledge, following the controversy on that subject raised by Mansel's *Bampton Lectures*, 1858. Despite the fact that Mansel took over his basic philosophic position from Hamilton, Campbell was opposed to the agnostic consequences for religion and took instead a very realistic stand. He developed the view that religious experience must be taken for what it really is, and that its irreducible given is the conviction of otherness or God which attends it. This realistic claim of religious experience is a claim of direct acquaintance. The experience is not describable wholly in terms of judgments, but involves an intuitive awareness ingredient to the experience of communion. Judgment and feeling are no doubt elements, but somehow neither by itself nor both taken together seem to do justice to the realistic conviction of the presence of God in spiritual fellowship. Campbell insists that this realistic import is essential to Christian faith, without which it becomes something less personal, and consequently

[14] Mackintosh, H. R., *The Christian Apprehension of God*, (James Sprung Lectures).

more deistic. On this view, the concept of revelation has a specifically religious significance and is not made completely synonymous with general enlightenment as gained in other fields of search for truth.

What check did Campbell have on revelation? What tests could be applied? This was not sufficiently analyzed, but it was considered. Revelation comes with an imperative voice, yet Campbell seemed to regard reason as the balance or complement to revelation. But even reason needed a moral handmaiden. Campbell had great confidence that "the love of the truth" was essential in the use of reason and alone could save us from partisan bias and sophistry. Truth in the realm of religion was related to moral goodness. Here Campbell came close to the idea of value judgments, a term which had not yet come into use. In its place he sought for the Christian norm in the nature of love discernible in the heart and mind of Christ, which had for him an ontological status. His elaboration of this view has left us an interpretation of Jesus which is one of the great Christian classics.[15]

The freshness of approach to problems of religion by Campbell should have been utilized much more than it has. As Pfleiderer has said, Campbell began a movement in Great Britain comparable to that of Schleiermacher in Germany. No doubt Campbell's empirical and realistic work would have been developed had it not been for the preponderant occupation, after his time, with idealistic applications to religion. But the very problems with which he was wrestling have been in the very forefront of modern attention.

This brings us to a final consideration of the synthetic quality in the work of Professor Macintosh. He is the most distinguished representative of the common sense tradition. He has endeavored to do justice to the realistic claim of religion for direct monistic acquaintance with God; to accept what is valid in the Ritschlian value judgment approach; to utilize pragmatism for all that it is worth; to draw

[15] Campbell, John M'Leod, *The Nature of the Atonement.*

certain metaphysical inferences from reasonable postulates; and, finally, to attain, if possible for theology, some scientific verification.

Coupling monistic realism with the Ritschlian value judgment, we find Professor Macintosh ready to agree that the religious judgment is a value judgment, but that religious experience is not reducible to value judgments—

. . . vital experiential religion has always meant by the distinctively religious quality or value something not quite identical with the intellectual, the aesthetic or the moral value, whether taken singly, or all together. . . .[16] It is important to note that social or moral value, however significant for the testing of religious value, does not exhaust the whole content of religious value.[17]

Here notice is taken of Rudolf Otto's view of the immediacy of the "holy" or numinous factor in religious experience, but it is not regarded as a sufficient guide by itself.

Not the subjectively numinous is necessarily in every instance the truly divine in the full sense of the word, but rather the spiritual, the value-producing process in the universe. Historical religion has often gone astray and suffered religious illusion in being guided too exclusively by subjective numinous feeling.[18]

Nevertheless, the realistic immediacy is adhered to and is brought out in the following passage from *The Pilgrimage of Faith*:

The awareness of the Divine Factor which results from dependably successful religious adjustment conforms to the general character of empirical intuition, or perception in a complex whole of experienced elements. As a result of acting intelligently on the hypothesis of the existence of a God great enough and good enough to justify our absolute self-surrender and confident, appropriating faith, there comes a

[16] Macintosh, Douglas Clyde, *The Pilgrimage of Faith*, p. 162.
[17] *Ibid.*, 167.
[18] Macintosh, Douglas Clyde, *Religious Realism*, p. 379.

religious experience of spiritual uplift and emancipation in which, as a complex of many psychological elements, there can be intuited empirically, or perceived, the operation of a Factor which we evaluate and interpret as divine, because of its absolute religious and spiritual value.[19]

At this point one runs athwart the radical pragmatism of modern times which would banish existential import from religious experience and from value judgments. The Ritschlians described religious experience in terms of value judgments, but they made room for faith in an existent God. The radical pragmatists, however, eliminate the existent God and worship at the shrine of practical value. This is consistent with the pragmatic view of truth, which is regarded as entirely a relative term without any absolute validity even as an ideal.

There is a less radical form of pragmatism, however, which is really a necessary accompaniment of religious realism. It accepts, on the one hand, the pragmatic claim "that the test of truth about reality is ultimately practical," and on the other hand, that truth has also an objective reference to reality itself.

Truth is representation of subject-matter by predicate, of reality by idea, as intellectualists have always insisted; but the test as to whether this representation of reality by idea is such as to merit the epithet "true" is found in the practical test of acting upon the idea, being guided by it, in adjusting one's self to the reality in question. The judgment is finally made in the light of the consequences of such experimental action. What is taken as true is whatever representation of reality by idea is held to be satisfactory for the practical purposes considered. If the judgment is mistaken, it must either be because the idea or predicate was not really satisfactory for the purposes considered, or because some important purpose or purposes did not receive adequate consideration. . . . This representational or realistic pragmatism shows that the way is clear for a religious

[19] *The Pilgrimage of Faith*, p. 223; cf. *Religious Realism*, pp. 375 ff.

pragmatism which will affirm the independent reality of the
Object of religious interest and yet find in practical religious
value an indication of validity and truth.[20]

The utility of pragmatism for religion lies in the support
which it brings toward the construction of reasonable religious beliefs or philosophy of religion. One of these reasonable beliefs which may thus find pragmatic justification is
the assurance of the moral freedom of man inferred from
the consciousness of moral obligation. It is similar to the
inference made by Kant. Following a line of argument much
the same as that of Kant, there is also postulated the existence of God and immortality of the soul. With Kant it is
held that these are reasonable inferences from moral experience. But Professor Macintosh would like to go further in
"changing the form of these latter inferences from what
ought to be to what is."[21] Can he really take this further
step? He thinks so, provided it is possible to affirm moral
optimism with reference to the cosmos. In order to establish moral optimism, it is shown that between pessimism and
extreme optimism there is the midway position of meliorism,
which allows for the possibility of improving life and increasing human values. William James is appealed to as one
who has developed the pragmatic justification for a moderate optimism in which human effort is devoted to the
cause of moral ideals. Racial experience has already given
us sufficient evidence that human progress is conditioned
upon such a practical attitude toward life. This modified
optimism as pragmatically justified for moral living is next
given a cosmic status which provides the basis for the step
from moral postulation to rational metaphysical inference.

If then we evaluate this form of religious meliorism which
we have called moral optimism as valid, and adopt it as our
attitude toward reality and destiny, is there anything that
in strict logic we can infer from it with reference to the

[20] *The Pilgrimage of Faith*, p. 184.
[21] *Ibid.*, p. 195.

nature of reality? The answer is simple and ought to be obvious. If moral optimism is valid, the cosmos, ultimately considered, must be on the side of the spiritual. In other words, the God we imperatively need exists. If we define God as a superhuman Cosmic Factor great enough and good enough to justify an attitude of moral optimism on our part, it is undeniable that the metaphysical proposition that God exists is logically implied in the value-judgment that moral optimism is valid.[22]

To be sure, "If moral optimism is valid" and if we define God as he is defined above, then the proposition that God exists may be evoked. But we cannot overlook the fact that such a conclusion is hypothetically grounded. Moral optimism is no doubt pragmatically justified to the man who will use the pragmatic argument as a basis for faith. But it is still faith. It is faith in a metaphysical optimism based on a pragmatically justified moral philosophy of life. A humanist may accept moral optimism and affirm that all we can actually claim is that if moral optimism is a pragmatically valid view of life, then the world in which we live is the kind of place in which moral optimism may be justified. This is good ground for adventurous faith, but in our judgment a doubtful basis for confidence that we have actually passed by logical necessity from what ought to be to what really is. It has occurred to us that the application of common sense in religion does not require this further step.

A great deal has been gained if we can give reasonable grounds for the religious convictions that grow out of moral and religious experience at its best. In other words, belief in the existence of God, freedom, and immortality are reasonable and permissible. It is a question in many minds whether we can really go further, except as, through religious practice, we do deepen our conviction about God as "a divine-value producing factor." But it is just here that Professor

[22] *Ibid.*, p. 200.

Macintosh introduces the idea of scientific verification. What he would do is, "go on to transform some part at least of this doctrinal content from practically justified belief to scientifically verified knowledge."[23]

There has been some objection to the term "scientific" as applicable to theology. The religious attitude seems to suggest personal relationships rather than "scientific" ones. Further, value judgments seem to imply a different kind of procedure. What Professor Macintosh has been at pains to declare is that in religion there is a reliable factor in the cosmos which can be depended upon to respond to religious need, and that such response comes most completely when the right religious adjustments are made. Experimental religion reveals the presence of a value-producing factor or God. But the revelation of this presence is in terms of religious experience which it is difficult for us to consider as amenable to scientific procedure. To be sure, on the other hand, there is much to be said for the statement that religious evolution has really provided us with a living laboratory of experimental religion.[24]

Thus progressive experimental religion has been becoming at once more rational and more moral, more spiritual and more scientific. This is not to say as yet that the religious man really does get, through religious experience, any scientific knowledge about an independently existing God; for the present I am satisfied to point out that, within the limits of his realistic religious presuppositions, the religious man, in becoming more critically empirical and logical, is becoming less unscientific and more scientific, and that certain results of his religious experience and logical thought naturally seem to him to yield genuinely verified knowledge of a really existent God. Man seems to have been finding out through experience what he can depend upon religion (or reality through religion) for, and how he must relate him-

[23] *Religious Realism*, pp. 374 ff.
[24] *Ibid.*, pp. 316 ff.

self to reality in religion, if he is to be able to depend upon it for the results desired.[25]

The above statement does summarize the process that has taken place in the forward movement of religion, and as stated and as viewed externally in perspective, it seems to suggest the experimental approach to religion. Yet if we view the experience from within, we recognize that all the great insights and forward steps came first in the souls of profound spiritual minds, who sustained a deep sense of personal relation with God. It is our view that this fact of personal relationship is the most distinctive characteristic of the Hebrew-Christian contribution to religion. The insights that came were as the voice of God, imperative revelations to which the whole nature of man responded. We may say, of course, that wherever these revelations proved fruitful, there must have been a right religious adjustment. This is doubtless true, but the right religious adjustment is not in itself, strictly speaking, a scientific attitude of mind, nor is it subject to scientific treatment. The terminology of science does inadequate justice to the realm of religion with its intimate personal relationships. We do not usually consider personal relationships amenable to scientific method. We offer the suggestion of Campbell that in the realm of religion, as distinct from the realm of science, the character of God is relied upon as the dependable factor, and that character relationships escape inclusion within scientific procedure.

Perhaps the interests of common sense are best served if we try not to prove too much. It has seemed to us that the common sense approach is valid, but that it does not require extension to quite the lengths to which Professor Macintosh has applied it. We believe that he has provided excellent common sense foundations for realism, both in general knowledge theory and in religion. We feel that his critical realism and pragmatism afford an excellent intellectual basis

[25] *Ibid.*, pp. 322-323.

for Christian faith. It is also our view that Christian religious experience will never be long satisfied with anything less than a pragmatically justified critical monism. In this respect we believe that Professor Macintosh has done a great service and rightly exercised a wide influence.

II

THEOLOGY AND RELIGIOUS EXPERIENCE

By

Vergilius Ferm

Professor of Philosophy, The College of Wooster

Experience, we are told, is a weasel word. This remark quoted widely as though it were a startling discovery turns out to convey a philosophical platitude. Professional philosophers have long been aware of the fact that the woods are full of weasel expressions. It is not so certain, however, that philosophers and theologians do not need an occasional warning as to their use of words; occasions justify the suspicion that philosophical platitudes are not always recognized as such.

It was one of the major lessons of the Socratic teaching that words in general are weasel. One cannot, nor should one take them at face value. Meanings frequently are not sufficiently precise; or, meanings change in the course of time and even during a single discourse; or, where no definition is implied, anything may be implicated. The critique of Socrates was levelled not alone at the man on the street for his mishandling of words; his shafts pointed directly to the professional teachers who unwittingly had been deceived by their own use of terms. Current professional literature is bringing home the validity of Socrates' warning. Terms are still toyed with even in high places. We are supposed to know what is meant by such terms as "science," "religion," "evolution," "God," "mysticism," "humanism," "idealism," "materialism," "realism," "orthodoxy," "Christianity," "church," "liberalism," "spiritual,"—to name but a few from the philosophical and theological stock-in-trade; a closer critical analysis of the use of such terms, however, will provoke one to set down the interrogation point on the margins of many an author's pages.

Quite evident is it that a writer's privilege is sacred at least at one point. He may use important words as he chooses, but then he must frankly avow the meaning he has given them, stay within that meaning, and take the consequences. If we choose to disagree with him on such definitions, for us the Achilles' heel to his system of thought will be found to lie at that point. Systems of thought are as strong or as weak, other things being equal, as the defensibility of the use of terms implicit in them. The crux of criticism, in other words, lies in the use of terms.

Whether or not the existence of Deity can be demonstrated depends upon the meaning of the term Deity and what is taken for demonstration. Whether or not humanism can be made compatible with theism depends upon the validity of definitions. Whether or not a theology can be considered empirical, or even a science at all, depends upon the meaning given those and other related terms. Whether or not an idealist is a realist, a materialist an atheist, a behaviorist a psychologist or biologist, a religious liberal or a fundamentalist a Christian, an epistemological dualist an epistemological agnostic, an absolutist a theist or pantheist, a monist a believer in free-will, a positivist a metaphysician, a vitalist a pseudo-scientist, a conservative a dogmatist, depends very largely upon the adequacy of definitions. Pertinent to this discussion is the question of what and how much is involved in "religious experience." If "experience" and "religion" suffer as weasel words, by a simple arithmetical process "religious experience" is a double weasel expression. Since this term has for decades carried an amazingly heavy load, especially in connection with theological systems of thought, it is in need of careful scrutiny. He who gives to it his own definition does so at a great risk; not to give it a clear-cut definition (if the term plays any significant rôle in one's systematic thought) involves a risk much greater.

What shall we say about the rôle played by this allegedly weasel expression?

It is common knowledge that liberal Protestant theologians for decades have been bent upon a quest for certainty. With the breakdown of the traditional biblical basis as a norm of unquestionable authority, they have been searching here and there to find an impregnable rock upon which to rebuild the tottering theological edifice. The suggestion of Schleiermacher, that the basis is to be had in the kind of experience later called "religious experience," was heralded by those who followed as the solid base of a re-orientated and respectable theology. Schleiermacher has been rewarded by the title of "father of modern theology"; more specifically, he has become the father of the modern theology of religious experience. American theologians of the more liberal school began to take this lead seriously about the end of the nineteenth century. One after the other set up systems of dogmatics which were alleged to rest upon that unassailable foundation: religious experience. Viewed from a contemporary perspective, many claims as to what is involved in that experience, particularly of the so-called "Christian" type, have turned out to be spurious. What happened (as we now see it) was the tacking on of much traditional theological lumber—doctrines alleged to have grown as trees from the nourishing soil of that experience. The quest for authority outran the truth. One could not possibly experience all that the theologians said was involved in such an experience. The quest for certainty which ended in "religious experience" has revealed itself to be a quest for a newer apologetic for the older faith.

The more cautious theologians sensed the danger. Distinctions were drawn. Fundamental or essential doctrines were distinguished as experienceable from the less fundamental out to the borderline of the adiaphorous. The further course in this development led, it would now appear, in the direction of a movement away from vindicating the traditional theology; a contemporary's "religious experience" is acknowledged as not at all points coincident with what had supposedly been handed down as a normal and normative experience; one by one theological doctrines were discarded as transitory ideational and social vestiges, which were of significance only in certain environmental contexts. The quest for certainty by way of an alleged experience turned out to be a peeling process: fewer doctrinal certainties emerged. The day of reckoning for this trend in modern theology was bound to come. It is now here.

Many factors have brought about this unexpected turn. Three are conspicuous: the influence of psychological investigations and theories; the wealth of material brought to light by researches in comparative religion; and the methodology of the historical-critical-social approach that is now expected of investigators. The effect of such studies as the psychology of religion has been cumulative rather than fruitful at one point. There remains no one conspicuous authority or point of view in this field. The earlier statistical and questionnaire methods brought shocking disclosures to theologians; though now found wanting and in need of revisions and a new series of inductions, psychological studies have contributed enormously to revised conceptions of the concept "religious experience." More especially influential was the rather recent and significant development of studies in comparative religion. Long kept from coming to its own by traditional biases and by the dearth of qualified scholars, the younger member of the family of related disci-

plines has finally come to claim its birthright. A long process
of painstaking research lies ahead, though enough results
have appeared to change the older notions of the relation
of theology to "religious experience." The term itself demands a more adequate definition than had been given to it.
If theology is confined to its Christian expression—as it has
been in Western thought—then the verdicts of the historic
critic upon basic materials come to be of indispensable importance.

The case of Ritschlianism is pertinent here. The Ritschlian
appeal to Christ and an alleged Christian revelation as an impregnable rock upon which to construct and shape a theology was headed in two opposing directions: back towards
an historic norm and forward towards a normative type of
mystical experience. In the one case the Ritschlian way led
back to the researches of the historic critic, to a properly attested historic fact, the historic Jesus, as the basis; in the
other, the way led, in spite of the Ritschlian protests, to
mysticism of the clearest type, an alleged spiritual *rapport*
of the individual with the alleged inner life-quality of Jesus,
the Founder. In the one case the seal of approval must come
from the critic who is to say what the experience ought to
be if it is to match the Founder's; in the other case the seal
of approval is stamped by one's own value-judgment; in the
one a disputable deliverance and in the other an unmistak-
able form of subjectivism; in either case: a dilemma. Ritschlianism disclaimed the latter as its ground for certainty and
it tried to avoid the implications of the former. The certainty turned out again to be but a species of apologetic
hope.

It was but natural, in the quest for theological certainty
within the field of religious experience, that epistemological
considerations should come to the fore. In the philosophical
field the reaction against traditional idealistic orthodoxies
became reflected in newer epistemological schools: realists
of different kinds with their corresponding variations of in-

terpretations of the world and of mind. The term "realism" is taken to refer to those views holding the world somehow or other to be an independent order, extra ego-mental in character, a world which can be disclosed (directly or indirectly) to the mind, however alike or unlike that order it may be. Epistemological realism asserts this independent order and its knowability. The wider implications of this view were drawn and applied: may not that "experience" which is distinctly "religious" make corresponding assertions as to the knowability of an order of things which does not depend for its existence upon that knowing relation, an order which for all theoretical and practical purposes corresponds to what on other grounds may properly be called Deity? Thus realism came to be recognized as an ally to the cause of a theology linked with religious experience. Theology thus grounded may lay claim, at least at that point, to be scientific, since such a claim is analogous to the realism implied in the natural sciences. If one may be certain of an objective order through general experience, why may one not be certain of an order apprehended by a particular kind of experience? Of course, there is always the possibility of mistaken identity, subjectivism, wishful thinking, etc., but this is not peculiar to one area of experience; rather it is a possibility open to any kind of experience. Realism thus becoming "critical" and allied with other criteria becomes the answer to the quest for certainty—for theology.

The way opened by a religious critically realistic epistemology, however, has not met with the general approval that one might expect among theologians. Objections came in the form of disagreement with definitions, with epistemological and ontological theories, and, what is more, with a growing tide of despair over the possibility of reaching any grounded certainty so long sought in traditional thought. New movements had already taken place in the philosophical field which were to find their counterparts in the theological. New theological rifts, commitments and alignments

swept into the scene. The tough and secular-minded pragmatists had popularized their short-cut solutions of theoretical puzzles and were winning ground in sacred areas.
Humanists had turned from a bewildered theocentric gaze
to the more promising anthropocentric focus with fresh
enthusiasm; after all, nothing is of more interest and importance than man himself. Metaphysicians and theologians
have had their day; the truer humility is to be had in positivism, which concerns itself with the creature rather than
the creator. Or, again: the truer optimism lies in an *ethical*
culture.

The spirit of despair has further shown itself in many
contemporary movements within the theological field. All
along there have been protests against a theology built upon
religious experience. The contemporary neo-Thomistic
movement has added its positive scorn and repudiation of
that development and for reasons which are consistent with
the great Thomistic tradition. Conservatives of the fundamentalist school have joined in the same chorus. After all,
Christian theology, it is said, rests not upon passing individual experiences but upon an objective revelation. Dressed
up in a more recent type of philosophical garb this older
current has expressed itself afresh in the Barthian vogue;
certainty comes by way of a determined avowal of belief
in revelation and in supernaturalism; there are two distinct
worlds joined only by threads reaching out from one direction; whatever certainty there is, it does not come by way
of "religious experience" but by way of an humble faith
supernaturally conditioned. The general revival of traditional doctrines, the return toward liturgical forms with the
disavowal of an intellectual emphasis, the Anglo-Catholic
movement, the apathy toward theological formulations (expressions of some recent cults, *e.g.*, Buchmanism), religious
quietistic movements old and new—these are symptomatic
of a general despair of any fulfilment of the kind of promise
of theological certitude contained in that modern theologi-

cal movement supposedly developed from the suggestions of Schleiermacher.

The case for or against a theology of religious experience rests very largely upon the validity of definitions. Can so-called "religious experience" carry the heavy load placed upon it by many modern theologians? Can Deity be cognitively affirmed in such an experience in a way unique from other types of experience? Can Christianity be vindicated, and be made philosophically and scientifically respectable by an appeal to the court of such experience? Can theology thus grounded be made empirical and thus escape the charge of being wholly speculative? What is this thing "religious experience"?

If the term "experience" is held in the widest sense as including anything that happens to the human mind, and if "religious experience" be defined (as it so often has been) as that mind in commerce with Deity (conceived after the pattern of a theistic theology), then the way may be paved for an empirically grounded theology of the traditional sort. However, if "experience" be taken to mean that phase of mental life which is akin to the sensory responses as distinguished from the imaginative and theoretical phase (as, *e.g.*, "empiricism" has historically been distinguished from "rationalism") and if "religious experience" be taken to have reference to something much more general than is implied by the theistic concept of God, then the way becomes much more rough for a theology which is supposed to link itself with traditional concepts and dogmas. Let this be made more specific.

Attempts to define the religious frame of mind have made clear a number of errors. The Christian theologian's attempt has, on the whole, revealed a striking case of the question-begging fallacy. The definition has implied a conclusion contained in the premise, *viz.*, that there is no "religious experience" without an awareness or recognition of Deity (conceived after a certain theological pattern); what is more: such a Deity, thus supposedly recognized, takes on the character and likeness of the Deity presupposed by the Christian interpretations. The same general type of error may be seen in terms of another fallacy: mistaking the part for the whole. Comparative studies in religion have revealed that it is necessary to extend the category of "religious" to certain attitudes and practices plainly not involving any clear-cut concept of Deity. The implied definitions of these theologians of religious experience, accordingly, are in need of such broadening as to make their cause most hazardous.

It has been said that to call a type of attitude or behavior involving no god-concept "religious" is to widen the term to the point of meaninglessness. Undoubtedly there is force to this charge. More specifically, it has been suggested that the Toda dairy-priests, for example, who repeat their ceremonies quite unconscious of any god-concept, are "religious" only by proxy, *i.e.*, they are "religious" only by reference to a prior situation which was religious; that if they have no god-concept it is a case of degeneration from what was once a religious practice to a case of sheer habit which in itself is not religious. In reply to this it may well be admitted that all behavior exhibits the force of custom plus an expression of various social and psychological activities; the question is how one is to characterize *this* particular behavior from other types. For every genus one must find a species, if one is to formulate a meaningful characterization and classification. The more specific question here is not whether the Toda-priests are social animals and creatures of custom—all men are that; the question is: how is this particular activity as a form of custom and social practice to be distinguished from other activities coming under the same genus? Back and underneath the crust of social habit there may well be a frame of mind to which, for purposes of classification, it is necessary to give the special term "religious," even though the participant in social exercises is unable to make clear either to himself or to others the meaning or wherefore of his behavior. Unprejudiced observation will show that it is necessary to apply the category of "religious" to certain frames of mind and behaviors not tied to theological meanings—if, for no other reason, than that other categories fail adequately to qualify. This being so, the way is opened for a religious type of "experience" and behavior which appear to have little to contribute directly to a theology (in the strictest sense of that term).

It need hardly be pointed out that many other mistaken notions in definition have been held. The identification of the religious frame of mind with ethical behavior is so patently unsatisfactory as to need no elaboration. It is as much connected with unethical as with ethical conduct; to use the two categories interchangeably is to violate the law of parsimony. A common error, however, is the failure to maintain the distinction between a normative and a descriptive approach; the question, in these matters of definition, is not what the religious frame of mind ought to be, but what it is and has been.

The weasel term "religious experience" must be defined, then, with a conscience sensitive to such considerations already mentioned. What appears to this writer as a valid approach to a defensible definition of terms is that of making a distinction between the adjective "religious," the concrete noun "a religion" and the generic "religion." If one were to seek a name for this approach one would call it the positivistic, nominalistic, naturalistic, humanistic; at least, there is no theological bias presupposed.

An individual may be said *to be religious* if in some vital manner he reacts to whatever he takes to be of serious and ulterior concern, however dimly apprehended. The attachment naturally implies a cognitive element, however dimly cognized, of something worthy of more than passing interest or allegiance. Potentially, anything that comes in the way of observation either through the senses or through imagination or reason may be the object of that attachment. Historically, that is what has happened. The imagined god or the sensed idol—if it be a god or idol—may be anything; but neither the god nor the idol standing alone as an object is of the essence of the religious spirit; it is rather the feeling toward, of mattering, of concern, of making-a-difference-to, that is of the essence of that frame of mind.

What then, it may be asked, is the difference between a person who is religious and a person who makes much of his profession or business? The question is not at all embarrassing for the simple reason that they have much in common. "To make a religion out of one's business" is an expression of genuine significance. A person would be religious if his concern toward his business were of serious and ulterior concern. Though there is a psychological one-to-one correspondence between the religious individual and such a business man, and though there is no theoretical difficulty in employing the category "religious" to both, there is a practical consideration that compels a differentiation. However great the concern of the business man may be over his business, he will find that the field of possible and probable concerns is always wider than that of his immediately pressing interests. In other words, the world presents an area much wider than our immediate horizons, and it is to such wider possibilities as attachments that it seems best to delimit the category of "religious." There are two considerations that compel the limitation of that concern to "ulterior" possibilities: first, man *can* and does normally react to conditions (imaginative or real) which lie beyond the field of his commonplace interests; and, second, there presses upon him the reality of that larger area which, though at times it may seem far removed from and unreal to him, becomes for him something significant. A man's reactions consist not alone in terms of bread and butter; he is so psychologically constituted that he is capable of converting intangibles into tangibles, and of bringing the remote very near. The poetry and the music of the world are symbolic, if of nothing else, of man's power to recognize (however dimly) things ulterior. And what is of complementary significance here is the fact that the world in which he finds himself is one that reveals the reality of things remote, wider ranges which upon occasion do seem to play into even the most commonplace. This is a world of wind and weather, of uncertainties and perplexities, where the dim future plays a part in the cruel present. There is much that lies quite outside the touch of hands aching to manipulate; life throbs with situations that call forth concerns ulterior. If man lived in quite another kind of world, and if he were other than he is (with his mechanisms of response reaching out beyond the immediate), it would be doubtful if he would be the kind of religious animal that he now is, or even if he would be religious at all. The religious frame of mind is natural and normal though it may be transitory.

An individual's religion consists in the body of crystallized meanings and behaviors which have reference either actually or potentially to this religious spirit. A huge percentage of it—if not all of it—in terms of practices and beliefs is a borrowing from the extant or preëxistent culture. Conceivably a man may be religious without a religion, *i.e.*, he may have the attitude above described as religious without giving to it concrete form. Practically, however, this is highly improbable for the simple reason that a thousand social forces play upon him to aid him give expression to what he thinks as somehow bound up with that spirit. Looking back to the dim past, we should, accordingly, find that the religious spirit came before a religion; looking toward our own past as individuals, most of us, who have been born in a culture embedded with religions, will find that we were first given a religion about which we were expected to become religious.

The abstract noun "religion" is but a name covering specific religions. There is no such thing as religion-in-general. When we talk about the conflict between "science" and "religion" we commit the fallacy of the reification of abstractions, for "science-in-general" is as non-existent as "religion-in-general."

We speak of religious objects, such as a cow, a cross, beads. This usage is permissible. Any object, performance or event is religious if it has reference to individuals who in turn are either actually or potentially religious. It follows that a person may act in a religious manner even though he may not himself be religious. He may perform the religious ceremony and be wholly concerned with an interest devoid of religious significance. The ceremony is religious by proxy; it is religious only in so far as it refers, directly or indirectly, actually or potentially, to a person who is religious. If such a ceremony should become totally divorced from this reference the thing ceases to be religious.

Psychologists to-day are wary over the division of mental life into the tripartite division of feeling, knowing and willing, and for the reasons given, justly so. There is always the danger of artificiality and abstraction in analysis especially in matters which concern the dynamic. And yet, not to make such a three-fold division of mental life is to slur over what apparently are definitely characteristic phases of mental phenomena. It may well be that the three are bound together in the actual ongoing of mental processes; and yet, there is something really distinctive about mental processes as feeling, as knowing, and as willing. Whatever else may be involved, the religious frame of mind belongs predominantly on the side of feeling. It is difficult to define adequately what is taken to be feeling for the very obvious reason that any definition must of necessity translate it into rational categories. What in essence is non-rational, cannot be rationalized. A workable suggestion is to say that feelings are fundamentally "organic commotions." The commotion may be and is associated with something apprehended, but it is in itself *characteristically* not that apprehension. In religious feeling the commotion is concerned with or attached to some object of serious and ulterior concern. Strictly speaking, the apprehension is on the intellectual side; the feeling is related to organic disturbance. In religious feeling there is a disturbance, vivid, fresh, intimate, "colorful," warm, over what is noticed as of ulterior significance.

The concept "God" is to be considered in reference either to the intellectual or to the emotional phase of mental life. The God of the theologian and philosopher is set in a framework that is emphatically intellectual; the God of the genuinely religious individual (if there be any God) is set in a framework that is emphatically emotional. The God implied by religious feeling is that which is taken to be supremely significant within that totality which is felt to make a difference. To chisel out in conceptual form that which appears to matter most is to go a step or more beyond the religious feeling itself. Conceptual formulae as such are always a step removed from the emotional phase. Definitions of God are then for the most part constructions of the intellect. We should accordingly expect very little in the way of definition of God from the area of religious feeling.

What is taken to be "religious experience" belongs on the side of feeling rather than on the side of sense-perception (which psychologists rightly or wrongly have linked to knowledge) and knowledge. One may presumably know God without being religious. Conversely, one may presumably be religious without knowing God in the sense of having any theoretically satisfactory God-concept. So-called religious conceptions of God are for the most part nonreligious concepts. The process of borrowing from intellectual, social and cultural sources unwittingly goes on. Religious feeling has very little to contribute toward a purely intellectual construction; the latter is the work of the intellect.

The term "religious perception" has been employed to suggest the close affiliation of "religious experience" to sense-experience. This, of course, is a matter of terms. Plainly, the motive here is to justify the premise of making out of the "religious experience" a state of mind correlative with that of sense-experience, and thus presumably to establish ground for a peculiar and unique way of asserting the knowability of the divine object and ground for scientific respectability. A closer analysis of such use of the term reveals the questionable thesis that feeling *as such* is cognitive. This extension of the category of feeling to cognition (it has already been indicated) is a slur upon terms. Feeling is feeling, and cognition is cognition; though they may be interlocked in the ongoing process of mental life they imply distinctive phases of that life.

The definitions above outlined are in need of much further elaboration and possibly of defense than can be here given. Of immediate concern are some of the implications of the definitions for theology.

Theology, supposedly, is a study or theory of God and related matters. It is just that: a theoretical system. Its relation to "religious experience" is the relation, if any, of intellect to feeling. Conceivably, it may have as little to do with the religious life as a study of the physiology of living forms has to do with living itself. One may live without a physiology. One may be religious without a theology and have a theology without being religious. There remains a clear line between the two.

The theologian of religious experience in his quest for certainty has assumed the unique cognitive significance of "religious experience." To make his case appear more secure he has employed that dubious word "experience," which is taken to mean an alignment with sense-experience (above defined) and knowledge. It is not only conspicuous but significant to notice that preference has been made for the term religious *experience* in place of religious *feeling*. One is on the ground of cognitive *un*certainty when one employs the term "feeling." To emphasize feeling at the expense of experience (with the implied connotations) is to jeopardize the cause of cognitive certainty.

The mistake of theologians of religious experience has been to overload religious feeling with intellectual constructions in the interest of the kind of certainty desired. The Catholic theologians have rightly protested against this confusion; their insistence upon rendering unto intellect the things that belong to intellect and to feeling the things that belong to feeling should not have gone unheeded. Feelings, we have indicated, are in themselves non-rational though linked to man's rational nature. There is no special feeling that is religious any more than there is a special instinct that is religious. If there is a special cognitive significance to religious feeling (as has been so widely maintained) there should be *quid pro quo* a special cognitive significance in the feelings associated with art and play! Feelings, however, are all of the same weave; we give to them special names only when they are associated with certain characteristic interests. What makes a feeling religious is its association with an ulterior concern. There is no unique way of knowing; all knowing is of the same weave. The supposed unique knowledge of the mystic turns out to be nothing more than can be explained as the work of ordinary imagination and knowledge and sense-experience coupled with feeling. The law of parsimony forbids the use of new entities unless there is an absolute necessity. There is no necessity in setting up an organ of knowledge different in kind from the usual ways of knowing. The lead taken by theologians of religious experience is thus a mistaken one prompted, it may be repeated, by an apologetic hope.

Theology is purely an intellectual construction. It is the artistic work of reason. A religion may have its theology, or to put it in another way, there may be a religious theology (in the sense above indicated); but, religious feeling as such moves in a realm or upon a plane other than that of theology, even as feeling is qualitatively different from knowing. The theologian's base lies in the realm of the intellect and not in the dynamic non-rational side of human nature. If the theologian desires, accordingly, to make his discipline "scientific" after the pattern of the natural sciences, and "empirical" after the pattern of the realism implied by a theory of sense-experience, he will have to do it —following the above definitions—not by appealing to religious experience as ground, but by linking his discipline to the rational work of the natural sciences and by cutting loose with them from that intimately personal phase of mental life associated with the term "feeling." The truth of his system should be as coldly formal as the truth of any systematic information presented by the natural sciences; its ideal of objectivity compels the continued avoidance of appeal to the realm of feeling.

Moreover, the kind of certainty that has been sought by the theologians has outrun in hopes the kind of certainty that is now asserted by the natural scientists. The natural scientist no longer speaks of the absolute, the final, the assured, the non-revisable. A natural science can maintain its respectability without an appeal to absolute certainty; should the theologian ask for more? A more humble hope would be a system that is reasonable and probable rather than unassailably absolute or final or sure. The historic position of the Christian ecclesiastical theologian has been to make faith seem reasonable and rewarding; to make faith certain is a contradiction in terms. The theologian of the future may well return to a more modest hope and join hands with other interpreters and systematizers in seeking at his present level of understanding and reflection what appears to be most probably true about his world of circumstance.

A rational theology and not a theology of religious experience contains the more promising and reasonable hope. A theology of religious experience represents a detour away from the main thoroughfare of historical theology. It reflects an age searching desperately for a newer and more satisfying type of apologetic. When viewed from the perspective of the age which produced it, an age unsettled by the tremendous transitions of thought, one sees in the attempt the highest *motif* on the part of such theologians; when viewed, however, from a contemporary time which, though it remains quite as unsettled, has the advantage of a longer perspective for an appraisal, that commendable *motif* is seen to have contained a hope which outran possibility and a movement which in its embryo contained the seeds of its own dissolution.

III

A REASONED FAITH

By

GEORGE F. THOMAS

Professor of Philosophy, Dartmouth College

THERE is a very real doubt on the part of many as to whether knowledge, in the ordinary sense of the term, is possible in religion. In general, knowledge arises when an object is presented and a judgment made about it by means of categories. But it is most difficult to determine when or whether the religious object is present to the mind. To identify an object as present is to distinguish it from other objects. But God may be in a sense present in any or every object since He is the Ground of all objects; and it is possible that He is never present by Himself alone.[1] How, then, can He be identified if He is present everywhere and nowhere? And, even if He can be identified, how are we to make judgments about Him in terms of categories whose primary application is to finite objects? These difficulties, real as they are, are not to be our main concern. Religious people may even be tempted to dismiss them as unimportant. They have always been certain that God is present to them in some experiences more fully than in others, but that He can be found by the faithful in every aspect of their experience. They do not, however, expect anyone to give a literal description of Him in terms of human cate-

[1] Smith, Norman Kemp, *Is Divine Existence Credible?*, 1931.

44

gories. It is sufficient if they can trace His lineaments in His creation and find analogies from their finite experience which are not wholly unworthy of Him.

But there is always serious danger that the complexity of religious knowledge may be underestimated and that God may be sought by a method too narrow and exclusive. The rationalist may try to demonstrate God by an appeal to scientific evidence; the voluntarist may insist that we can know Him only by a "will to believe"; while the romanticist may claim that He can be apprehended only through feelings of dependence and trust. But if true religion involves the response of the whole self to the whole of reality, any such attempt to base the knowledge of God upon a narrow foundation is bound to impoverish it. If so, it may be worth our while to examine critically some of the "methods" that have been used to gain religious knowledge and to suggest lines along which the most fruitful synthesis of them may be made.

Let us begin with *empirical* theology. The essence of the empiricist's position is that religious experience not only presents God to the worshipper but also certifies the truth of certain beliefs about Him. Religious experience must, of course, be critically analyzed before its authentic religious character can be accepted. But, once this is done, it can provide the primary data both for the science of religion and for the philosophy of religion. This position has often been accompanied by emphasis upon psychological analysis of the "varieties" of religious experience and by a polemic against theological speculation, as in the case of William James. More recently, however, empiricists have appealed to a realistic theory of knowledge to substantiate their trust in the validity of religious experience. Professor D. C. Macintosh is the best-known representative of this type of empiricism. Analysis of religious experience, he argues, reveals a dependable connection between a specific human "adjustment" and a specific "response" from reality.[2] If the desired "response" is to be obtained, the "adjustment" must be "right." The desired "response" is the support and increase of moral and spiritual value in our lives. How do we know what "adjustment" will lead to this end? By the study of the results of active religious experimentation by others and by ourselves. The history and psychology of religions describe the experimental adjustments of men to the reality upon which they have depended for conservation and increase of their values. They show that reality can be depended upon to further moral and spiritual values and that a specific adjustment to reality must be made to that end. And we can verify this by experimentation for ourselves.

So far we are at the "phenomenological" level. Presumably, we are not yet certain that a religious reality is active in the "response" we experience. Since religious men commonly make the assumption of such a reality, however, our phenomenological analysis has yielded us an hypothesis. Since "the test of the true hypothesis is perception, immediate experience,"[3] the principle by which this hypothesis can be tested is that "if we have any direct experience of this divine reality, we have some genuinely verified or scientific, religious knowledge."[4] Now, according to the true theory of perception, "critical monism" or "critical realism," an object may be immediately apprehended as it is, though not necessarily in its full nature or with perfect accuracy. On the basis of this theory Professor Macintosh argues that we may apprehend the reality and nature of God through His effects upon us in the religious "response." We may have scientifically verified knowledge of Him as a factor producing and increasing spiritual values in us.

[2] Macintosh, Douglas Clyde, *Religious Realism*, 1931.
[3] *Ibid.*, p. 332.
[4] *Ibid.*, pp. 332-333.

This knowledge forms the "laws of theology as an empirical science."[5] Thus scientific analysis of religious experience with the aid of "critical realism" leads to "theological laws." Of course, the deliverances of any given religious experience must be weighed carefully before we accept them. If the mystic, for example, claims that God is the sole reality, that the physical world, the finite self, and evil are all unreal, we may suspect him of "hallucination under the influence of self-hypnosis."[6] But the important thing is that we can have scientific, verifiable knowledge of God as a spiritual, value-producing reality. For, once we are certain of the actual working of this reality in direct experience, we can go further and develop "reasonable beliefs" and "surmises" about it by means of philosophical analysis and speculation. Thus, philosophy will be able to construct upon the secure foundations laid by experimental science and critical realism a religious "ontology."

What are we to say of this religious empiricism? (1) We must concede the usefulness of the "experimental" method in establishing a science of religious experience. By means of it, generalizations can be made concerning the religious feelings and attitudes of men as well as the results of such feelings and attitudes upon their lives. Moreover, these generalizations may be of great practical value in guiding our religious efforts. In all great religions men have been urged to "seek" if they would "find"; but men must know *how* they shall seek and *what* they may expect to find. Since the individual may verify for himself the value of the "right" way to God as established in his religious community, he may come to recognize more clearly his solidarity with and dependence upon that community. The science of the religious life as practiced, for instance, by members of the Christian church may provide principles for a practical

[5] *Ibid.*, p. 379.
[6] *Ibid.*, p. 358.

Christian discipline. Thus, experimental religious science may direct religious practice.

(2) But the dependableness of the connection between "adjustment" and "response" must not be taken to prove more than it actually does. Since both "adjustment" and "response" differ widely in different religions, we must be certain of the rightness of our adjustment before we can hope for the best response. But how are we to know what adjustment or response is "right"? To Professor Macintosh, "right" seems to mean "Christian," as is shown by his emphasis upon moral aspiration, self-surrender, trust, love and the like. For the Buddhist, however, the "right" adjustment would doubtless involve attitudes considerably different from these. Which is right about the "right"? Or are both right or partially right? The question suggests that a non-scientific assumption must underlie any science of religious experience, insofar as it claims to know the "right" or "normative" religious adjustment and response. For descriptive science knows nothing of norms. It may, of course, be held that critical study of all the historical religions demonstrates the ethical superiority of the Christian adjustment and response to all others, but such a demonstration is clearly impossible by the methods of descriptive science alone. It follows that the "laws" of theology as an "empirical science" can have no normative character. They may be scientifically certain descriptions of various sequences of adjustment and response, but they can never determine which of these sequences is the "right" one.

(3) Moreover, the attempt scientifically to establish the *divine source* of the response to man's adjustment must also fail. The subject-matter of science is the order of phenomena, and the activity of a non-phenomenal being must be inferred from its phenomenal effects. As Professor Macintosh puts it, it is a matter of "inferring what a factor is from what it does."[7] It is obvious that such an inference is

[7] *Ibid.*, p. 380.

justifiable, if at all, not on scientific but on philosophical grounds. If so, neither the reality nor the nature of the Divine Object can be proved by the science of religion, though it may suggest hypotheses concerning the Divine Object. This may be the view of Professor Macintosh himself, for he insists that the "phenomenology" of religious experience alone cannot yield knowledge of the Divine Object.

(4) He seems to hold, however, that by interpreting the results of religious "phenomenology" in terms of "critical realism" we can be certain at least of the existence of a "spiritual, value-producing" process acting upon human life. But it is very dubious whether a realistic affirmation of the direct and identifiable presence of such a process to the human subject enables us to escape the difficulties of "scientific" theology. Whatever may be said of "critical realism" as a theory of physical perception, it has dubious value when applied to religious perception. Even if God can be directly presented to the knowing subject, the knowledge of His "what" as distinguished from His "that" involves a process of conceptual interpretation. This would suggest that knowledge of God, as distinguished from experience of God, is more akin to philosophical than to perceptual knowledge. Even the knowledge that the object of the religious experience is a "spiritual, value-producing" process is interpretative, *i.e.*, it is an inference resting upon the philosophical assumption that a non-phenomenal cause must in a measure resemble its effects in human experience.

(5) This is doubtless why Professor Macintosh supplements the conclusions of "empirical theology" by "reasonable beliefs" of a philosophical nature.[8] It is not our purpose to discuss these "reasonable beliefs." But it is significant that a pragmatic argument is used in establishing the most important of them. Since "empirical theology" does not necessarily imply the personal God of theism, Professor

[8] *Ibid.*, Section on "Ontology."

Macintosh calls in moral considerations to justify that implication. "How," he asks, "can we morally surrender ourselves to an impersonal power as dependable, aiding us in the production of spiritual values? . . ."[9] We have a right to believe as we must in order to live as we ought, if we can—logically and psychologically."[10] Now, the use of this pragmatic argument for theism raises the question whether moral and religious motives may not have been present from the beginning to influence the conclusions of "empirical theology." Indeed, it is difficult to see how a purely scientific, objective approach to religious experience would be possible; or, if possible, how it could yield conclusions important for religion. How can the "right religious adjustment" be made save by one who seeks God out of a conscious need for Him? How can the "response" of God be sought save by one who is predisposed to believe that there may be a divine reality capable of responding? In short, the method of religious empiricism can yield religious conviction only to those who already possess religious faith or at least are conscious of a religious need. The volitional and emotional attitudes which constitute extraneous factors disturbing to scientific experiment are vital conditions of religious experiment.

Thus religious empiricism has great importance insofar as it emphasizes the necessity of consciously seeking religious experience if one's faith is to be made deeper and more fruitful for life. But it cannot by itself yield religious knowledge. Professor Macintosh, in supplementing his "empirical theology" with an essentially philosophical "ontology," bears witness to its inadequacy when taken alone.

Must we, therefore, conclude that religious experience is of no value in establishing religious knowledge? There

[9] *Ibid.*, p. 402.
[10] *Ibid.*, p. 405.

are those who do not hesitate to draw such an extreme conclusion. F. R. Tennant argues that *philosophical* theology
should be based upon non-religious data alone. Suspicious
of the attempt to separate theology from the "profane"
sciences by basing it upon unique data of its own, Tennant
argues that a "natural theology" starting from the data and
conclusions of the sciences can secure adequate religious
knowledge without the aid of religious experience. He
seeks to show by three closely related considerations that
religious experience cannot yield such knowledge. First,
there is "acquaintance-knowledge" of "concrete qualities
such as color only," whereas the object of religious experience is characterized, not by any such quality, but by "its
agency, which is not an object of immediate apprehension,
in causing or evolving a specific kind of valuation or subjective attitude."[11] Second, the object of religious experience is not a "quasi-impressional datum, uniquely apprehended with genuine immediacy, but rather a derived and
mediated image or conception which is interpretatively read
into perceptual or ideal objects."[12] Third, since religious
experience contains no unique elements that do not enter
into other kinds of experience, its uniqueness must be attributed to the interpretative idea of God which is introduced
into it. In short, God cannot be directly apprehended as a
simple quale. He can be known only mediately by interpretative conceptions.

Now, all of this seems to be true, as we have ourselves
implied above. It is obvious that experience of God could
never take the form of apprehension of a specific quale such
as a color, for God is not a sensible quale nor indeed a
quale of any kind. It is clear, also, that experience of God
cannot be immediate in any sense that would exclude the
influence of past experience and interpretation, for we come
to no experience with passive and empty minds. And, pri-

[11] Tennant, F. R. *Philosophy of the Sciences*, p. 171, 1932.
[12] *Ibid.*, p. 174.

marily, an experience is known to be uniquely religious, not by the presence in it of a unique psychological element, but by its reference to a religious object. But do such considerations possess the importance Tennant attributes to them? Doubtless they need to be insisted upon as against empiricists who would assimilate the knowledge of God to the immediate experience of a simple quality or object. But they do not destroy the evidential value of religious experience; they merely make it clear that we do not sense God in such experiences as a quality and that we require concepts in order to know Him.

The deeper ground of Tennant's objection to the theological use of religious experience lies, of course, in his general theory of knowledge. Direct apprehension of the actual, he holds, is limited to that which can be perceived by sense. General ideas are formed by processes of abstraction and idealization from data so apprehended. We may have knowledge of metaphysical entities such as God only by a process of interpretation, using categories which are not absolute but relative to the human mind. Since in religious experience God is not perceived by sense, such experience cannot provide data for religious knowledge. If it is objected that the restriction of data to objects of sense is sheer dogmatism, his answer is that the sciences require such a restriction. The "profane" sciences, he says, use as their primary data only the "sensorily perceptual"; and even the "sciences of valuation, such as ethics, ultimately presuppose sensory data. . . . Sense-givenness is the sole certificate of actuality."[13] From such premises he concludes that "theology must be an outgrowth from ordinary knowledge of the world and man."[14]

It is not within the province of this paper to deal with the general theory of knowledge. As will be indicated in a later section of this essay, it is my view that sense percep-

[13] *Ibid.*, pp. 167-168.
[14] *Ibid.*, p. 168.

tion is not the only method of direct apprehension, but that prophets and poets are right in believing that intuition gives us an initial, if not a complete and infallible insight into moral and spiritual reality. What we must point out here is that Tennant's view would rule out of "philosophical theology" even the "revelation" that comes to the religious genius unless it is completely "assimilable" by reason.[15] He seems to fear that the appeal to "revelation" must always lead to the setting up of religious dogmas, *e.g.*, the Trinity, once and for all "beyond reason." The only way to avoid a petrified orthodoxy and a disjunction of faith from reason is to cut natural theology forever free from religious experience and revelation. Moreover, he regards revelation as essentially a coercive inspiration or impartation of truth by God and holds that it would violate the ethical freedom and dignity of man. Man must discern truth by his own unaided efforts, if God's purpose to create real creators is not to be nullified. He seems to think that what is thus discovered must be capable of complete rational "assimilation," *i.e.*, of statement in terms of "philosophical theology." That prophetic intuition may grasp and religious imagery may express what cannot be stated fully in the conceptual language of theology he seems not to see.

Now, quite apart from the fact that this view rests upon a false conception of revelation as an external and arbitrary impartation of truth, it would lead to a great impoverishment of the religious imagination. The rich symbolism, liturgical, sacramental, and creedal, of historical religions, would tend to be sacrificed or treated as mere historical accretions. If we would avoid an evil so fatal to the life of religion, we must resolutely insist that religious knowledge, though incapable of demonstration by appeal to religious experience alone, has its roots in, and must continually be reinforced by religious experience. Religious knowledge is, in part at least, a development from religious faith, and reli-

[15] Tennant, F. R., *Philosophical Theology*, II, Ch. 8, 1930.

gious faith can be maintained only in the closest connection
with religious experience. The nature of the intuitions of
faith we shall discuss later. We shall see that, though they
may not be regarded as providing us with verified religious
knowledge, they give us intimations of a divine activity
which may be critically examined in the light of further
evidence. "Revelation" must be understood in the same way.
Psychologically considered, it is simply the process of creative intuition in the soul of the religious genius. As such, it
differs widely from the discursive reason of "philosophical
theology": it is not argumentative but declaratory. It is for
that reason dogmatic, if taken as self-warranted and self-
warranting. But it is none the less the germinal principle of
new and vital religious faith. And its insights can never be
completely stated in philosophical terms.

We must, therefore, reject Tennant's contention that
"philosophical theology" should be based upon the "sensory
data" of the "profane" sciences without the aid of distinctively religious experience and "revelation." But his insistence that theology must be philosophical, if it is not to
fall into dogmatism, is of great importance. A "philosophical" as opposed to a "dogmatic" theology must, as he argues, be developed in close connection with the natural
sciences, though it should never restrict itself to their assumptions, methods, and conclusions. Since the collapse of
the "high *a priori* way" of "speculative philosophy" in the
early years of the century, it has been clear that philosophy
must build its conceptual interpretation of the world in
such a way as to go beyond rather than minimize or contradict the sciences. This does not mean that philosophy has
no unique method of her own which distinguishes her from
the sciences. For it is no mere "totality" or "synthesis" of
scientific knowledge that is required of her, but a vision of
the ultimate significance of a whole which includes data
that defy exact scientific analysis. As Professor Whitehead
has recently pointed out, the only cure for scientific ab-

stractionism and the naïve naturalistic metaphysics that is based upon it, is to develop a conceptual system that shall adequately explain subjective aims and satisfactions as well as external events.[16] Tennant's insistence that "philosophical theology" shall be continuous with the natural sciences, that philosophical "explanation" shall be regarded as a legitimate extension of scientific "description," puts undue emphasis upon "external events" at the expense of "subjective aims," but it serves to throw into high relief the ideal of religious knowledge grounded in a natural and reasonable interpretation of genuine data. That is the significance of Tennant's contention that the theistic hypothesis, if it is to be accepted at all, should be accepted because it commends itself as the most "probable" and "reasonable," if not logically and scientifically "demonstrable" explanation of the data.[17] For religious experience and faith alone can never yield adequate knowledge of a God who has revealed Himself in the natural creation as well as in the spirit of man.

There is another aspect of Tennant's theology that must commend itself to all those who have abandoned the *a priori* method of rationalism. The "proofs" for the existence of God, he argues, are not to be regarded singly and separately, as if each constitutes an independent demonstration by itself. Rather, they are to be taken cumulatively. We are not to suppose that the cosmological proof establishes a First Cause, the teleological proof an intelligent Designer, and the moral proof a good and just Lawgiver. In fact, the cosmological argument merely leads up to the question whether the ultimate cause of the orderly and intelligible system we call nature can be anything short of an intelligent and purposive will. And as the cosmological argument serves to introduce, the moral argument completes the teleological argument. In short, the traditional arguments are simply aspects of one complex and cumulative teleo-

[16] Whitehead, A. N., *Nature and Life*, 1934.
[17] Tennant, F. R., *Philosophical Theology*, Vol. II, Ch. 3.

logical argument. The intelligibility of the natural order to human reason, the fitness of the natural environment for life, the course of organic evolution as a whole, the adaptiveness of natural beauty to our subjective faculties, and the reality of moral values in human life rooted in nature—all of these evidences seem to suggest "an intelligent Creator designing the world to be a theatre for rational life."[18]

One may object to the way in which Tennant interprets these evidences and relates them to one another. More important, one may question whether his preference of the teleological to the moral and religious arguments is justified. Norman Kemp Smith has pointed out that the chief impression of nature upon many minds is not one of beauty and adaptiveness but of indifference and cruelty; and he argues that, like the Hebrews, we are not likely to find evidence for God in the creation until we have come to believe in Him as a result of religious experience.[19] And Paul Elmer More seems to think that the hypothesis of cosmic teleology arises primarily from an intuition of purpose in the moral life of man.[20] It may be, therefore, that the teleological argument depends upon moral intuition and religious experience for its origin and for its persuasiveness. If so, Tennant's statement of it will have to be modified. But his emphasis upon the "cumulative" nature of the empirical evidences is of permanent value. If God exists at all, we must be able to find evidences of Him throughout the whole range of His creation.

We turn now to a brief consideration of *ethical* theology. It is obvious that judgments of value must play a large part in religious knowledge. Macintosh, for instance, points out that religion, since it affirms a certain relationship be-

[18] Tennant, F. R., *Philosophical Theology*, Vol. II, Ch. 4, p. 105.
[19] Smith, Norman Kemp, *Is Divine Existence Credible?*, 1931.
[20] More, Paul Elmer, *The Skeptical Approach to Religion*, 1934.

tween reality and value, takes its rise not only from "reality-feeling" but also from "value-feeling." Tennant, though he strongly opposes the exclusive reliance of theology upon judgments of value, makes use of them in his argument for cosmic teleology. Religion, if it is to be more than a mere shudder at the awful power behind phenomena or a philosophical assertion of the Absolute, must affirm God's eminent goodness and his concern for the moral life of man. For this and other reasons many religious thinkers since Kant have based their beliefs exclusively or mainly upon value arguments. Of these value arguments, A. E. Taylor affords the most interesting recent example in the first volume of his Gifford Lectures.[21]

Realizing that any argument from moral data to metaphysical conclusions must rest upon the close relation of the ideal to the actual, Taylor affirms the objective reality of value as an integral constituent of the real world. It is no mere ideal or imperative issuing from the reason of the individual, no subjective and arbitrary addendum to reality; rather, it is experienced as a quality of real existents. It can, therefore, throw at least as much light upon the nature of reality as do the physical and organic systems described by the natural sciences. Now, true goodness turns out upon analysis to be something very different from what it at first sight appears. The moral life is a temporal process whose real aim is eternal, a quest for a plurality of goods which can be fulfilled only by one supernatural Good, an earthly pilgrimage of self-perfection which must be completed in an immortal life. Since neither the temporal process nor its eternal goal should be slighted, the secret of the moral life is a proper balance between "attachment" and "detachment," "practicality" and "other-worldliness." All high moral endeavor must, therefore, be at once practical in expression and religious in spirit and aim. By itself it is incomplete and imperfect. The goods men set up as ends of

[21] Taylor, A. E., *The Faith of a Moralist*, 1930.

moral effort possess a transitory, fragmentary, incoherent character which leads a sensitive mind to the idea of an immutable, complete, harmonious Good which contains them all in perfect unity. And certain supra-temporal experiences, such as the enjoyment of a musical theme or the contemplation of a system of truths, are pledges of the reality of the Eternal Goodness. Thus, the objective moral values we discover in experience and the demand of the soul for a Good that includes these finite goods in perfection, suggest theism to the moralist.

It is to be noted at the outset that Taylor is interpreting the moral consciousness, not of ordinary good men, but of men of deep spiritual life. Indeed it might be plausibly argued that he is not describing the moral life of the good man as such but that of the good man who is also religious. In a sense, the "faith" of such a man both derives from the fact that he is a "moralist" and determines the kind of moralist he is. This is illustrated by Taylor's insistence upon the necessity of a religious motivation for morality. Rational ethics, he argues, cannot provide the strength and incentive necessary for high moral achievement; even simple courage and fidelity require resolution of will and insight into good that seem beyond the power of man. What he needs is, not a mere ideal, but an efficient cause that can illuminate his reason and give power to his will. Hence, moral effort can succeed only with the aid of Divine Grace.

Now, we would fully admit the great value to morality of a conviction that a "divine initiative" inspires and carries forward our moral efforts. But it is not true that rational moral effort without such a conviction is powerless. Mere recognition of the moral law as an imperative of reason is not the only non-religious motive of rational morality. Other motives, such as moral reverence, love of our fellows, desire for social harmony, and the hard logic of facts strongly reinforce such recognition. We are never left to our own unaided efforts in the moral life, for we are bound to our fellows by a thousand ties of sympathy and common interest. It is, of course, true that such natural and social forces cannot always be depended upon to provide adequate motivation. But this should not lead us to disparage rational morality as powerless. Indeed, if we find impotence in the moral ideals and efforts of men who are without faith, the validity of the inference from morality to theism must to that extent be called into question. If the only morality that can provide a basis for faith is one which is already shot through with faith, it is not likely that men without faith will be persuaded.

Another danger of moral theology is the ease with which moral notions can be turned to account by the Christian apologist. Consider Taylor's "ethical" defense of the orthodox doctrine of the Trinity.

The divine, infinite and eternal can only communicate to the created and finite so much of itself as the creature can receive without ceasing to be a creature. Hence, if the world of finite creatures is the only object on which the divine activity of giving can be exercised, the riches of the divine nature must remain as good as uncommunicated; in its foundations, the divine life must be egoistic. To make room for the ethical we have to think of the divine even apart from its relation to the creatures, as having a life in which there is, within the Godhead itself, an object adequate to the complete and absolute reception of an activity of giving which extends to the whole fullness of the divine nature, so that there is nothing which is not imparted and nothing which is not received.[22]

Here the Christian apologist seems to have overpowered the moralist in Taylor. It is difficult to believe that a reading of the plain facts of human love could reinforce the speculative doctrine of an eternal distinction between three Persons of the Godhead. The assumption on which Taylor's argument is based is that God can pour out the full-

[22] Taylor, A. E., *The Faith of a Moralist*, pp. 248-49, 1930.

ness of His love only upon "an object adequate to the complete and absolute reception" of it. But this assumption is questionable. It is, of course, true that man seeks a worthy object of his love and that much of his capacity for love may be unfulfilled if he fails to find such an object. But conditions which are necessary for the fulfillment of man's love may not have relevance when applied to the love of God. It is true that "the world of finite creatures" is unworthy of God's perfect and infinite love; but it is possible that He may manifest the riches of His love most fully in His dealing with it. Does not Jesus imply such a love when He speaks of the joy in heaven over a repentant sinner?

But the most serious weakness of Taylor's argument is his assumption that inferences can be made from the "ought" to the "is" without the examination of the nature of the world as a whole. Tennant's criticism of this assumption by ethical theologians in general seems to me conclusive.

We can only argue from needs and aspirations to their fulfilment when we have established, as a major premiss, that the world is reasonable or "rational" in the sense of the teleologically ordered. . . . What is initial fact or premiss is that the world is more or less rational in the sense of analytically intelligible. But such rationality does not imply that the world is so perfectly harmonious a whole that no serious error in human judgments or no frustration of the noble and more permanent human hopes is incompatible with it.[23]

Now, Taylor has made no attempt in *The Faith of a Moralist* to meet this objection to the primary assumption that underlies his inference from the many, temporary, and imperfect goods of the moral life to the existence of one, eternal, and perfect Good. It is true that at the outset he insists upon the objectivity of moral values as a ground for believing in their metaphysical significance. But it is not enough to establish moral objectivity and significance in

²³ Tennant, F. R., *Philosophical Theology,* Vol. II, pp. 94, 95.

some sense, for one might grant this and yet deny that the existence of God follows from it. It is, therefore, most important that the moral argument should be developed not in isolation but in close relation with a general theory of the nature of the world. Whether one begins with natural evidences of teleology and brings in moral evidence to supply "the coping-stone of a cumulative teleological argument," as Tennant urges, or whether one starts with a moral intuition of purpose in man and develops therefrom a teleological theory of the world as a whole, as More suggests, is not perhaps of the greatest importance. What is important is that man's moral ideals and aspirations be related to the purposive order of nature. Otherwise, the religious implications of morality are bound to appear arbitrary and discontinuous with nature and reason alike.

The positive value of ethical theology lies in its recognition of the fact that religion is in its origin and aim closely linked with the effort to realize a higher life. In its purest form, religion arises out of a human need which is perhaps more spiritual than moral. It is one of the chief merits of Taylor's book that it shows how men's deeper moral experience tends to pass over into spiritual experiences of a "supra-temporal" nature. Le Roy has given striking expression to the thesis that religion represents man's effort to rise above the "restlessness" (*inquiétude*) of his natural existence to a spiritual life.[24] Not only is man always at the mercy of natural forces which will one day claim him in death, but his knowledge is limited, his will weak and unstable, his passions at war with each other. To escape this *inquiétude*, as well as to attain joy in creative life, one must discover and yield oneself to the demands of one's deeper will. From the "profound will" alone, meaning and direction can be given to the "empirical will." But though it is the basis of

[24] Le Roy, E., *Le Probleme de Dieu*, 1929-39.

the moral demand, it is essentially spiritual in its activity. Its aim is liberation from conflict and passion. By its movement upwards and outwards, it seeks a progressive enlargement or expansion of the self. Thus, its direction is towards a goal infinitely distant but present in the "aspiration" that draws men to it.

This movement of the "profound will" towards spirituality constitutes the original ground of religious faith. For the action by which we identify ourselves with that will is also the action by which we "insert" ourselves into the creative life of the universe, which is continuous with the human spirit. Faith in God is at the outset not so much a belief as an affirmation that arises from the depths of man's soul. It is an intuitive recognition of spiritual destiny and an act of self-devotion to that destiny. Thus, it is not primarily a product of reasoning, since it involves aspiration and affirmation of life rather than mere judgment upon it. There must, of course, be a rational interpretation of the spiritual principle affirmed by faith, and it must meet the tests of critical thought. But we must never confuse our symbols of God with the hard and fast dogmas of theological rationalism. Finally, growth in religious insight is possible to the extent that man, in accordance with the truth he already perceives, responds to the advances of the divine initiative, gives himself to the ideal which solicits him, in short, enters actively into reciprocal relations with the Divine.

There are several important truths in Le Roy's view of the origin and nature of religious insight. In the first place, his analysis reminds us that vital religious faith arises normally when one has "become a problem to himself." It is only when one becomes aware of an incompleteness in his natural life, however well adjusted it may be externally and internally, that the question is likely to arise: what is the ultimate status of my life and its values? Out of the anxiety aroused by that question religious faith may be born. On the other hand, one who is kept by pride, poverty of imagination, or sensuality from facing the imperfection of his natural life is incapable of true faith. For faith springs from need for a higher life. In the second place, faith arises from an intuition of the existence of a spiritual nature struggling to realize itself in our lives. Since this spiritual nature meets with resistance from our lower nature and seeks to overcome that resistance at whatever cost, we know that it is no mere ideal of our imagination, but a creative force rising out of the depths of our nature. Moreover, since we recognize the existence in others of the same creative spirit, we are led to believe that through it we and they participate in a universal spiritual life. And in the third place, the development of these intuitions into reasoned convictions is dependent, in part, upon non-rational factors of will, feeling and action. We must not only act faithfully on the limited knowledge we possess, but we must, with absolute sincerity, open mind and heart to every intimation of truth that experience may suggest. This requires far more than an occasional rush of romantic, aesthetic, or mystical feeling; it requires a single-minded desire for the best and a willingness to strive for it at all times. This is the real significance of the view that religious knowledge is primarily a product of willing rather than thinking, a moral rather than an intellectual achievement. For though the will is not an organ of truth, the growth and refinement of religious truth are dependent from first to last upon sincere desire for and surrender to the Sovereign Good. In the same manner, feeling, whether positive or negative, is an important condition of truth. For as the anguish of *inquiétude* or guilt betokens the alienation of the soul from its spiritual destiny, so joy bears witness to the presence of God, the fulfillment of religious longing. Thus, feeling is both a sign of the partial possession of truth and a stimulus to seek further truth.

Our examination of Le Roy's theory has thus yielded important positive conclusions as to the origin of faith from spiritual aspiration and affirmation, the intuitive recognition of a spiritual principle, and the necessity of joyful and single-minded devotion of the will as a prime condition of further truth. We must stress the fact, however, that we cannot always remain at the level of faith and its intuitive affirmations. The function of intuition is to furnish insights which can be critically examined in the light of physical, biological, and other data. For instance, the spiritual principle whose reality we experience in ourselves cannot be shown through intuition alone to be present in nature as a whole. It must be established that "man is organic to nature,"[25] *i.e.*, an integral part of her life, if his spiritual aspiration and activity are to throw light upon her original source and ultimate purpose. Thus, we can rationally justify our intuition of a cosmic purpose akin to our own spiritual ideals only by means of a philosophy of nature and of man. In the same way, the intuition that Spiritual Being transcends both nature and human spirit although immanent in them must be tested philosophically. If spiritual aspiration is regarded as an exclusively natural phenomenon, it can warrant no inference to a spiritual reality outside man's mind. But spiritual experience, though conditioned by the organism in which it rises, appears to be directed towards a perfection that transcends the organism and its needs. Human spirit, natural in its conditions, may yet be transcendental in its intention. This view of spiritual experience will, of course, have to defend itself against naturalistic metaphysics and psychology. And it can do so only in terms of a philosophy of mind and its world which will show that it is as legitimate to believe in a transcendental Object of spiritual experience as in the objects of our ordinary experiences.

We have arrived at the conclusion that, while religious faith is intuitive in origin, it must be developed and sup-

[25] The phrase is Pringle-Pattison's.

ported by philosophical analysis of nature and man. Religious beliefs are beliefs concerning the Whole and its Ground. This means that they are metaphysical in nature and that complete certainty about them is unattainable. But the fact that we can never wholly verify our religious beliefs need not drive us into Kant's (theoretical) agnosticism. His mistake lay in the assumption that a "Whole-idea" must either be capable of complete verification or must be relegated to the status of a "regulative" principle. For there is another possibility, namely, that it may be progressively verified as our experience unfolds. All that need be demanded by the rational man is that his religious beliefs shall withstand the test of his limited experience of the whole.

But why, it may be asked, do religious people appear so certain of their beliefs? Why do they object when philosophers treat religious beliefs as if they were only probable? To be of any practical value, must not such beliefs be held with an intensity of feeling and a degree of conviction which is lacking in the calm regions of philosophy? Is it not academic to "entertain" or accept "provisionally" a belief of which one is not certain? And is it not downright insincere and theatrical to "stake one's life" on an "hypothesis"? Religious belief, if it is to transform life, must be something more than a speculative theory or a useful fiction.

This commonsense view of religion is nearer the truth than that of many philosophers. God is not commonly discovered at the end of a speculative process carried on in cool detachment from the moral and religious needs of men. He must be sought after with the strength of the whole self as the Sovereign Good without whom man cannot truly live. Exalted feelings, high aspirations, and fleeting intimations of harmony and holiness cannot be rejected as insignificant, however much philosophers may scorn their evidence as merely "subjective." Moreover, judgment cannot be indefinitely suspended if one is ever to gather the fruits of religion. To refuse to decide for God is in effect to decide against God, as in the moral life continuous omission to act is often as deadly as commission of many evil acts. The spirit of religion is the spirit of trust. The critical, skeptical attitude must be a necessary element in the religion of the reflective man, and at least an occasional intruder in the life of simple piety; but it cannot be the daily bread upon which religion feeds. Hence, religious belief cannot be indefinitely treated merely as a plausible hypothesis about the world. At some point it must be accepted as valid or rejected as invalid; and that fateful choice, like the moral choice between a good and an evil life, cannot be too long postponed without impoverishing the whole spiritual life. That is why religious communities emphasize the importance of commitment through initiation, conversion, or confirmation. Indeed, an initial affirmation of some kind may be an essential condition of the verification of religious belief. For though the "will to believe" can never be a logical ground for belief, the commitment to attitudes and actions required by belief may open up evidence for it that would otherwise pass unnoticed.

Thus, to say that religious beliefs resemble philosophical beliefs in that complete certainty about the Whole can never be attained is not to say that we can indefinitely take a purely theoretical attitude towards them. Indeed, it is doubtful whether philosophy itself is as critical, tentative, and purely theoretical as some of its rationalistic exponents would have us believe. A constructive philosophy must, like religion, spring from a governing intuition, verify that intuition by reflection upon experience, go beyond the evidence by a kind of faith, and yield conclusions for practical life. In any case, faith, once questioned, must be transformed into reasoned belief, or it will be lost. Honest doubts must be honestly faced by reason. It will not do to answer them by asserting a subjective feeling of certainty, when what is wanted is an objective ground of certainty. In truth, there is no need for faith to be blind. We are not required to commit ourselves at any time to a belief that is not strongly indicated by what we have seen and felt. Faith must, of course, outrun the evidence if it is to be faith at all; but it rests upon, and is continuous with the best evidence we have. Thus, it neither begins in utter blindness, nor eventuates in utter certainty. We "see" from the outset, but "in a glass darkly" to the end. The Divine can never be known by one who refuses to identify himself with what he can see of its creative purpose. But, if he commits himself to the Good, his conviction of its reality and sovereignty may become progressively deeper and more reasonable. To the end faith will have to go beyond reason. But more and more reason will be found to justify faith.

IV

CAN RELIGION BECOME EMPIRICAL?

By

JULIUS SEELYE BIXLER

Professor of Theology, Harvard University

"LET empiricism once become associated with religion," wrote William James, "as hitherto, through some strange misunderstanding, it has been associated with irreligion, and I believe that a new era of religion as well as of philosophy will be ready to begin." The era foretold by James with such expectancy has now dawned. Our religious empiricists are at work upon a philosophy of religion which, it is hoped, will be sufficiently critical to meet the objections to empiricism and sufficiently constructive to throw new light upon the religious scene. True religion, they claim, employs the empirical method both by taking experience as it comes and proceeding inductively, without passing judgments in advance as to what experience should bring forth, and also by appealing to a special kind of datum which is either itself sensuous, or else of such a sort that it can be substituted for sense as a means of contact with reality. This trend is illustrated in the thought of three recent American writers.

It begins, as do so many of the important trends of our time, with James himself. James's criticism of all rationalism and all dogmatism, and of all dependence upon other than experiential factors, made him turn in his "radical empiricism" to "experience" itself for the formal relations which "reason" or "mind" had been supposed to supply. Along with his stress on the exclusive right of experience to act as a basis for knowledge in general, James threw out a number of hints as to its bearing upon religious knowledge. In line with his idea that "knowledge of acquaintance" is the highest type of knowing activity, he invoked the notion of the "subconscious" to show how religion might avail itself of an extension of the ordinary channels of sense experience and thus find an expansion of the field of the given. Religious experience, he said, may be analogous to memory in that it effects a lowering of the threshold of consciousness such that data once sensuously perceived are made to form a sort of "fringe" of significance surrounding the usual conscious field. Developing the idea further, James described the "subconscious" as extending beyond the limits of the individual's memory and merging with a vast "cosmic reservoir" of consciousness or panpsychic continuum. Religious experience thus became an extension of the perceptual experience of the individual to include data once sensuously present, and also to include relations with further ranges of consciousness leading out into the unknown immensities of the cosmos itself. James was indecisive about the nature of the Deity to which this seemed to point. God, for him, was limited, but the limitation was perhaps that of an ideal tendency operating as one part of the vast scheme of things. Yet he was certain that the experience was authoritative for the person having it and also that its quality was perceptual. "Mystical experiences," he says, "are as direct perceptions of fact for those that have them as any sensations ever were for us. The records show that even though the five senses be in abeyance in them, they are absolutely sensational in their epistemological quality . . . that is, they are face to face presentations of what seems immediately to exist."[1]

The next important step was taken by Professor D. C. Macintosh who, through a careful analysis of the processes

[1] James, William, *The Varieties of Religious Experience*, pp. 422-3.

of ordinary knowing, showed that its factors were not unlike those to be found in religious knowledge. Professor Macintosh argued for a critical monistic realism by pointing out that in knowing we proceed through a complex of psychical experiences to perceive physical objects, and also the self and consciousness. In the case of our awareness of God we have the same "perception-in-a-complex," the only difference being that our data are not sensuous. We know a physical object or a person through a complex of attributes. In a similar way, when a man has made the "right religious adjustment" and has cultivated the right kind of receptivity, he is able, in the midst of a complex of feelings, volitions, and purposes, to apprehend the Object which we call God. When the proper tests are made the experience is seen to be as trustworthy as scientific experience itself. The one difference is that the data are not sensuous and the response on the part of the individual is a response, not of sense organs, but of volition. Religion invokes different hypotheses from those of science but none that are illegitimate. Its data are as truly verifiable as those of science, and lend themselves as naturally to the building of demonstrable laws. Theology, in other words, can be made into an empirical science. The appeal to experiences other than those of sight and sound need mean no lessening of the rigor of scientific procedure, but merely an extension of its application.[2]

A further step in the identification of religious with scientific knowing has been taken by Professor H. N. Wieman. Recognizing the danger of arguments for God which are purely conceptual and have no necessary connection with existence, and the corresponding difficulty in applying scientific methods of observation to anything else than sensuous material, Professor Wieman yet asserts that science and religion can be made compatible since religion, like science, deals with strictly sensuous data. Protesting against the emphasis on religious experience as "immediate," and

[2] Cf. esp. D. C. Macintosh, *Theology as an Empirical Science.*

claiming that experience must be interpreted before it can become knowledge at all, he maintains that interpretation is possible because the data of religion are as sensuous as those of science. It is true that it is a somewhat disorganized sense-experience to which he points us, since his illustrations are taken from experiences of bafflement and frustration. But the important part for knowledge, he insists, is the fact that while the responses are random, the stimuli are present in sensuous form. "Either God is an object of sensuous experience, or else He is purely a system of concepts and nothing more."[3] So far, then, as its problem is the knowledge problem, the task of religion is that of clarifying its notion of sensuous data and of the role which they can be expected to perform.

It is impossible not to sympathize with the motives which have prompted this attempt to bring religion and science into alignment. The conflict between the two has lasted long enough to show that we have a real dialectic on our hands. That attempts should be made to bring religion within the scientific fold is not surprising in view of the astounding success which science has to its credit. The fitness of the empirical method to meet the specific religious claim for richness and concreteness of experience is also noteworthy. Further, empiricism has made outstanding contributions to epistemology. We follow Locke in rejecting innate ideas. We follow the empirical *motif* in Kant in believing that knowledge must come through the senses. Since Kant's time we have acquired a horror of confusing validity with knowledge, consistent thought with cognition of actuality. The tests of logic we apply as checks upon given data, and not as in themselves positive revelations of the world in which we live. Yet the question remains of the possible loss to religion from too slavish an imitation of science. We do not want to throw out the religious baby

[3] Wieman, H. N., *Religious Experience and Scientific Method*, p. 28.

with the dogmatic bath. Further, we live too near in time to the first flush of enthusiasm over the victories of science to be sure that its method is universal even where ordinary knowing is concerned. Science can tell us about matters of fact, that is, about matters of sensuous perception, and to these religion can never be indifferent. But, at the same time, religion can not allow its interest to be centered exclusively in the factual world, nor can it forget that the bridge between the world of fact and that of meaning must take its form from the ideal as well as the real. Our enthusiasm for the Kant of the first *Kritik* should perhaps be tempered by the memory of Plato. Our need may be less to make religion scientific than to make science religious. While we are freeing ourselves from thralldom to rationalistic dogmatism we should not allow empiricism itself to become a dogma.

With this in mind let us return to the empirical trend just sketched and examine it more closely. We should notice first of all that the path from scientific to religious empiricism lies through James's emphasis on the interested will. Scientific empiricism, James showed, means not merely the passive acceptance of data as they appear, but an aggressive attempt to make them appear. On the basis of his interest the scientist selects certain hypotheses to submit to the test of experience. What he finds depends in a very real sense on what he is concerned to find. But this mood of attachment as contrasted with detachment is the very mood with which religion is concerned. By showing the subjective and emotional factors which enter into scientific empiricism James thus made religious empiricism, or the dependence on inner emotions, seem a less arbitrary thing. That which enters into the inner life becomes, with this treatment, as legitimate a component of experience as the external "given" itself.

But when this stress on the interested will is seen to be a connecting link between scientific and religious procedures, we should go on to observe that certain elements in the experience which he studied as a scientist are notably lacking in the experience which interested James as a religious man, so that the application of the term "empiricism" to religion contained an ambiguity of which James himself seemed hardly to be aware. Of James's work in general we may say that he took from biology and applied to epistemology the situation presented by the interplay of organism with environment. But with the change from biology and psychology to ethics and religion the significance of the figure changed. For when the organism is thought of as functioning according to biological laws, and the environment is physical, the test of adjustment is survival. But when the organism is a reflective human being, and the environment includes the world of spiritual values, adjustment means something quite different. Notice the contrast between the essay on "The Moral Philosopher and the Moral Life," and the other on "The Will to Believe." In the former, survival is a test of the rightness as well as of the competitive strength of a value.[4] In the latter James continues to talk, as a good pragmatist, about beliefs as means to practical adjustment, but the nature of beliefs, adjustment, and survival is not the same. The adjustment of the sensitive spirit to the world of spiritual values is quite different from the adjustment of the instinctively competitive organism to physical nature. And at least half the time when James talks of the demands of the practical life he means the demands of spiritual ends adopted by a critical conscience. It is hard to resist the impression that the real reason for his saying *solvitur ambulando*, and for his willingness to let ideas and values work out their truth in the long run, was his confidence in their validity from the start. He was content to apply the test of survival because he believed in advance that, in a critical world, what would survive and what should survive were the same. And the judgment seems a fair one that, in this

[4] Cf. James, William, *The Will to Believe, etc.*, p. 195.

respect, James set limits to his own empiricism. Of empiricism it has been said that it offers no negatives, but accepts
impartially all that is thrust upon it. But James, instead of
remaining passive, insisted on imposing upon the flux of
experience certain convictions of value which could not
meet his own biological tests, and which failed to reflect the
competitive struggle from which his original figure was
taken. Validity may depend upon results where the standards are those of animal life; where critical insight is concerned the case is different. In this sense James was more
nearly an apriorist with ideas to which experience must
conform, than a pragmatist waiting for the practical outcome before deciding on questions of truth. The fact is
that his spiritual insight was so keen and his hold upon the
world of values so secure, that the right seemed to him
perforce the natural and powerful, and the good not only
the desirable, but the actually desired.

Indeed, James's loyalty even to the empirical idea of a
necessary basis for knowledge in sense experience seems
open to question. It is not clear from what he says that
knowledge of acquaintance must be sensuous. One may cite
his treatment of mysticism, and also a remarkably "Platonic"
passage in the chapter on "The Reality of the Unseen."[5] In
the part which he assigned to volition, also, James was di-
recting attention away from the Kantian *a priori* of perception and toward an *a priori* of conation which, in its stress
on the transformation which data must undergo at the
hands of subjective interests, is at a far remove from sheer
empiricism. His pragmatism, with its emphasis on the active
influence of "passional" factors in knowledge, is in fact

[5] James, William, *The Varieties of Religious Experience*, pp. 54 ff.
Cf. *The Will to Believe*, p. 86, where James makes religious knowledge depend on inference from volition. It is interesting, further, to
observe that James's lecture on immortality expounded a view so
much nearer to absolute idealism than scientific empiricism, that
James was forced to write a special preface for the second edition of
the lecture explaining why he did not mean to be idealistic!

better fitted to serve as an explanation for the religion which creates than for the science which copies what it finds.

While our question with regard to James, then, casts doubt upon the thorough-going nature of his biological empiricism as well as of his sensationalistic tendencies, in the case of Professor Macintosh we would ask whether theology as an empirical science can be either a new kind of science or continuous with the older theology. The strength of Professor Macintosh's position lies, first, in the parallel he suggests between the position of the religious believer and the common sense realism of the plain man, and second, in the persuasiveness with which he defends the realistic view. Professor Macintosh maintains that the belief of the ordinary man in the non-mental, yet essentially knowable character of his world is justified, not indeed as naïve realism, but by a theory of critical realism in which it is shown that while not all that appears is real, there is sufficient identity of what is real and what is perceived to validate the claim that the object is actually known. But the very care and skill with which Professor Macintosh defends this view epistemologically leads one to question its pertinence religiously. By the success of his attack upon the older idealistic view, Professor Macintosh would seem to have freed religion from the preoccupation with epistemology characteristic of the logical analysis of idealism, and to have opened the way to a religious apologetic based on an analysis of value. Yet actually the relation to values is made less clear by the close alignment insisted on between the defense of religion and the defense of a critically realistic theory of knowledge. The stage has been set for an interpretation in terms of feeling and will, since God is a dependable Factor in our lives and Source of redemption, but the players have retreated so far into their epistemological background that their distinctive characteristics scarcely appear.

As we have noted before, the attempt to work out a

theory which will show the kind of knowledge which religion can hope to attain is itself highly desirable. We must know whether or not as religious men we can know. But is what we know in religion comparable to what we know when we know the external world? Are not the hypotheses of religion different in kind from those which either scientist or plain man must use in positing an external world? Is the bulk of the verifying testimony as clear-cut in the case of the God of religion as it is in the case of the physical world? Does not psychology make us dubious about the externality of many of the forces which influence feeling and will, and does not history with its conflicts and vagaries make us question our ability to derive an unanimous verdict from the religious tradition as it stands? The contrasts in the history of religions do not suggest an analogy with the verifiability of sense-experience. The mystics themselves claim that the experience of God is neither describable nor communicable, and further, that it is not dependable, since the "right religious adjustment" is often made without positive results. Have we in religion anything like the control which in science we can exercise upon the objects of our experiments? "It is the work of the educated man," Aristotle reminds us, "to look for precision in each class of things just so far as the nature of the subject admits." Indeed, do we find, or believe it desirable that we should find the uniformity and identity in repetition which scientific verification requires? Further, as science pays more attention to the averages of statistical probability and discovers meaning in mass conceptions, it would seem to be turning its back on the uniqueness and intimacy which are for religion its heart and life. Religion, we feel, can permit standardization no more than can art.

The question whether our experience of God is verifiable as is our sense experience brings us to the flat statement of Professor Wieman that religious experience is itself sensuous. Yet is it not true that as religion has become less primitive it has become less dependent on sensuous imagery? The fact today is that the more sensuous our religious perceptions become, the more we distrust them. What of the themes with which religion deals—guilt, purpose, courage, faith, tragedy, evil, death, mystery, absoluteness, infinity, immortality—can they by any stretch of the imagination be made objects of sensuous experience? "God being infinite," warns Leibnitz, "he can never be entirely known." Professor Wieman's own description of God as "the widest and fullest environment, past and future, possible and actual," removes him completely from sense-perception. The truth is that if the sense-content of religious experience is the same as that of other experience, presenting nothing new as sense which is to be construed as specifically religious, and on Professor Wieman's reading of the question this seems to be the case, the distinctively religious element must appear not in the sense-content as such, but in the interpretation given to it. Scientist and religious man deal with the same data, but in different ways. And an analysis of the sources of our religious knowledge will do better to inquire into the bases on which we make the special religious interpretation of ordinary sense-data, and to discover what constitutes their rightness, as well as their separateness from ordinary knowing, than to look for light on religion in our apprehension of sense-data as such. The article on "Twenty Minutes of Reality," by Margaret P. Montague, a description of an intense religious experience, frequently quoted with approval by writers on religion, stresses the point that the physical objects were the same during the experience and after, the differences lying in the significance, the feeling, the joy. The angels which Blake saw in the trees were, it is to be presumed, not angels sensuously perceived. Even if we say that knowledge of God, like all knowledge, must be derived, indirectly if not directly, from sense-data, as causation though "imperceptible" is known through our motor sensations, it is still possible to reply that knowledge of God, as the religious man has it, is not of this sort. If I infer, from evidences sensuously perceived, that God is at work in nature, I have not necessarily had a religious experience. To hold, on the basis of scientific evidence, that a power for good is seen in phenomena is not, *ipso facto*, to be religious. As James remarks: "Knowledge about life is one thing; effective occupation of a place in life, with its dynamic currents passing through your being is another."[6] To say that God is, is not necessarily to say what He is for me, and the latter is the fundamental religious question. Furthermore, it is the fundamental question for Professor Wieman, since it is his expressed wish to save the intimately irreplaceable intuition of reality which comes only with perception, and to prevent religion from degenerating into a series of abstract concepts. Dilthey saw the difficulty when he tried to define the non-sensuous basis which sciences of the spirit must have. He came to the conclusion that in the *Geisteswissenschaften* sense-perception plays only a symbolic part. Expressing it in the phraseology of the schools, we can say that religion, in so far as it is intellectual, is and must be an ontological and not a critical discipline. Indeed, one has but to appeal to the great tradition in religious philosophy to suggest that much which it contains can only with difficulty be reconciled with our new enthusiasm for the empirical method. Plato, we recall, is, to say the least, sceptical about sense-impressions, and in the *Timaeus*, representative of the more sophisticated view of the later dialogues, shows that the physical is not to be stressed in our knowledge of the divine. Eros is not sense-perception, but a principle of motion like the lure of the ideal. Spinoza compares our knowledge of God to our insight into the meaning of a mathematical relation. In the "Introduction" to the *Glaubenslehre* Schleiermacher expressly dissociates the idea of God from any "perceptible object." Emerson describes the experience of the Oversoul

[6] James, William, *The Varieties of Religious Experience,* p. 489.

in terms of the working of ideal laws in our own inner nature.

Further, the appeal to science to substantiate religion seems the more peculiar as we observe the limitations of science itself with its much heralded experimental method and the tenuousness of its hold upon its own proclaimed sense basis. It is all very well to be experimental, but what is new in our modern experimentation is not relevant to our problem, and what is relevant is not new. Sociology is one of the newest of the sciences, and its data are only very indirectly those of sense. And in the physical sciences themselves what do we find? On the one hand, a reduction to a system of pointer readings, which abstract from the supposed richness of empiricism; on the other hand, a substitution for mechanical models sensuously perceived of mathematical equations intellectually formulated. The conceptions of finite, empty, expanding, and four-dimensional space are all "structures of pure thought." The appeal to the methods of a scientific positivism is, in other words, already dated. Sense-perception, we now understand, gives us workable materials largely at the cost of over-simplification. It offers us a blotchy impression where reality is made up of many parts, a gray mass instead of the vibrations of the humming-bird's wing, a steady note in place of the discontinuities in nature. The clear and the simple and the definite no longer have the place, even in science, that was once ascribed to them. And when we step outside of science the great part played by interpretation is even more evident. *Wissenschaft* cannot be *Weltanschauung*, and the sooner we realize this, the better will be the service which each can perform.

But if *Weltanschauung* is not *Wissenschaft*, what is it? Whatever else it may be, a religious experience is a response to an essential rightness in the realm of truth, beauty, goodness, or in all three. It is an acceptance of the demand of the world of things as they should be, a sense of the presence of the absolute value. That this experience cannot be divorced from the experience of empirical fact is most obvious on all counts, but it does not follow that its own essential insights will come as does our knowledge of empirical fact. What we seek, as we strive to view the world religiously, is an awareness of that which we recognize as making an absolute and undeniable claim. We want to know "that which holds good no matter what," to feel "the eternal greatness incarnate in the passage of temporal fact," to do the thing required by the relationships which are intrinsic in the situation which we confront. The interest of our religious knowledge, in other words, is that of grasping the *Sollen* as contrasted with the *Müssen*, and of discovering our relation to those parts of reality which exert a categorical demand because they are themselves among the validities which are final. It is not the sense-experience which our behavior shares with lower forms of life, but the experience of validity in which we participate as reflective minds to which we must here turn.

An interesting feature of the present philosophical scene is the inquiry carried on by the German phenomenologists into the nature of valid relations. A brief sketch of some recent developments here will help us to see a possible alternative to empiricism. The quest of phenomenology is for "that which holds good no matter what," for the absolutes of logic, ethics, and aesthetics, for a finality which is thus of a religious type. Specifically, phenomenology is in line with religious inquiry, first, in its interest in an order of values which like logical essences are *a priori* and free from empirical conditioning; second, in its belief that values can be known otherwise than through the senses; and third in its concern with a type of absoluteness which upon examination turns out to be at least part of what religion has always meant by the absolutely holy.

The phenomenologists claim that if we are to have a science which is free from presuppositions we must leave psychology and empirical sense-experience behind us and enter the realm of pure or transcendental consciousness. This can be accomplished by what they call the phenomenological reduction, through which one deliberately eliminates all connection with the world of space and time, or with the world of sense-data as it is psychologically experienced. As phenomenologists their concern is not with what any individual sees or feels but with the natures of things as they would shine forth before a consciousness viewing them in their "essential" relationships. Harking back to Brentano's theory of the "intentional" nature of consciousness and the view that consciousness is always "of" something, and never without an object, that, for example, A and B can agree only because their ideas intend the same object and *mean* the same thing, they claim that an analysis of pure consciousness will reveal what *must* be there, and so display the essential natures or characteristics of the concepts and things with which we have to do. Corresponding to each "noësis" or subjective pole of consciousness is the "noëma" or objective pole which reveals itself as what *must be*, that which "holds good no matter what," that which would be there for angels and demons as for men, and indeed, if angelic and demonic and human and all other kinds of existences were blotted out. Certain things are thinkable; certain other things are unthinkable, not empirically, as golden mountains, but in the sense in which mountains with no elevation or four-angled triangles are unthinkable for any consciousness whatsoever. To explore this realm is to invade the world not only of logical relationships, but of that which lies back of logic itself. We should be able not merely to draw logical inferences, but to intuit immediately, without the aid of logical processes, the data which make logic what it is. When our phenomenological reduction is complete we shall see without mediation, without even putting the data into propositional form, that the manhood of Socrates must mean his mortality.

While Husserl has pressed this inquiry upon logical problems, others, like Scheler and Hartmann, have pursued the phenomenological quest into the field of values. For Scheler the problem is that of showing the freedom of values from empirical considerations without making them formal. He argues[7] that a philosophy of ethics can have no historical, psychological, or biological basis, but that all experience of good and evil presupposes a knowledge, founded on a phenomenological intuition of essences, of what good and evil are in themselves. Moral values must be *a priori* yet material. This is possible since the *a priori* is not, as Kant would have it, the formal, but rather, the intuitively perceivable as that which necessarily must be so. A proposition is *a priori* true only because the data with which it deals are *a priori* given. But these material data of ethics are apprehended, without symbolism or other mediation, as in themselves evident. Even the senses are less sure than this. We have been so largely dependent upon sense-experience, Scheler thinks, because we have asked "What can be given?" instead of the simpler question "What is given?" Even in ordinary life what is given is the experience of the thing itself, not the opaqueness of a part of it in our present perspective, nor its appearance under present conditions, nor even its sense-data. These are the results of later analysis. Only by believing that the object is itself given can we understand the meaning of thing, power, movement, similarity, and also value. Values have an *a priori* order of their own, independent of any intellectual construction or empirical observation —an order which Scheler takes great pains to analyze, and which he believes should be clear when we have sufficiently purified our insights. Loving and hating refer to an order which is as little dependent upon the specifically human realm as is logic itself.

Working along the same lines Nikolai Hartmann in his

[7] Scheler, Max, *Der Formalismus in der Ethik und die materiale Wertethik*, pp. 40 ff.

Ethics argues[8] that values are not prevented from being objective by the fact that they are *a priori*. In the spirit of Scheler he claims that we suffer from a prejudice which leads us to identify objective with sensuous. Yet geometrical relations are none the less objective by the fact that they are not derived from drawn figures but at best illustrated by them. The causal relation is objective though not sensuous. The categorical imperative hovers before the moral consciousness independently of its actualization in real life. Conscience gives us the bridge between the ideal world of values and the real world of man's emotional life, and values are the *prius* of conscience, the conditions of its possibility. We must free ourselves, Hartmann urges, from the Kantian identification of the *a priori* with the subjective. In the sphere of value we may say that our fundamental experiences of approval and of preference rest upon an intuition of that which has a claim upon us because it is prior to the experiences themselves. Values are thus absolute. Consciousness can grasp or miss them; it cannot spontaneously decree them. It is true that not all men see them clearly, but then, not all men can see at once that $a° = 1$. Insight into the nature of values may indeed change, but this is merely more evidence of the permanent quality in the values themselves, and of the need of raising ourselves to the point where we can see them as they are.

One other author with phenomenological leanings may be cited, Kurt Stavenhagen, who in a suggestive book called *Absolute Stellungnahmen* has made a critical inquiry into the nature of religion. If you make a distinction, Stavenhagen claims, between the religion of the Hottentot and that of the educated European, you do so on the basis not of empiricism, but of an *a priori* idea. Our insight into the nature of such ideas is not sensuous. That one object lies near another is sensuously perceived, but that three is greater than two is an *a priori* essence (*Wesen*) into which one

---

[8] Hartmann, Nikolai, *Ethics*, English translation, Vol. I, pp. 162 ff.

sees (*einsehen*). Further, the essence or spirit (*Geist*) of a person, situation, or object is grasped by inner perception, as when one discerns joy in the face of a friend, austerity in a landscape, or fate in a work of art. This inner perception is as little the creation of the intellect as it is sensuous. It is prior to both, a basic intuition. If we analyze the attitudes implicit in these intuitions we discover the kind of absolutistic quality which they may possess. There is, for example, an attitude of absolute love, in the sense of an attitude embracing all thinkable love. The object of this love is the absolute good. There is also absolute humility before the absolutely holy. Absolute goodness and holiness are in the realm of pure possibility. They are uncovered by immanent, phenomenological inspection, not deduced, logically, as that which can be inferred, but described directly as that which can be conceived. Following Reinach we must say that in the *ontisch* realm, the realm of pure thought, absolute attitudes, capable of no increment, are to be found correlated to absolute objects, and that religion is concerned with the fact that in our human experiences of reverence and love such attitudes and objects are implicit.

These illustrations from Stavenhagen may help us to see into the heart of our problem. The difficulty which faces all *a priori* philosophies is that of showing how the world of meanings can be anything else than relations among conceptions or intuitions and can establish a connection with the world of empirical fact. The contrasting difficulty which faces an empirical religion, as we have seen, is that of showing how it can leave the world of fact and enter the world of meanings at all. The question which we would raise is whether the ends of religion, and through them of truth as a whole, are not best served by concentrating on meanings, which are the distinctive portion of religion, and discovering such connections as they may have with the realm of fact, instead of proceeding in the other direction. Should we not, for example, begin with an analysis of the meaning of the holy, uncovering its conceptual and intuitional possibilities, and then examine the connections which such meanings make with our psychological experience, instead of starting with reactions to what uncritical men have supposed to be the holy, and passing on to discover how these experiences seem to have worked? The dilemma is a real one. If we begin and end with the world of fact we have a stable basis in knowledge for our religious experience, and the advantages here are not to be gainsaid. On the other hand, if we begin and end with fact in the sense of empirically observable and verifiable fact, we have reduced religion to the status of a science, and against this the whole religious tradition rises in protest. That religion must not contradict science is obvious. But to identify religious belief with scientific assertion is like making aesthetic experience consist wholly in the acceptance of certain truths about the nature of line and color. On this point, as on so many others, the insight of James was sure. In religion the feeling is primary, and the fact that its overtones are not completely reducible to scientific analysis is not to be taken as a denial of its validity in its own sphere.

The empiricist will of course raise the question whether we have a right to talk in this manner of a separate sphere removed from the conditions by which knowledge is bound. The answer seems to be that for purposes of method we must first isolate the realm of meanings in order to find out what they are, and then turn to the influence they may have on the world of space and time. The danger of erecting a dichotomized universe, is perhaps not so great as even the phenomenologists themselves at times imply. Stavenhagen, for example, is insistent on the fact that his analysis applies only to the *ontisch* world of conceivable objects. Yet he himself drops many hints as to the psychological effects of his analysis and its importance for life. Scheler lays so much stress on emotional experiences that it is impossible to believe that he considered them unaffected by the intuition of essences. For Scheler again, the fact that "being" is made a correlative of "knowing" leads one to suspect that the barrier between reality and thought is raised or lowered according to the pole from which one starts. Hartmann is clear on the score that we should turn to Plato rather than to Kant to find what reality is like. He protests specifically[9] against conceptualism as a misconstruction of Aristotle, and hails Hegel's notion of the essence as a return to the true doctrine. Husserl maintains[10] that while a science of essences is independent of sciences of fact, the independence is not convertible. "No fully developed science of fact," he says, "could subsist unmixed with eidetic knowledge, and in consequent independence of eidetic sciences formal or material." Heidegger goes a step further in his *Sein und Zeit* by developing what he calls his "anthropological" interest, studying man as the central figure in the problem of existence, and setting definite temporal limits to the validity as well as the working of insights attained on the phenomenological basis. In his book on Kant, Heidegger intimates that the problem with which Kant wrestled should itself be treated not as mere epistemology. Kant's problem, he claims is that of the nature and activity of man as he tries to break through the limits of human knowledge in the insistence of his drive for the absolute. Friedrich Heinemann, not himself a phenomenologist, but one who is in sympathy with the aims of the group, develops in *Neue Wege der Philosophie* his own suggestion of *Resonanz* or the response that can be made in time and space to the truths that are eternal. Indeed, we may ask whether a "pure possibility" which failed to apply to psychological experience could be even pure, and whether an analysis made by phenomenologists, who are also human beings, could be wholly free from application to psychological mechanisms without being unthinkable in a phenomenological as in every other sense. The notion of

[9] Hartmann, Nikolai, *Ethics*, English translation, Vol. I, p. 184.
[10] Husserl, E., *Ideas*, English translation, p. 63.

"evidence," however transcendentally conceived, must finally make its peace with psychological processes, even though it does not depend upon them for its status.

The world of being cannot, as Plato himself said, exist apart from life and mind "in awful unmeaningness." Nature gives us, as Plato also said, the objectification of abstract mathematical laws. Hegel bridged the gap between the two worlds by attributing empirical power to the Idea, Lotze by examining the meaning of *Geltung* or validity, and by discovering emotional suggestiveness in the ontological argument, Windelband by turning to the historical as opposed to the natural sciences, Rickert by his theory of the influence of values upon thought, Nygren by basing the claim of sense-experience itself upon the support offered by the religious *a priori*. The appeal of the transcendent good, never attained, but ever sought, is one to which psychology and history alike testify. The upward thrust of the evolutionary process and the increase in sensitivity which men have progressively shown is like the continuous turning of the sunflower to the sun. It implies both a sun to which to turn and a capacity in life to respond.[11] Even Professor Dewey, suspicious as he is of supernaturalism, has his doubts as to the emphasis which should be placed on *existence*. "The reality of ideal ends and values in their authority over us is," he says, "an undoubted fact." Justice and truth should not be encumbered with beliefs about existence "since all that Existence can add is force to establish, to punish, and to reward."[12]

The fact is that we are far from an adequate understanding of the influence which form may have upon content. Our universal judgments in logic are themselves not without bearing upon empirical truth. As Royce reminds us, to say that all A is B is to say that the real world contains no A's which are not B's. Deductive reasoning gives us more in

[11] Cf. A. Clutton-Brock, *Essays on Religion*, p. 78.
[12] Dewey, John, *A Common Faith*, p. 44.

the conclusion than is contained in the premises and may lead to the discovery of an indefinite number of new truths. The formal distinction between truth and falsity leads to special consequences in the world of facts. The form which guides our empirical wills appears also in our "metaphysical thirst for an absolute interpretation of the universe."[13] Professor Hocking lays stress also on the fact that the formal arrangement of the materials of a problem means the beginning of the solution and that the formal element of time, in spite of its seeming indifference, profoundly affects the content of events.[14] Recently Professor Boodin has called attention to the determining effect of space on physical and biological change, going so far as to suggest that space may be God.[15]

Partly under the influence of Professor Whitehead we are beginning today to understand the nature of the two interlocking worlds which we inhabit. One of these worlds is controlled by the laws of space and time, the other is under the domination of what we may call the lure of relevance. In events or occasions which are the units of reality we find a binding principle which Professor Whitehead describes as not unlike logical implication on the one hand or aesthetic compatibility on the other. God's purposes of relevance are working themselves out in so far as individual occasions achieve "subjective form," which is a kind of inner attraction and ability in turn to be attracted by the relevant. Now in this principle of relevance, which on the lowest plane is blind physical feeling, and in its higher manifestations is like logical necessity or aesthetic "rightness," we have a suggestion of the way in which the eternal principles are related to the physical and psychological im-

[13] Cf. Royce, Josiah, *The World and the Individual*, Vol. 1, p. 274. *The Problem of Christianity*, Vol. 2, p. 197. *Sources of Religious Insight*, p. 150. *William James and Other Essays*, p. 252.

[14] Hocking, W. E., *The Meaning of God in Human Experience*, pp. 197 ff.

[15] Boodin, J. E., *God, Three Interpretations of the Universe*.

pulsions of mankind. It is this Eros which expresses the lure of the ideal for mundane creatures and makes clear how "the eternal greatness" can become "incarnate in the passage of temporal fact." Just as Bacon's world must be supplemented by that of Plato, so the notion of brute force must yield ultimately, where the life of values is concerned, to that of persuasion. To use terms drawn from Euripides, Zeus must progressively be seen to be less like the compulsions of nature and more like the intelligence of mankind. The task of religion, then, becomes that of making persuasion triumph over force, by showing the control which a sensitive conscience may exercise over psychological and biological processes. The realm of essences which the phenomenologists have uncovered can become increasingly influential in human life as men discipline themselves to pay the price which is required of all who view them. If the essences exist in isolation it is because men have not understood what their own experiences of value imply. The connection will be made plain as men discover the reality in their own lives of the lure of the ideal. The atomistic logic in which much present-day phenomenology flounders will become organic as men find the necessary coherence implicit in the good life.

Religion is committed to the search for the holy as the absolute good. Empiricism can offer what men have supposed to be good. It must be supplemented if we are to find that by which degrees of good and evil are determined. The significance of the phenomenological quest for the absolute lies in its emphasis on the *a priori* with its corresponding stress on the fact that an *a priori* value need not be abstract but may be material and concrete. To the charge that a material value which is absolute may, by its own specific quality, breed intolerance in the man who holds it, the reply is that intolerance is the last thing that can result from the rigid preparation which the phenomenologists require for their intuitional approach to values, or from the careful exploration on which they insist before application is made to the world of fact. It is small wonder that we are afraid of an absolutistic philosophy when we see the havoc that has been wrought by the appeal to absolutes where data for knowledge is concerned. Science must ever be empirical in the sense that it must take its data without prejudice. But with values the case is different. Love is always good, even though men have had distorted notions of it, and cruelty is always bad, even though the nations are today preparing for it on the grand scale. That our empirical data must finally be brought into line with convictions of value, not by denying matters of fact, but by discovering the significance which values have for fact, e.g., the significance which a personal communication does not share with a rational demonstration, is the essence of religious faith. This is the kernel of truth imbedded in the paradoxes of such writers as Rudolf Otto and Karl Barth. The limitation in their case is that while Otto sees that the holy must be absolute, he yet allows it to depend upon psychological experience, so that it finally becomes obscured in the haze of mystery or pure negativity. With Barth the holy is placed so far above humanity that it can regain contact only through a miracle. Barth again loses sight of the meaning of the absolute by giving it the setting of a special historical tradition, thus making it an instrument of dogmatism. Lessing puts our criticism in the words: "Züfallige Geschichtswahrheiten können der Beweis von notwendigen Vernunftswahrheiten nie werden."

The strength of empiricism today lies in two factors: first, the cumulative testimony of the various sciences as to the genesis of mind and conscience in the natural world; second, the aptness of its theory of verification. In reply, religion can only point today, as it has in the past, to its fundamental conviction that a naturalistic view of mind means scepticism in the field of knowledge and unwarranted relativism in the field of values. With regard to the problem of verification it is clear that we lack today an adequate technique for the verification of our insights into what is good. Socrates believed that just as mathematical forms could be verified by measures of tangible things, so ethical forms would work themselves out in practice. But it is clear that our control of the processes by which we experiment with values have not reached the point where we can say that verification is possible. Yet even here we are not wholly without evidences. We cannot say that society has reached no measure of agreement as to the nature of beauty, or that honesty, courage, and love are values which make no appeal to the common conscience. As was said before, the fact that in and through the evolutionary process there has developed an ever greater sensitiveness to the lure of the transcendent ideal is our best clue to the power which values actually exert over temporal things.

Certain it is that the resort to empiricism in religion has raised at least as many problems as it has solved. The teleological proof cannot take the place of the ontological. The appeal from the brute facts of nature to a cosmic status for values is at least as difficult as the argument from the potentiality of the perfect Being to its actualization. Indeed the teleological proof is even more questionable for us than it was for Kant because of our increased scepticism about man's ability to put into practical effect the result of his growing insight into the nature of the good. Further, the only way to meet the agonizing questions raised by the experience of transiency, the fact that our values blossom but to die, is to point to the participation of our value experiences in a world which is significant because not limited by time. The problem of evil, again, becomes the more acute, the more we turn to empiricism for a solution. The problem is insoluble because it focusses attention on the control of existent things. Its answer will be found, if at all, by turning from this question, which is one of quantity, and asking what the qualitative aspect of life really implies. Finally, empiricism does not enable us to meet the issue of hedonism. But hedonism represents a philosophy of life with which religion never can compromise. Our surest insights reveal the fact that religious values can never be finally judged in terms of the pleasure they afford. Religion points us to a kingdom of ends, a realm of intrinsic worths, a world of values which bring not the peace of contentment but the sword of struggle. If we fear God because He can cast both body and soul into hell, we fear not God but a devil. Only as we feel the lure of that for the sake of which man must hazard all he hath, do we understand the symbolism of the Cross.

It is the chief glory of man that he finds himself able to respond not merely to the acquisitive, competitive demands of life, but also to the persuasive influences of reason and spirit. As he becomes not merely a creature of instinctive drives but a reflective human being with insight into the nature of things as they are, objects are for him no longer existences in time and space but bearers of an essence, a quality which illumines them with a light that never was on sea or land. When he steps outside the world of the empirically immediate and achieves a vantage-point for judgment in the world of the possible, man comes to himself. In doing so he does not escape his empirical obligations, but returns to them with a new sense of what they really mean. For the two worlds are, in human experience, ever present to each other. In the words of Riehl, the eternal values shine upon man in his progress upward as the stars accompany him in his journey across the plain.

V

VALUE-THEORY AND THEOLOGY

By

H. Richard Niebuhr

Associate Professor of Christian Ethics, Yale University

Since the time of Kant value considerations have occupied an increasingly important place in religious thought. Extremists, such as the left-wing Hegelian, Feuerbach, the left-wing Ritschlians, and modern religious humanists, have maintained that religious judgments are value-judgment. only and that the highest value, to which religion gives the name God, can be defined in terms of human wishes, desires or ideals without reference to a superhuman reality. More circumspect philosophers and theologians have admitted no such radical separation between value and being; they have maintained that value-judgments may be made the basis of religious postulates about reality, or that value and being are so inseparably connected that every religious value-judgment is at the same time an existential judgment, or—as in the case of American empiricism—they have recognized the priority of being to value, but have used value or a certain kind of value as the criterion by means of which to distinguish religious experience from non-religious, and the religious object from other objects in that experience.

In the earlier stages of this development ethical value alone entered into consideration and it continues to the present to occupy the place of primary importance in value theology. From this point of view God is defined in terms of ethical value—exclusively so by those who regard the word as only another name for the moral ideal, less exclusively so by those who believe that religion requires a reference to a reality, whether this be postulated or experienced. In the first instance, God is the good and what the good is may be stated without reference to God; in the second instance, God is the supporter and guarantor of such an independently definable good. This supporter of the good must be postulated, according to one mode of thought; he is directly experienced, according to another. In any case, what God must do in order to be God is determined by reference to ethical value.

A second phase of value-thought in religion was prepared by Schleiermacher and definitely set forth by Otto. For it religion is not dependent, directly or indirectly, upon ethics, but is an independent valuing function of men, akin in many ways to the aesthetic function. In man's religious relation to the world the value of the holy appears, as the beautiful appears in the aesthetic relation. God is the name which we give to that which has the value of the holy for us. As in the case of the ethical approach it is possible to offer various interpretations of this value-experience. It might be interpreted to mean that the abstract value, holiness, is the God of religious experience; or that whatever gives rise to the value-judgment, "This is holy," is God; or that, since we have this experience of holiness, it is necessary to postulate a reality which corresponds to the value-judgment; or that holiness is the criterion which we must employ in distinguishing religious from non-religious experience and in analysing the essential and the non-essential in the object of religious experience.

With the development in recent times of general theories of value, both ethical and religious value have yielded to the general concept in valuational theology. Such theology turns to the questions, whether the values—the old trinity of the good, the beautiful and the true, or the acknowledged human values of security, justice, harmony—in their totality and interrelation are equivalent to God, or require the postulate of a God, or offer the criteria by which the experience of God is to be distinguished from other experience.

The possibilities of choice and conflict between these various positions are illustrated by contemporary theological debate. Indeed, the shades of difference between the various types of valuational theology are much more subtle than our rough classification indicates. Yet there is one thing which all of these theories have in common: they assume that men have a knowledge of absolutely valid values which is not only independent of their knowledge of God but which is also in some way determinative of God. This is evidently true of those who equate value and God, since value is the primary term for them. It is true of those who deal with God as a necessary postulate. It is true both of those who regard value as dependent on human interest and of those who defend the transcendental status of values; for the former assume that there are no values worth considering save human values, and the latter regard values as offering us the keys to the understanding of being. It is true, finally, of those who make values the criteria by means of which the experience of divine reality is distinguished from other experience.

The last statement requires further defense and elucidation, for American empiricism—as represented particularly by Professors Macintosh and Wieman—arose in part as a protest against the dominance of value considerations in theology. Professor Macintosh regards the eclectic theology of the nineteenth century as unscientifically dogmatic, for it tends to believe that what ought to be believed, ought to be, and that what ought to be, is; it needs to be replaced by a scientific theology which will study the object of religious experience as physics studies matter and energy.[1] Professor Wieman wishes to "discuss God in terms of structure and process."[2] Yet both of these empiricists—and their divergences from each other do not now enter into the question—reintroduce the eclectic element which they wish to ban. Professor Macintosh does so by offering a double definition of religion as not only dependence on divine reality, but also as devotion to "divine" values, and by adopting as the criterion for the divine reality "eternal and absolute ideals, or values," such as "rationality, and beauty and goodness of personal life, individual and social, which we may reasonably regard as valid ends, always, everywhere, and for all persons." These ideals, he urges, are not only "qualitatively divine in the sense that they are worthy—as ideals—of our supreme and absolute reverence and devotion; it is also true that only as including them somehow could there be justly claimed for any being our absolute allegiance, worship and trust."[3] Knowledge of these values is an evident presupposition of theology. Professor Wieman proceeds somewhat differently, since his interest lies less in the analysis of religious experience. However he defines God as "that structure which sustains, promotes and constitutes supreme value" and defines value in terms of "the intelligent, self-conscious, goal-seeking activities of men," though nonhuman striving is not excluded.[4] In both instances—though less in the latter than in the former—empiricism is modified by an eclecticism and value takes precedence over being, despite the realistic interest. Empiricism—of the realistic sort—cannot be said then to have emancipated itself from

[1] Cf. Macintosh, D. C., *Theology as an Empirical Science*, pp. 13-26, New York: Macmillan Co., 1919.

[2] Cf. Wieman, H. N., "God and Value" in Macintosh, D. C. (editor), *Religious Realism*, p. 154, New York: Macmillan Co., 1931.

[3] Macintosh, D. C., "Experimental Realism in Religion," in *Religious Realism*, pp. 376, 377; cf. pp. 308 ff.

[4] *Religious Realism*, pp. 155, 156.

the value approach, though it is moving definitely in this direction.

Such a use of value considerations needs to be and is being questioned for three reasons: on account of its scientific inadequacy, its religious inaccuracy, and its philosophical dubiety. It has been recognized in the first place—most of all by the American realists—that theology cannot prosper as a science so long as it refuses to accept the disinterested method of all other sciences. A large part of the advantage of modern science over its medieval predecessors lies in its rejection of the interested attitude, for which the important question is, how any observed entity serves ultimate ends, defined in terms of man's terrestrial or eternal welfare. Empirical natural science has made much of its progress because it gave up the effort to fit "brute facts" into a prearranged rational or teleological system, and undertook, rather, to study them disinterestedly and in isolation. What was required before it could develop was not only the abandonment of a science based on a series of rationalist postulates about the world but also the elimination from observation of the interested attitude. Questions about value certainly remain in the empirical sciences, but the values which are studied are not those of the observer so much as those of the observed. The reference of value relations is sought in the entity observed and not in some external purpose or being. The value of the mosquito's sting is sought, not in a moral lesson it may convey to man, but in its function in securing the survival of the mosquito. From this point of view it may be said that the progress of modern empirical science was due in part to the substitution of a relative for an absolutist theory of value. Theology, insofar as it continues to use the value method, has remained or become medieval at this point despite its effort to adopt the method of the natural sciences. It has not inquired into the actual workings of God, irrespective of human wishes or ideals, but has defined or analysed his nature and functions in terms of a human value system. Schleiermacher is regarded by many as the founder of modern "scientific" theology, since he substituted the empirical for the rationalist and dogmatic methods. Yet his empiricism was dominated throughout by value considerations. The object of theology came to be, not God, but man's relation to God, and divine activity was explained, not as a function of the Godhead, but as a function of man's dependence on the Godhead for the purpose of maintaining his values as a person. Under Kantian influence Ritschl made explicit and developed to an extreme this tendency in Schleiermacher. What gave Ritschlianism its specific character was less the theory of value-judgments as such, and more the particular theory of value which is expressed in Ritschl's statement that what is sought in every religion "with the help of the superhuman spiritual power reverenced by man, is a solution of the contradiction in which man finds himself, as both a part of the world of nature and a spiritual personality claiming to dominate nature." In all of this theology the values of "spiritual personality" have been primary. Despite the scientific advance, then, which the empiricism of nineteenth century theology made possible in the history and psychology of religion—in which value considerations were largely banished and "brute facts" were studied disinterestedly—no similar advance was recorded in the field of systematic theology in which the interested approach prevailed.

It is frequently stated that philosophical agnosticism was responsible for this situation. Since the experience of God is always a mediated experience, only the mediators—religious feelings, Scriptures, church, tradition—can be studied as facts, while the existence of God himself remains as questionable as that of any *Ding-an-sich*. Hence systematic theology could not pursue the scientific method. Two objections may be raised to this interpretation. In the first place, the situation of religious knowledge does not differ formally in this respect from the situation of the knowledge of "nature." The latter knowledge is also mediated, and temptations to agnosticism have been quite as great as in the case of religion. Nevertheless natural science has been able to maintain its faith in the independent reality of its objects and to proceed objectively in its inquiries without turning aside to the study of the secondary qualities, or to the history and psychology of man's knowledge of natural things, and without referring the existence of its objects to the realm of postulates, or analysing the experience of objects in terms of their value for men. In the second place, it needs to be recognized that a positive influence was more effective in giving the direction indicated to empirical theology than was the negative influence of philosophical agnosticism. Science, like other human enterprises, is impelled by its beliefs rather than by its unbeliefs, by its certainties rather than by its uncertainties. In the empirical theology of Schleiermacher and Ritschl and their successors the fundamental certainty is the self-evident worth of human life or of personality. The explanation of God in terms of the human values is due less to uncertainty about God than to certainty about man.[5]

The consequences of this interested approach in theology offer evidence of its scientific inadequacy. The conflict of science and religion has, of course, other sources besides this one, yet the issue between interestedness and disinterestedness has been of great importance in it. Religion, as represented by a valuational theology, seeks to interpret the

[5] Far more radical examples of the interested method in theology than are offered by the varieties of empiricism may be found to the theological right and left—among conservatives who deal with God in terms of special providence and among humanists who find man wholly sufficient to himself. But neither of these positions can lay claim to scientific standing. The perpetuation of the interested attitude in empirical theology is selected for criticism just because this school acknowledges the necessity of scientific method in theology.

process of becoming as designed for human benefit, even when it substitutes a theory of creative evolution for that of creation in six days, and sometimes just when it does so. So it tends to substitute teleological explanation, in which mind, personality, spirituality are the final terms, for the scientific description of "brute facts." Such theology is interested in the freedom and immortality of human personality and tends to accept, reject or interpret psychological descriptions of human behavior by reference to its absolute values. Interested in the personal values, it expresses its discontent with the impersonal descriptions of natural processes or seeks to read into them ideas of a being who, as mathematician or as moralist, designs the world for intelligibility and human goodness. Conflict is inevitable under the circumstances and in the conflict theology has come off a second best, as wishful thinking must always do when it confronts objective description.

A second consequence of the valuational approach has been the loss of independence by theology. As medieval natural science became dependent on theology because of the predominance of the theological interests, so modern theology has become dependent on the prevailing systems of ethics. What has been required of theology is that it demonstrate the usefulness of religion and of God for man's search for security, justice, or the greatest happiness of the greatest number, for his endeavor to maintain his spiritual personality in conflict with nature or for his attempt to realize the transcendent values of truth, beauty and goodness. This situation seems as self-evident and logical to modern men as the analogous situation of natural science in medievalism. But the loss of independence is as disastrous in the one case as in the other. And science to be worthy of the name requires independence. As a science it can be interested only in the accuracy of its observations and descriptions, not in their value from some point of view foreign to its own. It may discern such values but it cannot make them its criteria. Hence the jealousy with which natural scientists guard the independence of their separate fields and methods is a great asset in the pursuit of knowledge, despite some disadvantages it brings with it. A theology which borrows its first principles from sociology, psychology or ethics has become a part of one of these sciences, and, since it has no independent point of view or object, the results of its researches have been determined from the start. It is vain to expect any new knowledge from such a science.

A third consequence of the value approach is closely related to the second. The law that the seeking of life leads to its loss has application in science as well as in morality. An interested natural science yielded few results of benefit to man; a science which does not concern itself with the "practical" bearings of its findings has been found to be highly beneficial to men and capable of wide application. It is not otherwise with theology. A theological science which is interested above all in serving the needs of men becomes a bad science incapable of supplying real benefits; but one which deals disinterestedly with its material may be of very great benefit indeed, as history indicates. For disinterested theology has been pursued at various times in the past, notably by the Hebrew prophets.

Value-theology is subject to criticism not only on account of its scientific but also on account of its religious unsatisfactoriness. "Unsatisfactoriness" is a value term and the criticism of value-theology as religiously unsatisfactory may seem to be itself a case of value-theology. This may be true in a sense, for, as we shall seek to point out later, there is no possibility of excluding value philosophy completely from theology. But the point at issue is whether man has knowledge of a system of values of absolute validity which he may make the basis of his religious judgments or employ as a criterion in the analysis of religious experience.

Now religion itself makes the same demand for disinterestedness in the observation and description of divine activity or reality that natural science makes in the case of its
objects. In neither case is this disinterestedness an uninter-
estedness. On the contrary, disinterestedness is possible in
science, as in religion, only when the object excites interest
for its own sake and not for the sake of any end external
to it. Religion demands that God be loved for his own sake
rather than for the sake of any value, high or low, material
or spiritual, which he is conceived to conserve, promote or
increase. That such values will be *added* to those who love
God for his own sake, is a belief, the validity of which experience may demonstrate. Nevertheless the original demand
remains in force. A theology which begins with values that
are logically prior to God or that are of greater value than
God, so that what is and what is not God may be determined by reference to them, makes him a means to an end
and confounds worship. It is unsatisfactory religiously,
therefore, for the same reasons that it is unsatisfactory scientifically; both religion and science must reject valuations
prescribed to them prior to their own valuations.

Along with the confusion of worship which takes place
in religion in consequence of the valuational approach, confusion in the description of God and in religious ethics en-
sues. Those elements in the Divine Being which appear
to be particularly relevant to the determining interests of
men are given a prominence which does not belong to them
from the disinterested point of view. Spirituality, personality, and moral goodness—in conformity with the particular
type of moral goodness which is prized at the time—are
regarded not as more or less pertinent categories which may
be employed in the effort to describe divine activity, but as
essential elements in the Godhead. Universality, power,
unity are described as of secondary importance. In consequence this theology faces increasing difficulties in explaining much of the divine behavior and needs to exclude a great

deal in human experience as irrelevant to the knowledge of God. A faith which finds in God the source and center of all value, which values personal existence only because it makes the enjoyment of God possible, and hopes for immortality only because it hopes for the vision of God, which founds its morality upon the sole value of God and the sacredness of his creatures because they are his creatures—such a faith must remain dissatisfied with an approach which, however disguisedly, makes him a means to an end, however noble the end in human esteem.

The religious unsatisfactoriness of the value-theology has been ascribed at times to the tendency toward religious Narcissism which is manifest among some schools of this group. This tendency is not a logical result of the value approach, but a close connection obtains nevertheless. For when religion is approached from the standpoint of values regarded as absolute apart from and prior to faith, the value-maintaining and promoting character of religion may become quite as important as the value-supporting character of the religious object. Furthermore, the by-products of religion, such as the feeling of awe or the sense of the holy, may come to be regarded as values, valuable for their own sake when the culture of the spiritual life becomes the highest task of man. But religion like morality is not interested in the values which it may have from the point of view of a spectator or a judge. It is directed away from the self toward a value or values. To direct its attention to itself is to pervert it. Moralism, the appreciation of the "moral values" or virtues and their pursuit for their own sakes, is inimical to morality which is not interested in virtue but in the values toward which virtue is directed. Moralism loves the love of neighbor, but morality loves the neighbor; moralism loves the love of truth, but morality loves the truth; moralism loves courage, but morality is courageous, preferring home, country or cause to physical life or ease; moralism loves the good will, but the good will loves the good. Similarly aestheticism loves the love of beauty, or the emotions which the beautiful inspires, but art loves beauty. So also what, by analogy, we may call religionism loves the love of God, whereas religion loves God. Religionism prizes religion either as an intrinsically valuable thing or because it promotes the values of the ethical, political or economic life; religion, however, subordinates itself and all these other values to God. Doubtless there is room in morality, art and religion for the love of "complacency"—to use Jonathan Edwards's term for the love of virtue—but it needs to be subordinated always to the primary value. To the extent that the value approach to religion has encouraged religionism it is religiously unsatisfactory.

Finally, the unsatisfactoriness of value-theology from the religious point of view is due to its tendency to neglect the principle of individuality in religion. It is the heir of that rationalism which sought to go back of the historical, individual faiths to a general, rational religion equally available to all men. As in the case of the previously discussed religious deficiency of value-theology, this present charge does not apply equally to all of its schools. It is less true of Ritschlianism than it is of American realism, and less true of the latter than it is of the idealistic interpretations. Nevertheless, to begin with universally valid and absolute values, discovered apart from religious faith, and to make these in any way decisive for faith is to seek the essence of the religions in the common criterion of all religions, and to make devotion to these values more fundamental than the worship of the individual beings with which the historic faiths are concerned. But religion, in spite of rationalism and such "axiologism," remains stubbornly individual. Judaism, Christianity, Islam, Buddhism not only claim individuality for themselves as historical events but demand that the individuality of their gods be recognized. For these religions, with the possible exception of Buddhism, are directed toward the particular God who revealed himself in an individual event or in particular events. Universal validity is claimed for these revelations not because of their correspondence to some system of valid values previously discovered by men, but because they are revelations of the universal power and reality to which man and his values are required to conform. The value-theologies tend to make the revelations incidental or unnecessary and to reduce the individual religions with their individual founders to the status of examples.

The philosophical inadequacy of value-theology appears in the first place in the dogmatism of many of the value theories upon which theologies are built. A theology which seeks to evade the dogmas of religion by founding itself upon ethics does not evade dogmatism, since every ethics rests at last upon a dogmatic basis. Kant's analysis of the moral judgment is one thing, but the assertion that there is nothing good save a good will is another. It is a dogma which claims simple acceptance and assumes universal recognition. The hedonist cannot go back of the self-evident goodness of pleasure; he asserts and can defend only by reassertion. The self-evident supreme value of personality is the confessed or disguised dogma of a host of theories, and again it is a first principle about which there can be no argument in the minds of its devotees. Those who exalt the supreme worth of the "transcendent" values of the spiritual life—truth and goodness and beauty—make their last appeal to the judgment of all right-thinking men, but who the right-thinking men are can only be determined by reference to the standard of rightness, that is, to the scale of values in which spiritual values are supreme.

Now it is quite true that dogma is unavoidable. Beginnings must be made and they can only be made in dogma. But the presence of dogma in ethics points to the fact that it cannot furnish a basis for religion since it is itself founded upon a religious faith. For whatever may be true of the dogmas of metaphysics, the dogmas of ethics are religious. They are assertions of faith, confessions of trust in something which makes life worth living, commitments of the self to a god. To found religion on such a basis or to criticize it by means of such a system of ethics is to found one religion upon another, or to argue in a circle, or to criticize one religion by means of another. It is not to found religion upon a wholly rational, undogmatic foundation or to criticize it by means of an impartial principle.

The philosophical inadequacy of value-theology is due, in the second place, to its failure to take the principle of value relativity seriously. This principle does not mean that values must be regarded as relative to desire or to consciousness, that there is nothing good or ill but thinking makes it so. It is generally recognized that objectivity of a sort must be provided for in any value theory, that the "ought-to-be-ness" of justice, truth and peace does not depend upon the fact that men happen to desire them. But it does not follow that values are independent on structure and process. Such independence can be maintained only by means of a vitiating abstractionism and the denial of the relative standpoint of the observer. There can be no doubt of the absolute claim which truth and justice have upon man, but to abstract them from his nature and to call them valid apart from any being for whom they are valid, to say that *they* ought to be, rather than that *man* ought to be truthful and just, is to abandon the realm of experience and to enter into doubtful regions of metaphysical abstraction. There is, however, another and more serious way of refusing to take the principle of relativity seriously in the field of value thinking. It consists of the exaltation of values recognized as relative to human structure into the final values of reality, in the assumption of the human standpoint as the last standpoint which man needs to recognize, or, at least, as the standpoint whence the values of universe become visible as an integrated system. Not many theologians have followed the idealist philosophers in maintaining the absolute, wholly independent and self-sufficient character of values, abstracted from the mind and nature of man. Ritschlianism recognized that the values with which it was concerned were relative to the spiritual life of man. The American realists, who employ the value criterion in the analysis of the experience of God, have committed themselves to the relativist position. Professor Macintosh speaks of the "obvious relativity of values" and defines value as "a quality which anything has by virtue of its relation to an end-directed process, that is, a process regarded as working toward an end, whether the end be consciously contemplated in the process, or not."[6] Professor Wieman adopts, with some modification, Professor Perry's analysis of value, which recognizes the relativity of value not to desire but to interest.[7] He concedes, furthermore, that value is not merely human "although it is always relative to humans"; it is a "characteristic pertaining to all the universe and to metaphysical reality."[8] Furthermore, Professor Wieman defines God as that structure which not only promotes and maintains but which constitutes value, and acknowledges that human interests are never final but need to be taken up into an over-arching and all-inclusive system. Nevertheless, human values remain the starting point of the system; it is required that these values be integrated in the system; and "God is that in the universe which will yield maximum security and increase of human good."[9] Professor Macintosh states the absoluteness of values relative to persons more definitely:

"The question whether, in view of the obvious relativity of values, there are any which may reasonably be believed to be absolute in the sense that they are universally and per-

[6] *Religious Realism,* pp. 308, 309.
[7] Wieman, H. N., *The Wrestle of Religion with Truth,* pp. 160 ff, New York: Macmillan Co., 1927.
[8] *Wrestle of Religion,* pp. 161, 163.
[9] *Ibid.,* p. 59; cf. *Religious Realism,* pp. 156, 161 ff.

manently valid for persons (whether recognized as universal and final or not), is ultimately the question as to whether there are any *processes* the value of which ought to be (or can reasonably be) recognized and appreciated as having positive worth, always, everywhere, and for all."[10]

And it is just these values, absolute for persons, which are made the criteria of the divine.[11] In the case of neither of these methods does it seem to us that the principle of value relativity is taken seriously enough, though evidently it is taken much more seriously than it is by those who simply postulate God. To make the values which are acknowledgedly relative to personality criteria of the divine is either to assume that the divine must be personal or to regard personality as the one wholly worshipful reality and God as a means to personal ends. To proceed from the values of persons to an integrated system of values, which overarches and includes them, is to assume a harmony of values similar to that one which liberalism assumed in the case of individuals and society. The confidence that such a harmony exists as a hidden reality and that, eventually, it will be made actual or apparent belongs to the essence of religious faith; that it is now so actual and apparent that one can begin with the values of the individual and proceed to declare the values of society identical with them, or with the values of the human person and proceed to the values of God is more than dubious. The ideal of all liberal philosophers and theologians, as well as of the Thomists, has been the definition of a unified system of reality and value in which thought proceeded from the lower to the higher, from the individual to the social and from the social to the universal. Gaps and conflicts may indeed be recognized but they are of secondary importance; they indicate how a system of values relative to a lower or less inclusive stage of reality needs to be corrected. But the assumption remains that the system rela-

[10] *Religious Realism*, p. 309 f.
[11] *Ibid.*, p. 375 ff.

tive to the lower, and defined from the point of view of the lower reality, offers the key to the definition of the higher. This assumption seems to us to be unwarranted in view not only of the relativity but also of the conflict and tragedy of values.

Dewitt Parker has been almost alone among value theorists in giving adequate attention to this conflict and tragedy. Yet it is an obvious fact to which daily experience bears witness. Only in occasional instances are the values relative to animal life included in the system of human values. The liberal faith that the values of the individual could be integrated into a system of social values has needed to give way to an inverted approach from the values of the society to the values of the individual. For in the former case the values relative to nations and groups were denied despite the faith; and it is evident today that when the beginning is made with values relative to the societies, the values of the individual, as conceived from the individual's point of view, must be sacrificed. The individual who now says, "I was born to die for Germany" or for Italy, or for Japan, or for the Communist Society, may indeed discover that his values are included in the values of society, but the included values are not the same as those which he defined when he made his beginning with himself and sought to proceed from the values relative to personality to the values relative to society. The social values require the sacrifice of the values of isolated personality and vice versa. If, then, within the system of personal and social life, and within the system of human and animal relations it is impossible to proceed from one set of relative values to another, or to use the interests of one type of being as criteria for the determination of the interests of another type, similar procedures in the case of human and divine values would appear to be even more precarious. It is not only possible but highly probable that human ideas of justice and goodness, as well as justice and goodness themselves as relative to isolated humanity, are out of line, so to speak, with divine ideas of goodness and justice, or with the goodness and justice relative to the divine nature, so that conflict and tragedy rather than progressive integration are to be looked for. The relativism which obtains within the field of values allows, at best, the development of an analogical argument; but the more the fallibility of human value-judgments about human values, the relativity and the conflict of values with consequent tragedy are recognized, the less will such an argument be regarded as offering certain assurance; the more it will be realized that it leads only to rather dubious probabilities.

The objections which must be raised on scientific, religious and philosophical grounds against value-theology indicate the fallacies in its approach. Realistic empirical theology, as represented in Macintosh and Wieman, has recognized these objections. In its endeavor to adopt the disinterested method of the natural sciences, in its recognition of the requirements of religion, and in its acknowledgement of the relativity of values it has taken important steps toward the development of an adequate theological method. Yet each of these steps remains incomplete, since values gained from non-religious experience are employed as the absolute criteria of theology. The completion of the steps requires the complete abandonment of an approach from values known as absolute prior to the experience of God. Only if this approach is abandoned can theology become truly disinterested, just to the requirements of religious experience, and philosophically consistent.

Because it is unsatisfactory to develop theology on the basis of value-presuppositions gained prior to religious experience, it does not follow that value-theory has no place in theological science. On the contrary, the new tendencies which have arisen in reaction to value-theology appear to be incomplete and unsatisfactory, partly, and perhaps largely, because they leave value-theory wholly out of consideration. Instead of recognizing their relation to Ritschlianism and value-theology in general, they deny that such a relation exists and seek to return to a type of thought which prevailed in early Protestantism. They make revelation their starting point, but by dealing with it as though it were a bolt out of the blue and by refusing to relate it to the value cognitions of men, they fail to give an understanding of the process whereby revelation is received. They insist upon the uniqueness of revelation, particularly upon the revelation of God in Jesus Christ, but by setting the unique revelation completely apart from other faiths, they fail to show the relation of various faiths to each other and to describe intelligibly how one faith supplants another. They make ethics dependent on faith, but, failing to make use of the principle of value, they tend to substitute the commandment for the love of God, and so run again into the danger of legalism and formalism. In each of these positions there is a large element of truth, not only in what is asserted, but also in what is rejected. What is asserted is the absolute priority of God, and what is rejected is the assumption that prior to God, or to God's revelation of himself, or man's experience of faith in him, the mind is in possession of a valid standard by means of which it can judge God and his revelation. The assertion and denial are true to religious experience, but assertion and denial are not enough in theology. The theologian is required to show where and how such denials and assertions have been made possible, and how they compare with the assertions and denials of other faiths. For this purpose a theory of religion, of revelation and of religious ethics are necessary and such theories—today at all events—cannot be set forth without reference to valuation and values.

It is possible and necessary to interpret religion as an affair of *valuation* without assuming that such valuation must or can be made on the basis of a previously established standard of values. The enduring contribution of empirical theology, from Schleiermacher to Macintosh, lies in its insistence on the fact that knowledge of God is available only in religious relation to him. In emphasizing this point, modern theology has not only made explicit an interest which was implicit in the Reformation doctrine of salvation by faith alone, but has developed it in a new and important direction. For while the Reformation contended against the fallacy of salvation by works, the new development was a reaction against the fallacies of salvation by belief, as in traditionalism, and of salvation by reason, as in rationalism. Religious knowledge has been shown to be unique, and this uniqueness has been shown to be due to the fact that it is a type of value-knowledge or valuation—as, indeed, all knowledge probably is. The knowledge of God, it has been pointed out, is not equivalent to the knowledge of doctrine or of a First Cause or a Designer. And its dissimilarity to theological or metaphysical knowledge is due not only to its immediacy—which may be questioned—but to its character as knowledge of a being having value of a certain sort. Empirical theology has seen that religion is an affair of valuation, analogous to morality and art. For as an action or a character may be known by the psychologist or historian without recognition of its goodness, or as a picture may be known by a chemist or a physicist without knowledge of its beauty, so the being which religion knows to be God may be known by philosophy, history or natural science without knowledge of its deity. And as the former cases can not be described as knowledge of the good or the beautiful, nor regarded as steps toward that knowledge, so in the latter instance there is no knowledge of God.

But it is in seeking to describe the value which God has for faith, or rather which he discloses to faith, that modern theology has encountered the difficulties described above. For in attempting to describe what kind of value God has as God, it has either identified deity with a quality, an ideal or an abstract value, or it has made religious valuation dependent on the subject, so that deity is ascribed to a being not on account of its intrinsic nature but on account of the attitude of the subject to the object, or—in the third place— it has taken its value criterion from an anthropocentric ethics and analyzed the experience of God in terms of non-religious value.

A more adequate value-theory would, I believe, be able to avoid these difficulties and fallacies. Such a value-theory would recognize, first of all, the relativity of values without prejudice to their objectivity. The interpretation of values as relative to structure and organic needs, rather than to desire and consciousness, provides for such an objective relativism. The value of deity would appear, on the basis of such a theory, to be quite independent of human desire and the consciousness of need, but not independent of the human constitution and its actual need. The situation may be stated positively in the terms of Augustine, that God has created us toward himself and that our souls are restless until they find rest in him. It may be stated negatively by saying that, while the Being men call God exists independently of the creatures constituted to need him, it is not possible to define his Deity without reference to his relation to his creatures.

Furthermore objective relativism in value-theory recognizes that value can be abstracted from the object as little as from the subject. Value has no existence save in valued beings, and they possess value not as an independent quality but by virtue of their character or constitution, as that which corresponds to a need. Truth exists only in true judgments and what is valued in a judgment is not truth as a special quality but the characters by virtue of which it is true. No devotee of truth seeks truth as such, but rather accuracy, consistency and consiliency. The abstract idea of beauty is neither beautiful nor real. It cannot be made incarnate by paying attention to it; attention must rather be given to those characters by virtue of which a work of art becomes, or is recognized as, beautiful. In the moral sphere the same situation prevails. An act or a person is valued as good not because it or he possesses goodness as such, but because loyalty to a standard and a system of preferences corresponding to actual needs are discovered. It is so in the case of deity. The idea of deity does not have the value of deity; it is no more worshipped than the idea of the beautiful is aesthetically valued or the idea of goodness morally preferred. Moreover, a being is found to have the value of deity not as a separate quality but by virtue of those characteristics which enable it to fulfill the need for deity. Hence the important question for religion is not the question, whether a god exists, but rather, what being or beings have the value of deity, just as the important problem of ethics is never whether there is such a thing as goodness but rather what action or character or society is good. The question about value as a question of the valuing mind or of the needful organism is always a question about being having value. To be sure, when all known beings fail to satisfy the needs of men, imagination may picture some being which will have the value of beauty, of goodness or of deity and which will become known or real in the future. Even so it is a being which is sought, not value as such, and the more disciplined imagination is, the less Utopian it will be, the more it will look for the valuable being in present reality with its potential value. The question about the existence or non-existence of the gods is a false question. The true query of religion is, "Which among the available realities has the value of deity or has the potency of deity?" And this question turns into the other query, "Which reality has those characteristics which are the foundation of the value of deity, or which fulfill the human need for God?"

Man's need for God cannot be described in terms of his feelings when he experiences the satisfaction of the need. It is not the need for an object corresponding to his feeling of dependence or his sense of the numinous. It would be quite as satisfactory to describe food in terms of feelings of repletion or of gustatory pleasure. Nor can it be described as the need for that which will conserve men's highest values, since in that case the uniqueness of the religious value-experience is sacrificed and its fundamental character forgotten. The religious need is the need for that which makes life worth living, which bestows meaning on life by revealing itself as the final source of life's being and value. The religious need is satisfied only in so far as man is able to recognize himself as valued by something beyond himself. That has the value of deity for man which values him. The valuation of which man becomes aware in religious experience is not first of all his evaluation of a being, but that being's evaluation of him. The latter evaluation does not need to be positive; on the contrary, in his experience of deity man frequently becomes aware of his disvalue, but he does not become aware of his unvalue. Religious experience includes an evaluation on the part of man, but primarily it expresses itself in the judgment, "This is the being which values me or judges me, by relation to which I have worth or possibility of worth," while reflexively it issues in the judgment, "This is the being of supreme intrinsic value, which corresponds to all my deepest needs."

Such a value-experience is primitive and original. It deals with that absolute source of all value by relation to which all other things have their value. To analyze this experience by reference to values known and regarded as absolute prior to the experience is to lose sight of this fundamental character and so to falsify it to an extent. That the experience of the supremely worthful being by reference to which all other things have their value should lead to ethical results by increasing man's devotion to his best interests is true. But what the best interests are cannot be decided prior to the experience of that which is the source of all value. The experience of the ground and source of all value leads to the criticism and reconstruction of the ethical system rather than to the support of one which has been accepted as absolute prior to the experience. In this case as in others the statement that all other things shall be added to those who seek first the kingdom of God is profoundly true.

The task of theology from this point of view lies then in the analysis of those characteristics by virtue of which a being has the value of deity for man, the examination of reasons for the failure of religions which attach themselves to beings which do not possess these characteristics adequately, and the description of the ultimate being, which as the supremely real and the source of all other being, is alone able by virtue of its character to satisfy the human need for God. No attempt can be made within the limits of this paper to develop even in outline the application of religious value-theory to these problems of theology nor to the further problems of revelation and religious ethics. It can only be suggested that there is at least a remote analogy to the unique fact of revelation in the "givenness" of all beings having intrinsic value and that the necessity of revelation is due to the fundamental character of the need and value with which religion is concerned. Furthermore, it will appear, I believe, that the content of revelation is not the self-disclosure of an unknown being, but the unveiling of the value of a known being. What is revealed in revelation is not a being as such, but rather its deity-value, not that it is, but that it "loves us," "judges us," that it makes life worth living.

The approach to theology through a value-theory of the type suggested will, I believe, overcome the difficulties which have beset modern empiricism and will carry forward the interests of American religious realism.

VI

THE TRUTH IN MYTHS

By

Reinhold Niebuhr

Professor of Applied Christianity, Union Theological Seminary

---

In the lexicon of the average modern, particularly in America, a myth is a piece of fiction, usually inherited from the childhood of the race. The scientific outlook of our mature culture has supposedly invalidated the truth value of these primitive stories in which gods and devils, nymphs and satyrs, fairies and witches are portrayed in actions and attitudes which partly transcend and partly conform to human limitations. They are regarded as the opulent fruits of an infantile imagination which are bound to wither under the sober discipline of a developed intelligence. Science has displaced mythology. A careful observation of the detailed phenomena of life and history yields more credible explanations of life's mysteries than these fanciful accounts of the origin of life or the genesis of evil or these fantastic pictures of the universe. When we have the conception of evolution we do not need the story of creation, and when we see man's slow ascent toward the ideal we have no place for a mythical "fall" to account for the origin of evil in the world. The reign of law revealed by science invalidates the miracles which abound in all religions; and the insight into, and power over, his own future given to the modern man through his intelligence frees him of the need to seek salvation in the myths of religion. Such are the convictions which belong to the unquestioned certainties of the modern man.

Since mythical elements are irrevocably enshrined in the canons of all religions it has become the fashion of modern religion to defend itself against the criticisms of science by laborious reinterpretations of its central affirmations with the purpose of sloughing off the mythical elements, apologizing for them as inevitable concepts of infantile cultures, and extracting the perennially valid truths from these husks of the past. Unfortunately the protagonists of modern religion usually fail to placate the devotees of the scientific method by these diligent but not too dignified labors. They are met by the contemptuous suggestion that they have been merely insinuating new meanings into ancient phrases, and that they have gained nothing for their pains but what might have been secured more simply by a scientific analysis of the known facts of life and existence. If science has the final word and authority about life, as many of those theologians who have been most anxious to adjust religion to the scientific world-view have assumed, this suggestion is plausible enough. Indeed some of the supposedly abiding truths which have been distilled from ancient myths by this process of reinterpretation have lost their religious essence so completely, have been flattened and deflated to such a degree in the process of adaptation, that the charge of the empiricists and naturalists seems perfectly justified.

The modern protagonists of religion made the mistake of retreating too far and too quickly when the exigencies of the cultural situation demanded a retreat. Their error was to disavow permanent myth with primitive myth. Religion had no right to insist on the scientific accuracy of its mythical heritage. From this position a retreat was necessary. That part of mythology which is derived from pre-scientific thought, which does not understand the causal relations in the natural and historical world, must naturally be sacrificed in a scientific age. But there is a permanent as well as a primitive myth in every great mythical heritage. This deals with aspects of reality which are supra-scientific rather than pre-scientific. Modernistic religion has been so thin on the whole because it did not understand this distinction and thus sacrificed what is abiding with what is primitive in religious myth.

What are the aspects of reality which can be stated only in mythical terms?

The most obvious aspect of reality which can not be comprehended in terms of scientific concepts is the aspect of value. It is true that the value of things for a particular individual can always be stated in terms of aesthetic myths. The aesthetic myth (such as "Hail to thee, blithe Spirit! Bird thou never wert," in Shelley's ode "To a Skylark") makes no claim about the ultimate value of a thing in a total scheme of purpose. It merely asserts value in terms of the moods and purposes of an individual in a given instance. The purely aesthetic and non-religious myth is therefore sceptical about values in the ultimate sense. "Poetry," declares Santayana, "is religion which is no longer believed." The aesthetic myth becomes transmuted into a religious myth when it seeks to comprehend facts and occurrences in terms of their organic relation to the whole conceived in teleological terms. For only if things are related to each other organically in a total meaningful existence can it be claimed that they have value. Religion, to transpose Santayana's phrase, is poetry which is believed. Religion seeks mythically to grasp life in its unity and wholeness. This unity and wholeness can never be expressed in terms of complete rationality; for reason only observes and deduces. What it observes is concrete reality in its multifarious forms. Its deductions are based upon the sequences which it observes in nature and history. But these sequences reveal nothing of the internal unity in all organic growth. For this reason scientific descriptions of reality always tend to a mechanistic interpretation of it. The facts of organic growth can be comprehended and described only by mythically transferring the inner unity of the human consciousness (where unity is directly experienced and apprehended) to the external world. A certain amount of primitive myth is always involved in this process (its analogy to animism of primitive mythology is apparent). But it is also permanent myth in the sense that it is permanently valid, since reality is actually organic and not mechanical in its processes.

A full analysis of the organic aspect of life reveals another quality of existence which can not be comprehended in terms of rationality and which might be defined as the dimension of depth in existence. If the relatedness of things to each other is more than mechanical, the source of their unity lies beyond, behind and above the observable phenomena. "The world of things as they are," to quote Professor William P. Montague, "is not self-explanatory; it bears the earmarks, if not of a manufactured product, at least of a thing which has been derived from something other than itself." Not only the secret of its unity but of its growth (the emergence of novelty) lies beyond itself. Sciences may carefully observe certain processes of life and history and describe how or under what concatenation of circumstances certain forms, biological or social, were transmuted into other forms. But it can only describe these processes after the fact, and it is forced to treat each new emergent as following necessarily from the forces which immediately preceded it. It is, therefore, constantly tempted to commit the logical fallacy of *post hoc; ergo propter hoc*. It is, in short, compelled to deny the idea of creation.

The idea of creation is a typical mythical idea. It relates the source of life to observable life in terms which defy rationality. The primitive myth speaks of God making man out of clay, and breathing the breath of life into him. But the idea of creation remains mythical even when the primitive myth is discarded. If the myth is completely rationalized the creator becomes the first cause. Inasfar as he is merely a cause, among many causes, creation is denied and every new fact in history is explained in terms of previous facts. Inasfar as he is a uniquely first cause the limits of logic in dealing with the problem of causation in history are recognized but the recognition is left in negative form. Thus when religion refuses to yield the idea of creation to the idea of evolution it is following an instinct for the truth. When, as has been frequently the case in modern religion, it apologetically declares that nothing but a difference in terminology is involved ("Some call it evolution and others call it God") it is erroneously yielding to the prejudices of a scientific age.

The myth of creation not only expresses dynamic and organic qualities in reality which can not be stated in rational terms, but paradoxical qualities which elude the canons of logic. The dimension of depth in life contains such a paradox. All life and existence in its concrete forms suggests not only sources but possibilities beyond itself. These possibilities must be implied in the source or they would not be true possibilities. God is in other words both the ultimate ground of reality and its ultimate goal. "Religion," to quote Professor Montague in a revealing phrase, ". . . is the acceptance of the momentous possibility—that what is highest in spirit is also deepest in nature, that the ideal and the real are at least to some extent identified, not merely evanescently in our own lives but in the universe itself."[1] The myth of creation, in which God is neither identified with the historical world nor separated from it, offers the basis upon which all theologies are built in which God is conceived as both the ground and the ultimate fulfillment of a meaningful world, as both the creator and the judge of historical existence. This paradox is really the only ground of an effective ethic because it alone harmonizes ethical and metaphysical interests and gives us a picture of a world

[1] Montague, William Pepperell, *Belief Unbound*, p. 6.

which is really a universe, but not so unqualifiedly a meaningful world as to obscure the fact of evil and the possibility of a dynamic ethics. Every dynamic ethics depends
upon the dimension of depth in life and upon a description
of this dimension, which neither equates the metrical and
mechanistic aspects of concrete existence with meaning and
value, nor completely separates the world of value and ideals
from the facts of concrete existence.

Efforts to describe the unity and meaningfulness of the
world and existence in purely rational terms must ultimately choose between a metaphysics which inclines to
monistic idealism (and may finally degenerate into a dualism) or a science which inclines to a mechanistic monism.
Most of the modern efforts to arrive at a unified picture of
life and reality have been under the direct influence of science rather than metaphysics. When science disavows both
myth and metaphysics it has only two alternatives, in its attempt to construct a total world picture. It may picture the
world and life as a mechanism, held together by the mechanical processes which it believes to have discovered by its
observations. But there is only superficial unity and no
meaningfulness in such a world. There is no place in it for
the kind of vital and organic unity which the self experiences in its own self-consciousness. The logical ultimate of
such a world view is found in behavioristic psychology
which denies the unity of consciousness as a reality. But
such an ultimate is self-destructive because it invalidates the
truth value of everything discovered by the conscious self
about the world in which it lives. It is furthermore destructive of human vitality because it is impossible to live with
zest if no purposes can be found worthy of our striving.
A purely mechanical world is bereft of purpose and meaningfulness.

The other alternative (more generally followed) is to
introduce mythical and transcendent elements covertly
(usually unconsciously) into the supposedly scientific ac-

counts of life and history. Our modern culture has maintained its spiritual life by such a covert myth: the idea of progress. It is possible to speak of progress in interpreting the endless changes of life only if some measuring rod of value can be found with which to gauge the process. But the rod must not be a part of the process. It must transcend it. The rod taken by modern culture has usually been some ethical ideal, inherited from religion. The confidence that the processes of nature support and contribute to the victory of this ethical ideal is really a rationalized version of the Christian myth of salvation. Unfortunately it is more optimistic and really less credible than the Christian myth. It derives its credulous optimism from the fact that it sacrificed the primary myth of creation prematurely and thus identifies the processes of history too uncritically with the transcendent ideal implied in these processes. It is only through the myth of creation that it is possible to assert both the meaningfulness of life and the fact of evil. To say that God created the world is to assert its meaningfulness; and to distinguish between the creator and his creation is to make a place for the reality of evil in the inevitable relativities of time and history.

Philosophy, before modern science made the futile effort to give a unified account of the world without metaphysical presuppositions, usually sought to comprehend the unity of life and the meaningfulness of existence by viewing all things from the perspective of the unity of human consciousness and bringing all forms of life under the categories of human reason. The world was declared meaningful because it is rational. While it is not exact to identify philosophical idealism with the method of philosophy as such and to equate naturalism with the method of science, such a distinction is roughly correct. Philosophy from Plato to Hegel was predominantly idealistic in interpreting reality in terms of rationality. The confidence that external reality conforms to the categories of human consciousness is itself a rationalized form of religious faith. It is true of course that men have partially validated this confidence by bringing the external world under the control of their practical purposes by acting upon their faith. But they would have been unable to do this if they had not initiated their efforts on the assumption that the structure of life is relevant to the forms of mind. Bertrand Russell is right, therefore, when he declares that philosophies which ascribe meaning and value to external reality are rationalized mythologies. He may be less correct in suggesting that the ascription of meaning to the world is always unwarranted.

The real difficulty with idealistic philosophies is that they are rationalized myths which lost their virtue in the process of rationalization. Idealistic philosophy is unable to do justice to either the heights or depths of life. It is unable to do justice to its heights because for it the transcendent source and goal of the meaning of life is still within the limits of human rationality. Thus the God of philosophical idealism is always less than a living creator. He is also less than the holy and perfect God of religious faith, though Plato overcomes this difficulty by frankly turning to myth and declaring "that the good is not essence but soars even beyond essence in dignity and power." The potentialities of life are in other words greater than can be comprehended in terms of the "essences" which are always the constructs of the human mind.

The God of philosophical idealism is always something more as well as something less than the living creator (the source) and the holy God (the goal) of existence: He is the totality of existence. Therefore idealism can not deal adequately with the problem of evil. By rationalizing reality it brings it into a premature harmony; for a rational universe has no place for the incoherence of evil. It discovers therefore that partial evil is universal good and lames the energy of moral effort. The real fact is that mystery of both good and evil in human life and in the world can not be completely comprehended or stated in perfectly rational terms. Every sensitive human spirit is conscious of belonging to an order of reality which embodies values beyond his achievements; but he is also conscious of incarnating forces of evil which mysteriously defy this order. When philosophy deals with the problem of evil it either denies the reality of evil by lifting all processes of history into the category of the rational and the divine; or it reacts from this monism and optimism, and culminates in an extreme dualism in which the entire concrete, physical, and historical world are either relegated to meaninglessness or equated with evil. This dualism is prompted on the one hand by the failure of monism to do justice to the dimension of depth in life (that is, to the contrast between the real and the ideal) and on the other hand to the basic difficulties of a rationalistic ontology. The totality of existence is first comprehended in rational categories; but since the facts of existence do not conform to these categories, those which are not rational are relegated to a lower order of existence. Finally this lower order of existence is pronounced either evil or illusory. This entire history is symbolized in the trend of thought from Aristotle to Plotinus. In Aristotle the material world produces a hierarchy of existence in which the pure being of God is the apex. In Plotinus the pure being of God is the only real being; it prompts emanations of mind, soul and body, each with a lower order of existence than the former. The logical culmination of such rationalized religions is to be found significantly in Buddhism in which the only reality is an eternal existence which has been freed of all the characteristics of historic and corporeal life and therefore of every conceivable content.

Neither the vital thrust of life, nor its organic unities nor its disharmonies nor its highest possibilities can be expressed in terms of logic and rational consistency. The dynamic and creative energy of life can be described but not comprehended by reason. The unities of life are organic, and reason can only logically assemble after analytically dividing, thus reducing the organic to a mechanical unity. The disharmonies of life are paradoxically related to its harmonies, as mechanism is paradoxically related to the world of meaning and purpose and every rational scheme of coherence fails to do justice to the tragic realities of evil and to its paradoxical relation with the good.

The dimension of depth in existence has thus far been dealt with only as if it were a fact in the world external to man. But it is really man, with his capacity of transcending the world and transcending himself, who comprehends this depth in existence, and feels it within himself. Man is a creature of both necessity and freedom. He is inserted in the mechanisms of nature and bound by them. Yet he also gains freedom over them by his capacity to envisage purposes and ideals more inclusive than those to which he is driven by nature's impulses. For him the problem of evil is therefore also a problem of sin. His freedom endows him with responsibility and his responsibility spells guilt. The impulse of nature is not evil in the beast because it has no alternatives. But every human action is a choice between alternatives. An external description of the act may prove that a particular action was inevitable because a dominant impulse or set of forces actuated it. But an internal description of an act of choice can never escape a comparison between the act and a higher possibility. It is for this reason that religion, which has a grasp of this dimension of depth, deals with the fact of sin, while science, with its external descriptions, always inclines to deny the reality of sin and the fact of human responsibility.

In spite of the fact that the responsibility of freedom enters into every moral act, purely moralistic descriptions of human sin are as erroneous as purely deterministic and external description of human conduct. The relation of man to freedom and to mechanism is paradoxical. His conscious self is never in complete control of the mechanisms of impulse with which nature has endowed him. Yet it is in sufficient control not only to check these impulses in the interest of a more inclusive purpose but to interfere with the harmony of natural impulses, and to transmute the harmless impulses of nature into demonic lusts and imperialistic purposes. It is, in other words, the nature of human sin that it arises at the juncture of nature and spirit and is as much the corruption of nature by spirit as the corruption of spirit by nature.

All this is darkly expressed in the myth of the fall in Christian theology, much more adequately than in rational explanations of human evil. In explanations which achieve full rational coherence, evil is either attributed to the ultimate source of being (as in various forms of monism), in which case the reality of evil is really denied; or it is attributed to the world of matter, nature and historical concretion (as in various forms of dualism) in which case the fall is equated with creation (in gnosticism for instance), and impulses of nature are regarded as the source of evil while the direction of mind is regarded as the source of all good. Modern liberalism, with its confidence in increasing virtue through increasing control of reason over impulse, is a particularly naïve version of this kind of dualism, though liberalism rests upon a metaphysical foundation of naturalistic monism. Against these rationalistic versions the myth of the fall expresses these ideas: that an element of human perversity is always involved in human sin since a degree of freedom enters into every human action; that nevertheless sin is inevitable since all men are inserted into the paradoxical relation of freedom and mechanism and can not escape the possibility of destroying the harmony of nature without achieving the ultimate harmony of spirit; and, finally, that this inevitability is not to be attributed merely to the fact of nature, finiteness and the world of concrete mechanism and physical impulse. The fact that the fall came after creation, and is not synonymous or contemporaneous with it, in the Jewish-Christian myth, has always saved Christian orthodoxy from falling into dualistic heresies, no matter how strongly tempted it has been in various periods of Christian history.[2] Modern theology has been scornful of the doctrine of original sin (a corollary of the myth of the fall in Christian orthodoxy), because in its moralism and optimism it imagined the possibility of escape from the paradoxical human situation of finiteness and freedom. Orthodoxy, leaning upon mythical insights, has been truer to the facts of the total human situation upon this point. The real situation is that man's very self-consciousness and capacity for self-transcendence is not only the prerequisite of his morality but the fateful and inevitable cause of his sin. It is because man can transcend nature and himself that he is able to conceive of himself as the center of all life and the clue to the meaning of existence. It is this monstrous pretension of his egoism, the root of all imperialism and human cruelty, which is the very essence of sin. To recognize all this is not to accept the story of the fall as history. The modern dialectical theology of Germany calls it *Urgeschichte*, and that is perhaps as good a term as any. Whenever orthodoxy insists upon the literal truth of such myths it makes a bad historical science out of true religious insights. It fails to distinguish between what is primitive and what is permanent, what is pre-scientific and what is suprascientific in great myths.

The religious myths of salvation spring from the same necessity as the myths of creation and the fall. The modern man thinks himself emancipated from the need of religious assurances of salvation. They seem to him theological and unreal. The only redemption in which he believes is moral redemption, the actual conquest of evil by the good. But he can regard the problem of salvation as so simple only because he has equated evil and sin with ignorance. Once the

---

[2] See, for an historical elaboration of this thesis, Williams, N. P., *The Idea of The Fall and of Original Sin.*

element of perversity in evil is recognized, salvation in the full sense is possible only if the will is changed (conversion), and if the guilt of the past is pardoned. In all genuine religious experiences of salvation there is a sense of new moral power and an assurance of pardon. This is in other words a transaction between a transcendent God, who is not bound by the iron laws of necessity in history, and a transcendent self, which also stands above these laws both in the evil that it has committed and in the moral will by which it overcomes its previous perversity. If sin is not merely imperfection and weakness but an act of the will, reconciliation is possible only through an act of the will of the Divine; and this can be revealed only if divine forgiveness achieves some form and symbol in history (the Incarnation). The absurdity of theologies which try to define the two natures of Christ and to distinguish between the temporal and the eternal in the mythical God-man, prove how impossible it is to bring essential myth into the categories of rationality. A completely rationalized myth loses its virtue because it ceases to point to the realm of transcendence beyond history, or, pointing to it, fails to express the organic and paradoxical relationship between the conditioned and the unconditioned. That is why, as Clutton-Brock observed, religion is forced to tell many little lies in the interest of a great truth, while science inclines to tell many little truths in the interest of a great lie. The great truth in the interest of which many little lies are told is that life and history have meaning and that the source and the fulfillment of that meaning lie beyond history. The great lie in the interest of which science tells many little truths is that spatio-temporal realities are self-contained and self-explanatory and that a scientific description of sequences is an adequate analysis of causes.

It has been previously suggested that the myths of art are related to those of religion. It could be claimed, in further elaboration of this thesis, that great art is bound to be

religious; for great art is more than the objectivization of a
particular sentiment or sense of meaning. It is a symboliza-
tion of the universal in the particular, to use Goethe's definition of great art. Its analyses of particular situations or its
objectivizations of particular sentiments contain suggestions
of the total human situation. But the very quality in them
which points to the universal or the transcendent, makes
them something more and less than a scientific description
of the facts.

A portrait is mythical as compared with the scientific ex-
actitude of a photograph. Though a wise photographer will
try to catch the permanent and significant rather than
the passing mood of his subject he is always limited by the
physical facts. The artist, on the other hand, falsifies some
of the physical details in order to arrive at a symbolic expression of the total character of his subject, this total character being a transcendent fact which is never completely
embodied in any given moment of the subject's existence. A
really great portrait will go beyond this and symbolize
not only the transcendent personality of the subject, but
will contain suggestions of a universal human mood. The
artistic licence of the artist belongs in the same category
as the artistic licence of religion. In both cases it is subject
to abuses. The artist may falsify reality and produce a
caricature of his subject rather than a true portrait; and
religious myths may falsify the facts of history and experience. But at their best, both artist and prophet reveal the
heights and depths of human experience by picturing the
surface with something more and less than scientific ex-
actness.

Critics of Greek literature are agreed that Euripides's
Electra is inferior to the *Choephori* of Aeschylus and the
Electra of Sophocles, all three dramas dealing with the same
theme, the vengeance of Orestes upon his mother. But the
prejudices of modern culture have made it difficult to give
the reason for this inferiority as simply as it might be given.

Euripides is the secularist among the three great dramatists. Under his pen the great myths are naturalized and secularized so that human actions and attitudes become the inevitable causes and consequences of succeeding and preceding actions. He thus dissipates the power of Greek tragedy; for at its best it fills us with a sense of the beauty and terror of life by suggesting that human destinies are woven by forces vaster than human wills. Greek drama at its best lies close to its source: Dionysiac religion. Like all great art, it shares with religion the intention and the power to illumine the facts of life and the course of history by pointing to sources of meaning which lie beyond the facts we see and the history we experience.

The ultimate problem of myth is always the problem of God. Myths may begin by picturing good and evil spirits and by personalizing the forces of wind and water, of sun and moon and the starry heavens. Since every natural phenomenon can be explained in terms of a preceding one the myth becomes useless when science discovers the chain of causation. But meanwhile mythical knowledge has been driven from the effort to seek the transcendent cause behind each phenomenon to the search after the ultimate source of the meaning of all existence.

The approach to the transcendent source of meaning confronts us with a problem which seems practically insoluble. If the meaningfulness of life points to a source beyond itself, how is it possible to say anything about that transcendence, and how can anything that may be said be verified as true? "The vision into the Absolute," declares Professor Morris Cohen, "is either into a fathomless depth in which no distinctions are visible or into a fulness of being that exceeds our human comprehension." Mysticism has usually insisted on the distinctionless aspect of the transcendent. By seeking the absolute through a progressive elimination of temporal distinctions it finally arrived at the knowledge of God: but the God it found was emptiness and void. It could say nothing about him but that he negated the reality of significance of temporal existence. The final logic of this method is consistently expressed in Buddhism in which the ultimate is a distinctionless reality which serves only to destroy the meaning of temporal existence. Something of the same logic is to be found in all mystic asceticism. Thus the search after meaning becomes self-devouring. An ultimate source of meaning is found about which nothing can be said except that it destroys the meaning of mundane existence.

Philosophical idealism has searched for the transcendent in terms of its "fulness of being"; but being jealous of the fulness which "exceeds our comprehension" it defined the ultimate in terms of totality and rationality. By defining the transcendent in terms of totality it obscured the fact that temporal existence reveals not only glimpses of meaning but suggestions of chaos which defy meaning and order. By defining the transcendent in terms of rationality it destroyed its transcendence; for human reason is a part and product of the temporal process, and a rational picture of the transcendent obscures the very qualities of transcendence and ultrarationality. Since, however, reason has its own transcendent perspective over the natural processes and even a degree of transcendence over its own processes (therefore a rational appreciation of the limits of rationality), the efforts of philosophical idealism to comprehend the meaning of existence are never without a measure of truth or without some suggestion of its own limitations.

The effort of modern naturalism to comprehend the meaning of existence by denying the reality or validity of any transcendence behind and beyond the temporal process, usually leads, as we have seen, to an unconscious ascription of transcendence to the processes of nature and therefore to an introduction of ethical meaning into the process. In ethical naturalism an ethical meaning is given to the historic process even more immediately and unqualifiedly than in philosophical idealism. Modern naturalism is thus an even more uncritical rationalism than philosophical idealism. Its fruits are invariably either despair in a meaningless world or sentimentality in a world too simply meaningful. Modern culture is torn by conflict between the two attitudes.

The inadequacy of purely rational approaches invariably forces a return to a purer mythical approach in which the transcendent is defined and ceases to be mere emptiness, but is defined in terms which insist that it is more (and therefore less) than mere totality. But the problem of religion is how it may define God without resorting to a dogmatic acceptance of whatever mythical definition a particular historic tradition has entrusted to a certain portion of the religious community. The modern reaction against naturalism and rationalism expressed in Barthianism fails, significantly, to escape dogmatism. It is superior to the older dogmatisms of orthodox religion in that it does not insist on the scientific and rational validity of the mythical details of its tradition. The Fall and the Resurrection are not conceived as historical in its theology. But the total truth of the Biblical myth is asserted dogmatically with no effort to validate Christianity in experience against competition with other religions.

How is it possible to escape this dogmatism? It is possible only if it be realized that though human knowledge and experience always point to a source of meaning in life which transcends knowledge and experience, there are nevertheless suggestions of the character of this transcendence in experience. Great myths have actually been born out of profound experience and are constantly subject to verification by experience. It may be simplest to illustrate this point in terms of a specific religious doctrine: the Christian doctrine that God is love and that love is the highest moral ideal.

The ideal of love is not a caprice of mythology. It is not true because the Cross has revealed it. The Cross justifies itself to human faith because it symbolizes an ideal which establishes points of relevance with the deepest experiences and insights of human life.

The ideal of love can be validated as the ultimate moral ideal because it stands in a verifiable transcendent relation to all rational idealism. It is both the fulfillment and the abyss of the rational ideal of justice. Justice is the highest rational moral ideal because reason must seek to deal with human relations and moral conduct in terms of the ascertainable causes and consequences of action. A good act must be rewarded and an evil one punished. The interest of my neighbor must be guarded; but my own interests deserve protection as well. Yet all rational justice constantly sinks to something less than justice. Remedial justice fails to "do justice" to the causes which prompted an evil act because it is ignorant of the operations of mind and conscience in that secret place where actions are compounded. If reason should grow imaginative ("Love is justice grown imaginative," declares Santayana), and make shrewd guesses about the source of evil actions, it will result in a fairer justice. But if it should become so sensitive as to recognize that the evil in the other has its source in the self or the self's society it will destroy every form of remedial justice. "Let him who is without sin cast the first stone." Thus love is both the fulfillment and the denial of remedial and punitive justice.

Love is related to distributive justice in the same manner. It is "right" that I protect my own interests as well as those of my neighbor. But an imaginative regard for the interests of my neighbor will be concerned for his needs even if they are in competition with mine. Such an imaginative concern for the neighbor's interest transcends all ordinary conceptions of equity and enjoins actions of generosity which no society can ever enjoin or regularize. But this same tendency toward the fulfillment of justice in love leads to the negation of justice by love. The neighbor's interests are avowed rather than my own and no effort is made to protect myself against the neighbor ("resist not evil"). Thus morality is fed by a realm of transcendent possibilities in which the canons of the good, established in ordinary experience, are both fulfilled and negated. That is why Jesus could symbolize the mercy of God through the impartiality of nature in which the sun shines on the evil and the good and rain falls upon the just and the unjust. The impartiality of nature is something less than human justice—and a symbol of something more, the mercy of God.

The Cross in Christian faith is the myth of the truth of the ideal of love. The Christ of Christian faith is both human and divine. His actions represent both human possibilities and the limits of human possibilities. But the possibilities which transcend the human are relevant to human experience and every moral experience suggests these ultimate possibilities. Therefore parental affection is a symbol of the love of God. ("If ye then being evil, know how to give good gifts unto your children, how much more will your heavenly Father give good gifts to them that ask him.")

The transcendent source of the meaning of life is thus in such relation to all temporal process that a profound insight into any process or reality yields a glimpse of the reality which is beyond it. This reality can be revealed and expressed only in mythical terms. These mythical terms are the most adequate symbols of reality because the reality which we experience constantly suggests a center and source of reality, which not only transcends immediate experience, but also finally transcends the rational forms and categories by which we seek to apprehend and describe it.

VII

IS SUBJECTIVISM IN VALUE THEORY COMPATIBLE WITH REALISM AND MELIORISM?

By

CORNELIUS KRUSÉ

Professor of Philosophy, Wesleyan University

WHILE subjectivism in value-theory cannot properly be regarded as the prevailing attitude of American students of value problems, yet the eminence and distinction of some whose study has led them to subjectivist conclusions has nevertheless, unfortunately, imparted a certain prestige to subjectivism. One of the most surprising facts in this connection is that subjectivism in value-theory, where found, is usually connected with realism in epistemology. Not that realism is by any means predominantly associated with subjectivism. Far from it.[1] Yet in each of the two important American schools of epistemological realism, new realism and critical realism, at least one outspoken and distinguished subjectivist is to be found, notably Perry of Harvard in the more monistic-realistic group, and in the more dualistic group, Santayana, whom we delight to count as being one

[1] Spaulding, E. G., *The New Rationalism*, pp. 498-9: New York: 1918: "*Ideals are real.* . . . This was the philosophy of Plato—his Idealism and his Realism,—and, also, is it modern Realism, with *its reality of ideals, and its ideal reals.* . . . Among values, as among non-values, there are both existents and subsistents, with the former subject to time and space, conditions, and the latter not."

of our philosophers, though by birth and recent foreign residence he has also other affiliations.

Now, one would surely be pardoned the expectation that the school whose chief polemic was avowedly directed against subjective idealism (mentalism)[2] in epistemology and who were at great pains to demonstrate that the ego-centric predicament in cognition, because of its ubiquity, could not be exploited for subjective conclusions in epistemology, would be quick to see disturbing analogies to what may be called the value-centric predicament. Such a supposition would be corroborated by the fact that conspicuous European realists, English and Austrian, like Russell, Moore, and Meinong were regarded as the "big brothers in Europe"[3] of the neo-realistic movement in America at the time of its inception. They, however, did not, at least at that time, nor do European realists today generally adopt a subjectivist attitude towards value (whatever may be the chameleon state of Russell's views today). Nevertheless, one of the most important members of the American group and the very thinker who created the famous term "ego-centric predicament" and expended much effort to show its neutrality in the epistemological controversy between idealism and realism, himself exploited this very predicament for a subjective conclusion in the field of value. In his important study of the nature of value Professor Perry reaches the conclusion, unexpected in a rep-

[2] "The escape from subjectivism and the formulation of an alternative that shall be both remedial and positively fruitful constitutes the central preeminent issue for any realistic protagonist." *The New Realism*, p. 10, Macmillan, 1912.

[3] Cf. *Contemporary American Philosophy*, p. 145, New York: Macmillan Company, 1930. William Pepperell Montague, relating the circumstances attending the launching of new realism, declares: "We set out with high hope of success, confident in one another and in the sympathy of our big brothers in Europe, Russell, Moore, and Meinong." Cf. also Meinong, "Für die Psychologie und gegen den Psychologismus in der Allgemeinen Werttheorie," paper presented at the 4th International Congress of Philosophy, Bologna, 1911. Logos, 1912.

resentative of a movement tending to pan-objectivism in epistemology, that value, in general, is purely subjective and exclusively dependent for its existence on the organism or subject. "That which is an object of interest," he asserts without qualifications, "is *eo ipso* invested with value. Any object, whatever it be, acquires value when any interest, whatever it be, is taken in it; just as anything whatsoever becomes a target when anyone whosoever aims at it."[4] It is true that Professor Perry distinguishes between a generic or perhaps minimal meaning of value in contrast with value taken "in the comparative or superlative sense."[5] Neither does he deny the existence of "standard" values. On inspection, however, these values are in quality like the others and differ only quantitatively from "primordial" or frankly subjective values. Values may be distinguished and arranged in a hierarchical order in accordance with his quantitative principle of inclusiveness, that is, the more values that can be harmonized, the better. These values, however, do not cease in their harmonization and in their being members of a larger group from being finally and essentially subjective. Harmonization of values is practically tantamount to integration of personality. It is neither chance nor irrelevance, then, that so much of Perry's important book on value is devoted to psychology. His treatment of values begins and ends in psychological subjectivity.

It is not without a shock of surprise, then, that one reads his contention, in his autobiographical sketch of the development of his philosophy,[6] that for him—in contrast with subjectivists—value-judgments are objective. The reader returns with perplexity to the well-known passages in which a subjective appraisal of values is clearly expressed No, there was no mistake, psychological interest is still avowedly held to constitute value. With continued puzzle-

---

[4] Perry, R. B., *General Theory of Value*, pp. 115-6.
[5] *Ibid.*, p. 19.
[6] *Contemporary American Philosophy*, Vol. 2.

ment the reader returns to the claim to objectivity. Then finally a light dawns. This "objectivity," upon second scrutiny, turns out to be simply the objectivity of psychological fact. It is a factual judgment *of* or *about* value as entertained *subjectively* by human beings. A hallucination would, of course, be no less a fact.[7] Such an "objectivity" may register idiosyncracies in human preferences, but would seem to hold itself entirely aloof from questions of validity and reality. The analogue of such "objectivity" in the realm of truth would be contenting oneself with merely collecting private opinions, no matter how diverse or bizarre, as if one should go into a madhouse and take careful note of what the inmates think. Such *descriptive* objectivity has its place in science and in a sociological account of value, but just as one does not get truth "by counting noses," one cannot achieve *normative* objectivity by collecting preferences. Now, curiously enough, in the realm of knowledge new realism holds that "things *are* just what they seem," but no trace of this extreme realism persists for Perry in the field of value. Over and over again the reader is told in Perry's writings that "interest" does not recognize value in the object, as perception clairvoyantly recognizes even secondary qualities in the object, but rather that interest of whatever nature is "constitutive" of value.[8] It is again of importance to emphasize that English realists, like Moore, Laird, and Alexander, as well as a number of American realists, reveal on the contrary a more consistent realistic attitude, at any rate finding, as does Montague, a "certain thinness" and "too formal" or "too restrictedly psychologi-

---

[7] *Ibid.*, pp. 202-3. "Attractiveness and repulsiveness are not those elements in an object *by virtue* of which it evokes feeling or will, they *are* the evoking of will and feeling and mean nothing apart from motor-affective response." But "in the *knowing* of value the *knower's* own will and feeling is no more involved than in his knowing anything else." (The last two italics are mine.)

[8] "In short, interest being constitutive of value in the basic sense, theory of value will take this as its point of departure and center of reference." R. B. Perry, *General Theory of Value*, p. 116.

cal quality in such an attitude" as Perry's.[9] It is, further-more, a matter of personal interest and satisfaction to the writer to find that Professor Macintosh, who has throughout the years of his writing and teaching held to a realistic position in epistemology, no less rejects subjectivity in the field of values. In his distinguished book *The Pilgrimage of Faith*, in which the reader finds summed up years of wide reading and profound reflection, critical realism is developed in full harmony with a religious realism, that is to say, with realism in a field that is universally acknowledged as dealing preeminently with values. The nature and status of values in the world of time is, it will be remembered, of necessity the most poignant question in religion. Professor Macintosh, so far from turning values into mere subjectively entertained interests, does not hesitate to call some values "universally valid," "eternal," and "absolute,"[10] namely, values "which all persons ought to appreciate, values worthy of being sought always, everywhere, and by all."[11] These values, furthermore, are for him not only universally valid, but also strongly supported by reality. True religion gives assurance not only that "God is the conserver of absolute values,"[12] but that in God "the absolute Ideal is already real."

The subjectivist attitude of a different type of critical realist like Santayana, on the other hand, should not occasion surprise, for his essences, by which independent reality under certain favoring circumstances may indeed be

[9] Montague, W. P., *Belief Unbound*, p. 33, Yale Press, 1930.

[10] Macintosh, D. C., *The Pilgrimage of Faith*, p. 277, University of Calcutta, 1931.

[11] *Op. cit.*, p. 276. To the usually recognized Platonic triad of values, the values of love and religion are added.

[12] *Ibid.*, pp. 257-8. It must not be forgotten that agreeing with Bergson and James in insisting upon the reality of events in time, on the one hand, and on the other with moral consciousness that manifestly the actual is not yet altogether ideal—far from it—Professor Macintosh holds that perfectly valid values are still in need of actualization in the realm of existence.

known, constitute nevertheless a world of "dream lights kindled by my fancy," "an innocent realm of ideas," a "wilderness" in which a disinterested mind "finds a very sweet and nameless solitude."[13] Now, if "essences" which "are indispensable terms in the perception of matters of fact and render transitive knowledge possible,"[14] should primarily "be welcomed for their fair aspect," values surely should not demur at being made to dwell in a world so insubstantial. But in contrast a more monistic realism can scarcely afford a similar long-lingering joy in impalpable being.

Moreover, the same arguments ably called forth to do battle with such telling power against the ego-centric predicament proceed, in spite of efforts to call them off, with equal enthusiasm and effectiveness against the value-centric predicament, as is clearly seen when the central polemical contention of realism against subjective idealism is translated into these value-correlates:

The result is either the redundant inference that valued things are valued, or the false inference that all valuable objects (values) are valued. The former is, on account of its redundancy not a proposition at all; and its use results only in confusing it with the second proposition, which involves a *petitio principii.*[15]

To be sure it is asserted that

Since the moral and aesthetic attitudes differ in *some* respect from the cognitive attitude, then they *may* differ in just that respect which is crucial as regards the implication of universal validity.[16]

[13] Santayana, G., *Skepticism and Animal Faith*, pp. 69, 86, 1923.
[14] *Op. cit.*, p. 80.
[15] *New Realism*, pp. 11-12. The first sentence in which I have substituted value-correlates reads as follows: "The result is either the redundant inference that all known things are known or the false inference that all things are known." The second sentence is presented unchanged.
[16] Perry, R. B., *General Theory of Value*, p. 94.

But it is surely not irrelevant to recall that bare possibility is not actuality, nor does it become probability unless more positive evidence is adduced than the usual reference to diversity in valuation, for the history of science amply displays diversity even of expert and considered cognitive judgments in matters of existence. Diversity in valuation need no more issue into subjectivism than diversity in cognition. To hold that it does seems surprisingly incompatible with an avowed monistic realism.

As a matter of fact there is a certain inveterate blindness on the part of some epistemological realists in failing to recognize the kinship existing between the value of truth on the one hand and the values of goodness and beauty, and one might add, the holy, on the other hand. It is sometimes even denied that truth is a value. Now, we can readily grant that these various values are not identical, and that each remains to the end sovereign in its own realm. But distinctness does not mean complete disassociation, any more than sovereignty involves a Chinese wall of separation. Such views can only lead to error. Of course if value is purely subjective, it is clearly understandable why in the interest of safeguarding truth's objectivity an attempt should be made to disassociate it from all values. But can this strategy be effective on any interpretation of value? If value is interpreted as any interest whatever, as Professor Perry does, it surely does not require labored demonstration to show that truth on this principle is most certainly itself a value. Or is there no "interest" in truth or is truth perchance "value-less"? Of course, truth is not really subjective, but it must be if all value is.

The oft-mentioned "disinterestedness" of science has beguiled not only the naïve that all human interest has been left behind in its pursuit. Nothing could be further from the truth. The dispassionateness of science is the passionateness of single-heartedness. Science is a jealous mistress and will brook no rivals. "Thou shalt have no other gods before me" is also her command. Ordinary people not overmuch interested in pure knowing feel only the denials of the scientist and not his positive affirmation, just as "the world" regards Christianity as purely negative because it denies "the world." Hence arises the myth that scientists are cold, when in fact they burn with singleminded and concentrated devotion.

This insistence on the concentrated interest brought to science by the scientist is not of course intended to discredit science. On the contrary! It is intended, however, to show that the interest theory of value not only fails to do justice to the values of beauty, morality, and religion but inevitably discredits science as well. On its own principles it cannot prevent truth from being swept away into the same maelstrom of subjectivity into which all other values have been committed. This is not the place to enter into a full discussion of the theory of value, objectively interpreted, but it would seem elementary to recognize that the undoubted presence of subjective aspects in all valuation, including devotion to truth, does not involve *ipso facto* a complete subjective characterization of all values, or else the ego-centric predicament would imprison scientists as well as lovers of the good, the beautiful and the holy in the prison house that would then be one's self. While the blurring of the distinctions between the various types of values is constantly fraught with injustice to each, the refusal to recognize their common kinship leads into errors that are even worse. In my father's house there are many mansions, distinct indeed, but with doors that open to each other.

The second part of this paper wishes briefly to consider whether subjectivity in value-theory, whether put forward by epistemological realists or by anyone else, is compatible with meliorism[17]—the popular doctrine, namely, that the world, though actually at present far from perfect, may be made to conform, especially through man's intelligent and devoted efforts, at least somewhat more satisfactorily to man's standards. Accepting the universe with resignation and simply remoulding our values to agree with what would happen any way, cannot be regarded as in keeping with the melioristic temper. Meliorism may be Promethean, or more persuasively aggressive, but it must assume that man's efforts at reform of himself and his world must have some efficacy. Readers of William James will recognize meliorism as an important part of his pragmatic doctrine. "Meliorism," he maintained, "treats salvation (of the world) as neither necessary nor impossible. It treats it as a possibility, which becomes more and more of a probability the more numerous the actual conditions of salvation become."[18] This attitude of meliorism is frankly adopted by Perry, positively, when he declares that realism "is theistic and melioristic in its religion," and negatively, when he attacks "absolute optimism" for attempting to show that this is the best possible of all worlds. Absolute optimism, as he holds, ends by supinely accepting the universe as it is. Such a position is rightly regarded as a pusillanimous surrender of one's ideals.[19]

But is it possible to adopt an attitude of meliorism with a

[17] It appears that it was James Sully (cf. *Pessimism, A History and Criticism*, p. 399, 1877, who popularized this term among philosophers as indicating a midway position between optimism and pessimism which would challenge human effort and keep hope for better things alive. Sully credits the English novelist, George Eliot, with having brought the term first to his attention. Spencer, who also uses the term, in distinction from Sully, depends for his confidence in the emergence of a progressively better world less upon human efficacy and more upon cosmic evolutionary forces.

Contemporary Review, July, 1884, p. 39.

[18] James, William, *Pragmatism*, p. 286.

[19] Perry, R. B., *The Present Conflict of Ideals*, p. 379 and pp. 243-4. Cf. also the entire chapter XVII.

purely subjectivist interpretation of values? All the traditional difficulties of a sharply severed epistemological dualism would seem to descend upon us to plague us now in
the field of value. If our ideals or values are merely *our*
fancies, *our* desires, it is difficult to see how they can become operative in the world of actuality. True, we are told
that we should study actuality, the better to find hospitable
acceptance for our ideals in it. Our desires must be schooled.
This is sound counsel, and has been throughout the ages
the teaching of wisdom. An objectivist in value-theory
would not hesitate to admit that there are errors and illu-
sions in valuation as there are in man's attempts to know
his world. But it is one thing to say, as Montague does, that
"we must stoop to conquer," or that we must in knowledge
conform to the world so that, in turn, we may conform
the world to our ideals if there is in the realm of actuality
a certain cooperativeness and relevance. It is, however, quite
another thing to expect the universe to respond to ideals
which are regarded, in principle, as at best simply the
results of integrated human desires. It is of considerable importance that Professor Montague, sensing, as it seems to
me, this embarrassing incompatibility of meliorism with extreme subjectivity, becomes critical of Perry's definition of
value which he declares himself willing to accept as far as
it goes. His reason for looking for a greater massiveness in
values is exactly mine. "They (such "utilitarian"-hedonistic
conceptions) are too formal and too restrictedly psychological; they cry out for a concrete ontological filling that
will integrate the thing called value with the nature of the
existence which it should qualify, and not leave it floating
mysteriously and relegated exclusively to a realm of its
own. My conception of the ideal as increment of the real,
the *ought* as the dynamic and growing aspect of the *is*, in
short, of value as the actualization of potentiality," he
rightly concludes, gives some reason for expecting that hu-

man ideals can enter into efficacious commerce with the actual world.[20]

What subjectivism in value, consistently maintained, finally issues into, may best be seen in the philosophy of Santayana, especially in its more recent development. In his earlier days a certain interest in meliorism was not absent for all of his native aloofness from social preoccupations, but in his later years he seems more and more to become a spectator merely of all life and existence, much resembling in this respect Oliver's father, Peter, in *The Last Puritan*. Santayana's gaze turns more and more away from interest in the world's amendment, and concentrates on contemplation of the fair objects in the realm of essences.

The whole of natural life, then, is an aspiration after the realization and vision of Ideas, and *all action is for the sake of* contemplation.[21]

Even in earlier days William James sensed this withdrawn joy in sheer contemplativeness, for though upon the reading of Santayana's *Interpretations of Poetry and Religion* (1900), he, as was characteristic of his generous nature, exclaimed, "the great event in my life recently has been the reading of Santayana's book," he could not refrain from adding, "But what a perfection of rottenness in a philosophy! . . . how fantastic a philosophy!—as if the 'world of values' *were* independent of existence. It is only as *being*, that one thing is better than another."[22] It is true that the conspicuous naturalistic trend in Santayana brings him at times rather close to the position of Dewey that values are the natural outgrowths of man's cooperative life with nature.[23] But this trend, though present, is, I repeat, yielding more and more to "a pious reverence for the nature of

[20] Montague, W. P., *Belief Unbound*, p. 33.

[21] Santayana, G., *Soliloquies in England and Later Soliloquies*, p. 227, 1922, italics mine.

[22] *Letters of William James*, Vol. 2, pp. 122-3.

[23] Santayana, G., *Winds of Doctrine*, p. 120.

things"[24] and to a joy in contemplation of Platonic essences which must not be regarded as reals. Plato's identification of the ideal and the real, in fact, is Santayana's only quarrel with his great master.

The poet in Plato had been entrapped by the moralist, the logician enslaved by the legislator. . . . Plato had grown forgetful of the ideas, and of the life of intuition; his gaze had become sad, troubled, and hopeless; he was preoccupied with making existence safe.

Similarly, Santayana mildly reproaches Berkeley for not simply "studying these ideas for their own sake with a steadier gaze."[25] It is very clear to the writer that it is Santayana's subjectivism which carries him along irresistibly to an eventual repudiation of meliorism as being almost somewhat vulgar.

But Santayana's growing Olympian aloofness from preoccupation with making existence safe or better, sounds like a counsel of despair to those who have not deeply tasted of his lotus flower. A better world in the making or still to be made will remain the hope and ideal of active spirits. But then any yielding to subjectivism in values must be frankly abandoned.

The whole point of the matter is that a well-founded meliorism depends upon the *possibility* of making the world over in some sense and to some degree. But it would be futile to hope, unless we were gods creating *ex nihilo*, that this sorry scheme of things *entire* could be broken into bits to be remolded closer to our heart's desire. No, it is very clear that possibility must mean, as James pointed out, more than bare possibility. "But most possibles are not bare, they are concretely grounded, or well-grounded, as we say." The possibilities, he continues, must be "live possibilities."[26]

[24] *Ibid.*, p. 116.
[25] Santayana, G., *Soliloquies in England and Later Soliloquies*, pp. 231, 233.
[26] James, W., *Pragmatism*, pp. 283-4 and 287.

As Schelling would say, taking "art" in the wide sense used by Santayana and Dewey as meaning effective human contrivance, nature must at least be unconscious art as art is conscious nature. James himself does not hesitate to speak of cooperative forces which include not only man's fellowmen, but "superhuman forces" as well.[27] "Is it not sheer dogmatic folly," he vigorously demands, "to say that our inner interests can have no real connection with the forces that the hidden world may contain? In other cases divinations based on inner interests have proved prophetic enough. Take science itself! . . . Hardly a law has been established in science, hardly a fact ascertained, which was not first sought after, often with sweat and blood, to gratify an inner need."[28]

One may account for this cooperativeness of reality with values which a well-grounded meliorism imperatively demands, in a variety of ways, as the history of philosophy and contemporary philosophical writings amply reveal.

A simple, perhaps the simplest way of accounting for it is exemplified in certain forms of naturalism, as, for instance, in the naturalistic monism of John Dewey. As is well known, Dewey holds that man is a child of nature, the wishes of whom, though often, indeed, in need of discipline, nevertheless bear nature's imprint and therefore deserve respect. Our deepest values are not simply our dream-fancies, but are solidly rooted in the nature that brought us forth. "Fidelity to the nature to which we belong, as parts, however weak," he insists, "demands that we cherish our desires and ideals till we have converted them into intelligence. . . . The belief and the effort of thought and struggle which it (this sense of unity with the universe) inspires are also the doing of the universe, and they in some way, how-

[27] *Ibid.*, p. 298.
[28] James, W., "Is Life Worth Living," in *The Will to Believe and other Essays*, p. 55.

ever slight, carry the universe forward."[29] A certain answering fitness of the environment must be assumed in all devotion to our ideal values, for "an ideal realm that has no roots in existence has no efficacy nor relevancy."[30] Though the philosophy underlying Wordsworth's poetry is by no means identical with Dewey's the following lines from Wordsworth's *Recluse* admirably express Dewey's fundamental mood:

> "How exquisitely the individual Mind
> . . . . to the external World
> Is fitted:—and how exquisitely, too—
> Theme but little heard of among men—
> The external World is fitted to the Mind."[31]

The ideal and the real in classical philosophy, so far from being separated, have often been frankly identified, as in the philosophy of Plato and in all subsequent philosophy that has borne the marks of his great influence, including the philosophy of Spinoza, for whom perfection and reality were by definition regarded as one and the same.[32] To establish this identity of the ideal and the real recourse often was taken to the famous ontological argument for the existence of God. This argument, too well-known to require restatement, even after having suffered apparently definitive disproof at the hands of Kant, nevertheless has shown an

[29] Dewey, J., *Experience and Nature*, p. 420.
[30] *Ibid.*, p. 416.
[31] *Recluse*, lines 816-20.
[32] Spinoza, *Ethics*, Part II, Def. vi. To turn Spinoza into a subjectivist in value-theory, as some have attempted, including Perry, seems a grotesque *tour de force* resulting from a total disregard of Spinoza's important distinction between the good as men conceive it anthropomorphically and capriciously, and the good as it is revealed through the use of intuitive knowledge. Any defender of the subjective interpretation of Spinoza's philosophy of value is invited to explain in a subjective way the definition cited above. The usual proof-text cited in favor of such subjective interpretation, namely, that things are good only because we like them and choose to call them so, surely has a bearing only on the "good" as conceived by man as yet not imbued with "the intellectual love of God."

unexpected vitality in post-Kantian thought even to our day. The secret of its vitality does not lie in the attractiveness or persuasiveness of its apparent logical legerdemain. Quite the opposite! In fact, so long as its logical husk preempts attention Kant's demonstration of its desiccated invalidity seems perfect. But one's whole attitude is changed if one penetrates into the heart of the meaning of the ontological argument and realizes that it represents really a magnificent, and even heroic, affirmation of faith that the ideal and the real in the nature of things do not fall apart—as pessimism is led to suppose—but that they gloriously and triumphantly belong together, even to the point of identity. The argument may be weak but the faith expressed is fine and strong. In our own day, objective or speculative idealism has most frequently taken delight in having recourse to this argument, but its rehabilitation, in modified forms, has been attempted by defenders of other philosophical positions as well.

There is, however, a danger for meliorism itself in the overeager readiness to declare the ideal and the real identical. Modern objective idealism, adhering as it does to the ontological argument, has had to defend itself against the charge that in the exuberance of its ontological faith it has made experienced evil unreal, or worse still, has called it good. The moral conscience of mankind has rebelled and will continue to rebel against declaring a premature armistice with evil. Here indeed is a paradox: if the ideal and the real fall utterly apart, as in extreme subjectivism in value, there can be no meliorism for pessimistic reasons, but if regarded as perfectly coincident, meliorism is no less impossible for optimistic reasons.

A final and more usual way of accounting for the cooperativeness of reality with values necessary for a vital meliorism which avoids the complete identification of the ideal and the real, may be found in most forms of theism. Professor Macintosh himself may be taken as an excellent representative of a critical theistic point of view. His position is the more interesting for the purposes of this study in that, firmly grounding his philosophy on realism, he, with admirable consistency, vigorously rejects any doctrine of meliorism unsupported by cooperating reality.

But mere meliorism would be singularly inadequate as a gospel. . . . The question is whether, if and in so far as man as a morally free agent does his best toward the triumph of right, even with the help of religious exercises, he can be wholly free from anxiety as to the ultimate outcome; whether when he produces values that are absolute, he can trust that throughout all cosmic changes these absolute values will be conserved.[33]

He rightly concludes that pessimism would soon crowd out any meliorism that was not supported by the assurance of a "Factor constantly favorable to absolute spiritual values as ends, to other values as means, and to human persons especially as bearers, actually and potentially, of moral and other absolute values."[34]

The outcome of the study so far is that realism in epistemology is logically incompatible with subjectivity in value. The natural affinity of epistemological realism with value realism is clearly revealed in the succinct joint statement of the whole cooperative group: "The neo-realist is also a Platonic realist."[35] Unfortunately not all who call themselves Platonists enter fully into Plato's realm. Perry, for example, declares: "Most modern realists . . . would go with Plato a part of the way. . . . They would accept . . . (however) . . . only the mathematical and logical part of Platonic realism."[36] The Platonic reals would on this interpretation include simply logical and mathematical entities. This would seem to readers of Plato's divine dialogues like remaining half-heartedly only at the mathematical por-

[33] *Op. cit.*, p. 199.
[34] *Ibid.*, p. 200.
[35] *The New Realism*, p. 35.
[36] *Op. cit.*, p. 371.

tal of Plato's grove. But previous references to other realists would show that the Platonic influence, once under way,
may easily spread to include other than logical value.

Another definite outcome of the study is that subjectivity
is incompatible with a well-grounded meliorism. It must be
abundantly clear by now that the reformer, eager to re-
mold reality, could never even have the heart to begin if he
believed simply that his values were his private fancies.
Though the universe of nature and of fellow-man may provide as resisting material as a sculptor finds in marble, yet
somewhat after the fashion of Leibniz's block of veined
marble in which the figure of Hercules was already vaguely
indicated, important potentialities must be discovered in the
material. Certainly, the success that meliorism demands requires at least a potential cooperativeness on the part of
reality that cannot be logically explained if we separate
dualistically the realm of value from the realm of reality as
subjectivism inevitably does.

In conclusion, apart from questions of realism's consistency with itself and with the creative re-formation of
the world that meliorism demands, we may cast a glance at
the final implications of the adoption of the subjective or
the objective attitude towards value. In the discussion of
meliorism we have seen how easily and naturally the objectivity of values leads to a consideration of a religious
background. What final bearing may the discussion of subjectivity and objectivity have upon religion itself?

To many moderns, religion, along with art, and sometimes
even morality, has been relegated to the *non disputandum*
realm of private subjectivity. The resulting gain in urbanity
and tolerance makes this attitude to values seem like wisdom's last deliverance. But if religion is but a cherishing of
idiosyncratic values, there is nothing to be tolerant *about*,
and if it becomes known and accepted that in religion values
are subjective merely, the wings of faith are clipped. However much one may justifiably deplore and reject a purely

humanistic value approach to a knowledge of God, as Professor H. Richard Niebuhr does with persuasiveness and logic, it is clear that unless values are objective there is no God. Why have causal arguments for the existence of God of whatever nature failed to lead men to God? For the simple reason that supreme existence—even granting that it could at all be reached by the causal ladder—stood stripped of any worth-imparting values. As Kant has shown, even where an Uncaused Cause or a Prime Mover proved to exist it would no more be God than a storm or a mountain is God, or, one may add, than in Eugene O'Neill's fancy a dynamo is God. The mere imputation of divinity to the dynamo by O'Neill's hero in the play by that name resulted in a tragic self-immolatory end for the hero. The religious person may well say: "Brute omnipotent power may roll on its relentless way, for all of me, I may even fear it, but I will not worship it!"

The humanistic value-approach to God is rightly spurned by the religiously sensitive, just as an artist will not brook the subjection of beauty to the services of utility or even of morality, because the supreme object of love of the religious person would then become an instrument for other human values rather than the source and fountainhead of all that can be precious to man. But when all that is said and admitted God remains a value nevertheless. Nay, even more so, for He has now become the supreme value to which all others lead by the mystic stairway of beauty, or by the stony *salita* of the good, or by the slow mountain-scaling way of truth. The religious person does not really repudiate value, else would his faith be but idolatry. With Spinoza and many other seers he insists that God be loved disinterestedly for His own sake rather than for the sake of any other value no matter how high otherwise. It is in this sense, if I mistake not, that one must understand Spinoza's statement that the love of God is the love wherewith God loves Himself.

A common danger in value discussions, which is really at bottom the reason for declaring all values subjective, is the tacit or explicit assumption that all human *wishes* are values. But not all wishes are values any more than all opinions are truths. The astounding thing about man is that he is not content to be himself—at least not as he finds himself at any given time. Nor can we glory in the world if we are it creators. This is perhaps the basic reason, usually unexpressed, why epistemological realists repudiate subjective or even objective idealism. Professor Montague in his confidential sketch of himself and his beliefs brings this underlying motive to full and candid expression by declaring that for all of his gratitude and affection for Royce he felt sadly obliged to repudiate his philosophy because it seemed to him based upon "the monstrous premise . . . that that great nature, in which we are such recent and humble participants, is itself the product of our social consciousness and of the funny little techniques of communication which we have developed."[37] Exchange, in Profesor Montague's moving statement, "that great God" for "that great nature," and one realizes at once how kindred it is to the religious spirit that must reject subjectivity in values even when it comes with the authority of social subjectivity.

The practical man may wish to control nature, the scientist wishes to be controlled by it. But it is not otherwise with the religious person, nor for that matter with the artist or the lover of beauty. What forces us to look for an escape from the private meaning of our experiences is that in the last resort, to speak with Fichte, we have experiences that come "with a feeling of necessity." Standards of excellence in the value-realm we experience with no less a feeling of necessity. If purely private meaning is intolerable in the one case, it is no less so in the others. It is not only the scientist who is subject to the inexorable discipline of a standard of excellence. The "ever-not-quite" both lures and

[37] *Contemporary American Philosophy*, Vol. II, p. 140.

baffles the artist and the "high calling of God" both exalts and humbles the saint. Let any one who believes that standards count only in science try to be either artist or saint. But are not standards our highest values? We may flaunt them, as Kant said of the categorical imperative, but we are none the less judged by them. Whence come these standards of excellence which imperatively judge rather than are judged? What is the source of their validity and authority? It is perhaps the writer's deepest conviction that the answer to these questions is the beginning, and perhaps the end, of the philosophy of religion.

VIII

THE SEMI-DETACHED KNOWER

By

Robert Lowry Calhoun

Professor of Historical Theology, Yale University Divinity School

---

This paper deals only with a certain aspect of the problem of knowledge: to wit, the status of the knower in a given instance of knowing. It seeks to establish a familiar and modest, but I think a very important conclusion regarding this matter, in opposition to the widely acclaimed doctrine called radical empiricism, which is here held to be untenable as an account of knowledge, religious or other. The present argument makes no attempt to go outside the limits of epistemological inquiry. It notices but does not examine, for example, the closely related question as to the intrinsic character of the knower, as physical, psychical, or what not. The boundary line is sufficiently clear, I trust, between the epistemological thesis here treated as demonstrable, and allied metaphysical problems which would need to be argued in a different manner. It appears to me, none the less, that if the conclusions of the paper be sound, they furnish reason for re-examining with care an issue of obvious moment for both philosophy and religion, which today is often dismissed as obsolete: the question whether and in what sense human persons should be called substantial selves.

By substantial self I mean an existing entity such that, among others, it would satisfy these conditions: 1) that it cannot be adequately described as a character, process, or function of some other entity (such as a physical system, or a World-whole), but must be described as itself a subject of behavior which has a primary center or frame of reference within itself; 2) that it exemplify characters or modes of behavior (such as sentiency, effort, and self-direction) other than those which the physical sciences now attribute to bodies as such; 3) that as subject of these and other modes of behavior, it be not completely open to observation, not even to introspection, but remain partly hidden, *i.e.*, non-phenomenal or non-apparent; and 4) that it endure through a period longer than a single "specious present."

The notion of man as substantial self has been formulated most clearly and made most familiar, so far as I know, in the thought of Western Christendom. To a considerable extent, no doubt, this development has expressed the growing individualism of Western culture. But in a more fundamental sense, it has been a natural transcription of moral and religious demands which are ingrained in Christianity as an ethical religion. Traditional Christian doctrine, indebted heavily to Hebraic and Hellenistic sources, but shaping its legacies from them in distinctive fashion, has clearly affirmed that each man is a being other than God, capable of acting within limits at his own initiative. Such affirmation has seemed necessary, to safeguard belief in the perfect goodness of God and the responsibility of man. The ultimate dependence of every man upon God for both his existence and his salvation has been affirmed no less clearly; but almost never, by well-trained thinkers, in such a way as to abrogate the basic conviction that each man and God are existentially two, not one—two between whom relationships both of communion and of opposition obtain.

To express this conviction, a variety of concepts have been employed in describing man: some primarily religious—servant, sinner, adopted son; some primarily philosophical—creature, subject, substantial self. Concepts of this latter sort were most fully elaborated and freely employed by the Schoolmen, from whose technical vocabulary these terms have come over into modern speech. But though we use much of their language still, we use it often enough in denials of their doctrines. In particular, the concept of substance has been subjected to widespread criticism, and many even of those who still find use for the notion of substance at other points reject the concept of man as substantial self. This rejection is defended now on philosophical, now on religious grounds. Some critics, that is, find intellectual difficulty in conceiving a man as in any radical sense independent of his environment, while some object primarily to assertions which might be construed as affirming human self-sufficiency over against God. For misgivings of both sorts I have deep respect. But summarily to close a question of such difficulty and of so far-reaching import seems premature, especially since the reasons offered for closing it now are for the most part not new ones, which might be conclusive, but old ones which have been ably debated on both sides for centuries. To examine these reasons is no part of our present purpose. We seek rather to call attention once more to one sort of philosophical considerations which point the other way. Analysis of the process of knowing brings to light what seem to me good theoretic reasons, in support of more practical religious and moral incentives, for careful restudy of this whole issue.

Since the days of John Locke, acute and intensive examination of human knowing has made familiar a number of verbal distinctions about knowledge. Given a human person taking cognizance of something, it is for example not difficult to distinguish in words, 1) a knower or subject, 2) one or more cognitive acts, processes, or events, 3) a datum or a configuration of data, and 4) an object or situation known. But that all these verbal distinctions reflect real differences is not self-evident, and perhaps more often than not, in recent years, two or more of the terms thus verbally set apart have been declared to be in fact identical. In particular, it is very often held that the subject or knower is simply and wholly identical with one or more of the other three terms noticed. The intent of this paper is to set in order a number of reasons, mostly familiar but in need of periodic rehearsal, for judging that on the contrary the knower cannot finally be identified *tout court* with any of the other three terms. It must be regarded instead as "semi-detached," as including one or more factors not identical with nor completely determined by object, datum, nor cognitive act, and not fully open to observation.

Until very recently, a short and easy way to dispose of any such view, in many quarters, would have been just to call it Scholastic. The epithet would be, as already implied, a not wholly unfair one, and to the minds of many in our day sufficiently fatal. For the tide of philosophic revolt which began to rise during the Renaissance against Scholastic metaphysics and epistemology by no means reached its height in Francis Bacon, nor in Locke, nor even in the men of the Enlightenment. Rather, it has gone on rising steadily, with the development of evolutionary naturalism, of Hegelianism and its derivatives, and more especially of positivism, phenomenalism, and radical empiricism which denounce metaphysics of all the older brands. A wholesome respect for observation, and skepticism about the unobservable, have led to impatience with any talk of transcendental or trans-empirical entities. In particular, the growing prestige of the natural sciences and of behavioristic sociology has raised high hope, not to say brought widespread assurance, that old-fashioned, elusive concepts like substance and soul can now be dispensed with. Eminent philosophers, at once alert to and helping produce these prevailing winds of doctrine, have worked zealously toward ways of conceiving all that goes on as a seamless fabric, through and through experienceable, free from the annoying discontinuities of natural and supernatural, appearance and reality, observed act and hidden agent, which an older metaphysics accepted as ineradicable. Even pluralists like James, and believers in novelty like Dewey, no friends of traditional singularism, have joined the hue and cry against discontinuity of the sorts implied by substantial selves and dualistic knowledge situations; and among their followers, "Scholasticism" has come to rank high as a term of reproach.

In other quarters, of course, a philosophic mood less shy of classical and mediaeval thought has begun to reassert itself effectively. Both speculative metaphysics in the grand manner and frankly dualistic theories of knowledge, *bêtes noires* of the radical empiricists, are making vigorous counter-attacks. But excepting Neo-scholastics, few contemporary thinkers even among personalists and dualists are inclined to welcome back anything like the old notion, say, of a substantial soul, nor even its paler offspring the "transcendental ego," for fear of being entangled once more in the "pseudo-problems" of unempirical, outgrown speculation. Avowed monists are of course at pains to affirm or to imply that knowing and knowers alike are wholly included within the area of what is immediately experienceable. Avowed dualists, with rare exceptions, give their attention mainly to establishing particular disjunctions between datum and object of knowledge, on the one hand, and generic unlikeness between physical and non-physical existents, on the other.[1] The further affirmation that knowing such as ours

---

[1] For example, the acute arguments of Lovejoy in *The Revolt against Dualism* (1930), to which I am heavily in debt, could be satisfied for the most part by some such theory as James's earlier version of "the stream of consciousness," without the "non-phenomenal Thinker" which James himself (*Principles of Psychology*, 1890, I.341 n.) kept provisionally in the offing, before his thought moved (with the provocative essay, "Does Consciousness Exist?") into what was for him the new phase of "radical empiricism." Here and there in Lovejoy's book are hints at the existence of a non-physical knower more unitary than a stream of consciousness, and more enduring than a single "wave" in such a stream. Thus, the phrase *"memini ergo fui"* (p. 305), or the parenthetic reference to "the organism *or mind* in which" a cognitive event occurs (p. 317, italics

seems to involve a unitary, enduring factor not fully open to direct inspection is still widely unpopular. It is this further affirmation that I wish to defend.

I have, indeed, no inclination to think of the subject or knower as a quite separate thing, sundered from and alien to the processes of knowing and the objects known; a wholly transcendent ego split off from the observable flow of events, unconditioned by them and indiscernible through them. Without holding so bizarre a view, one may think of the knower as semi-detached, in the simple sense that it cannot without contradiction be thought of as fully included among observable data, nor within any immediately observable series of cognitive acts or events as such. It will be thought of here as intimately and dynamically related to both, but not as fully identical with either, nor with both together.

The position taken is, if I mistake not, essentially akin to that which Kant defined in his discussion of "the original unity of apperception" as a synthesizing or unifying principle, without which human experience in its familiar forms cannot be clearly conceived, yet which is not itself a datum nor an object of experience. It is a "transcendental unity,"

---

mine), might suggest that to Lovejoy, as to James in his earlier mood, the question of a "non-phenomenal Thinker" remains open. But whereas Lovejoy argues strongly (pp. 267-302; *cf.* pp. 12-15) for the common-sense view that physical things have intrinsic, continuous, partly extra-empirical existence, he nowhere argues similarly about minds. Indeed, he expressly disclaims (p. 253) all concern to do so in this book. So too J. B. Pratt in *Religious Realism* (1931), p. 49, is content to speak of "the active unity of experience itself," and refers approvingly to James's account.

On the other hand, A. K. Rogers: *What is Truth?* (1923), pp. 168-170, declares: "the self most certainly appears to be something in addition to the actual processes that make up the stream of conscious experiencing," and proceeds to ask what more it may be. Of such affirmations, the most forthright known to me is that of F. R. Tennant: *Philosophical Theology*, I (1928), pp. 82-104, pp. 366-368, *etc.* He bluntly affirms belief in the reality of substantial souls, and argues the issue at length.

in Kant's well-known jargon, which is not simply identical at any moment even with the experienced *me*, the *myself* which is known. Behind the scenes and in the long run, "transcendental ego" and "empirical ego" may well be interpretable as two correlative aspects of one enduring reality.[2] The point is, they are two aspects, not one; and the distinction between them, somewhat like the distinction between *natura naturans* and *natura naturata*, must be kept clear, else confusion results. So definitely is the view here defended a kind of offshoot from the Kantian analysis that it seems convenient to introduce the thesis by paraphrasing Kant's statement of his case; then to consider in turn three versions of more or less radical empiricism in which the presence of a trans-empirical factor is disavowed; and finally to suggest the bearing of the argument upon our understanding of religious experience as involving relationship between God and men.

Two passages in the *Critique of Pure Reason*, one in each of the first two editions, may help to define more precisely what is meant here by a semi-detached knower, and why

[2] In one passage Kant, after calling attention to the "doubling" of the "I" in self-consciousness, goes on: "This does not mean a double personality: only the subject I which thinks and observes is the person, whereas the objective I which is observed by me is like other objects external to me, a thing." This distinction is elaborated in the two succeeding paragraphs. See *Ueber die Fortschritte der Metaphysik seit Leibnitz und Wolf*, in Kant: *Werke* (ed. Hartenstein, 1867-68), VIII, 531; and cf. *Kritik der reinen Vernunft*, B 155. (A and B denote, of course, the original paginations of the editions of 1781 and 1787, respectively.)

I am not forgetting here the warning of Professor Kemp Smith: *A Commentary to Kant's Critique of Pure Reason* (1918), pp. l-lii. The primary point of this paper is to insist on the positive considerations which he himself puts so vividly on pp. xliv-xlv of the same work; though it does deliberately seek to hold open also, as Kant did (*ibid.*, p. lii), the questions that arise concerning "a noumenal self." These constitute the metaphysical problem toward which this paper points, but which it does not attack.

such a factor seems involved in human knowing. Consider first a part of the stiff, painstaking "subjective deduction" of the categories in the edition of 1781, which holds that in a typical instance of cognition, say apperception of a straight line, synthesis or unification of three sorts must take place, in a single center. The successive parts of the line must be apprehended together in a unitary *perception* or sensory apprehension; but this requires that the prior parts of the line be summated with those perceived later, in a unitary *memory* or imaginative reproduction; and this in turn would be nugatory unless prior and subsequent parts be grasped in a unitary *intellection*, or conceptual recognition, as conforming to a common "rule" or pattern. These three syntheses, finally, must all be effected by one and the same unifying principle, which Kant labeled "the original unity of apperception," or more simply "the transcendental apperception," or understanding. It is grounded upon the hidden substructure of the productive imagination (*Einbildungskraft*), and operates directly upon sense data, in accordance with the familiar scheme of categorical patterns.[3]

Let us put aside here the obvious questions of detail raised by Kant's phraseology, and focus upon what he himself insisted on as central: the need for *unification* of a given field of experience with reference to a single viewpoint, if knowledge is to be forthcoming. There might, I judge, be fairly general agreement with him thus far. But it would be urged quite properly that unless further reason be shown, there is no obvious need to locate that central viewpoint outside the field of awareness itself; all the more since it is commonly agreed that such a field is in fact internally oriented about a focal area often called "the empirical ego," which both philosophers and psychologists readily recognize and acknowledge. Why look for a knower outside the field of experience when *prima facie* we find one within it?

To this question, urged by certain of his critics, Kant

[3] *Kritik der reinen Vernunft,* A 99-110, 115-130.

devoted a section in the 1787 edition of his *Critique*. His initial reason for holding that the knower must be transcendental was that its unifying apprehension extends not merely to the details of experience but also to its *a priori* conditions, the forms of space and time. Now the latter of these is basic, and therefore logically prior, to the experienced *me* (the "empirical ego") no less than to other experienced phenomena. But no simply empirical ego, any more than another phenomenon, can be thought to apprehend its own *a priori* conditions or groundwork. A "transcendental ego" is therefore logically indispensable. So much had already been intimated in the first edition.[4] The further defense of this view in the second edition lays especial stress on the essentially passive status of the empirical ego as such. It is a part of the content of experience, *i.e.*, of that which is experienced. By contrast, the true subject must be active, not passive; experiencing, not experienced. That which is itself *Vorstellung* or percept cannot be, as such, that to which the experienced manifold of *Vorstellungen* is presented; though it may, no doubt, be the authentic outward and visible sign of an active percipient whose self-manifestation it is—a *superficies cogitata* revealing the presence of a genuine *res cogitans*.[5]

So far Kant, with the general drift of whose argument on this particular question I find myself concurring. Its pri-

[4] A 107.

[5] B 155 ff. The phrase *res cogitans* is, of course, appropriate only to a part of what Kant writes; *viz.*, the part which Professor Smith calls "semi-Critical" (*A Commentary to Kant's Critique of Pure Reason*, index *s. v.* "Self," and passages there cited). But this "semi-Critical" bias admittedly "persists throughout the later forms of the deduction," as well as the earlier, because Kant "was irrevocably committed in his own private thinking to a belief in the spiritual and abiding character of the self; and this belief frequently colours, in illegitimate ways, the expression of his views" (*op. cit.*, p. 212). Which is another way of saying that Kant did not write what his able commentator can prove that he should have written in order to make his more radical departures from the older philosophy self-consistent. As Lovejoy has shown, this has been a common failing also among recent and eminent radical empiricists.

mary affinities, so far as I can judge, are with the more moderate sort of "Scholasticism," from Augustine to Leibniz, as against the neo-Nominalism of Hume and his successors. With the rise of positivism, radical empiricism, and various sorts of phenomenalism, however, Hume's prestige has reached new heights, and the portion of Kant's own thought which has enjoyed most favor (outside the ranks of speculative idealists) is that part which has least in common with the older metaphysicians and most in common with Hume; to wit, Kant's strictures on human knowledge of a real external world, rather than his more positive affirmations about the knowing and acting self. As we have already remarked, transcendental or trans-empirical entities are under suspicion just now; and efforts have been widespread to describe both knowing and knowers as wholly within the area of what is immediately experienceable. To an examination of three theories which seek to identify the knower wholly with something experienced or experienceable we now turn.

It seems well to begin with the simplest radical empiricism, of the sort worked out by Hume; not only because his seems to have been the first explicit formulation of such a view and the one which Kant undertook to confute, but because in this peculiary incautious, clear-cut form certain important characteristics of the general position are more easily recognizable than in the less unguarded statements of more recent thinkers. For Hume's theory, then, experience comes in a succession of discrete moments, no one of which is as such intrinsically connected with any other moment, either causally or by inclusion in a common psychical or experiential continuum.[6] Knowledge has no other ground

---

[6] This follows from the assertion (*Treatise of Human Nature*, I.ii.ii; Selby-Bigge's edition, p. 31, 1896) that "time, as it exists, must be compos'd of indivisible moments"; and in the Appendix which

than these separate point-events, and no other locus than that which they provide. They are at once knowers, knowing, and known.

At a given moment, then, Hume's "knower" can be nothing other than just that momentary experience which is then extant; and its "knowing" must consist simply in being what it is.[7] In the absence of temporal or other existential diversity within the single moment, there can take place within it no event or operation which involves the relating of two or more terms that are existentially external to one another. For two such terms cannot both be given within one such moment.

From this root arise unmanageable difficulties for such a theory as Hume sought to maintain. What is ordinarily thought of as cognition, *viz.*, that complex mode of experience which includes "interpretation and classification,"[8] involves precisely such relating of existentially sundered terms, through "symbolic reference."[9] Apart from such overpassing of existential gaps, no interpretation and classification can take place; for these operations involve relating

---

Hume added to Book I of the *Treatise* (Selby-Bigge, 636), it is explicitly affirmed as basic to his entire position "*that all our distinct perceptions are distinct existences*, and *that the mind never perceives any real connexion among distinct existences*" (italics in the original). It is necessary to keep this atomism clearly in view, in spite of numerous passages in which "connexions" of various sorts are spoken of without apology, to the confusion of the unwary reader. (See the next note for examples.)

[7] The radical isolation of each single moment is repeatedly obscured by Hume's unblushing references to "the mind" as "a heap or collection of different perceptions, united together by certain relations" (*Treatise*, I.iv.ii; Selby-Bigge, p. 207); or as "a kind of theatre" (*ibid.*, I.iv.vi; p. 253); or as "a system of different perceptions or different existences, which are link'd together by the relation of cause and effect" (*ibid.*, I.iv.vi; p. 261). All such evasions Hume himself flatly and finally disqualified by such emphatic statements as those quoted in the preceding note.

[8] Dewey, John, *Experience and Nature* (1925), p. 21, *etc.*

[9] Whitehead, A. N., *Symbolism, its Meaning and Effect* (1927), p. 7, *etc.*; *Process and Reality* (1929), pp. 255 ff.

what is now given (a present datum) to something which is not now given otherwise than symbolically. In ordinary perception, for example, various factors in a present experience are taken to represent, or symbolize, some aspect of a thing or situation that is not now existentially present. Thus, the datum a-luminous-red-circle-on-a-dark-field I interpret as meaning a stop-light fifty yards ahead, and set my brakes accordingly. To achieve this interpretation, it is not enough that I see the red-circle datum in relation with other present data accepted simply as data (*i.e.*, as phenomena naked and disembodied, like the Cheshire cat's smile); nor even with data taken as revealing present states of my body or mind. This present red-circle must be taken as related also to luminous red circles previously but not now experienced, to hidden mechanisms for traffic control, to automobiles stationary and moving, to familiar space-time-speed ratios, braking movements not yet performed, and a million other matters not now present as data, but presumed to have such existential status and practical efficacy that, though they are now and may remain always for me unseen, I dare not disregard them.

In such everyday, practical cognition, the envisagement of non-present factors through "symbolic reference" is most plainly involved. On the other hand, when a cognitive judgment has reference to present data simply as data, rather than as signs of more or less remote things and events, there may seem to be no necessary "symbolic reference" beyond what is given; and a way might then be sought for interpreting the former case in line with this latter one. But a closer inspection will make it clear that whenever present data are interpreted and classified in any way, not merely stared at or intuited, there must be reference also to what is not now present. For to interpret and classify means to say of a datum (yellow color, salt taste, or what not): "This is an instance of such or such a class of data." But to say this is forthwith to refer to other members of that class which are not present now, though some at least have been present on other occasions. Only by comparing the present datum with these others, as represented now by some datum—some verbal or other image—which *is* present, can I assign it to a class along with them. Even if the present datum under examination be adjudged unique, the sole member of a class which has no other members not now present, this judgment likewise involves recognition at least that the present datum is other than data not now present. Which is to say that a datum cannot be classified even as unique, except as it is classified also in such other ways as to affirm relations between it and non-present data. Comparison of this sort may be absent from simple intuition or awareness, but never, I take it, from the full-orbed cognition of which we are speaking. And whatever other modes of behavior and experience a theory of knowledge may deal with, it cannot leave this one out of account.

In the light of these considerations, now, Hume's version of radical empiricism must be adjudged untenable. 1) It fails most quickly and obviously as regards our supposed knowledge of an "external world." This failure Hume, of course, recognized in part, and insisted on as a kind of philosophic virtue.[10] But the full extent of its failure is masked rather than revealed by the general course of his argument. I find no intimation, from first to last, of awareness that the external world which cannot be known, on his terms, includes the whole of what lies outside a single present moment. Yet from his principles this consequence plainly follows. No one moment can be another. Neither can any part of the content of one moment be validly affirmed to "represent" or symbolize another moment, nor any aspect thereof; since,

[10] See the *Treatise*, Book I, Part IV: "Of the sceptical and other systems of philosophy," which is in fact a lively defense of *both* skepticism and animal faith (cf. Selby-Bigge, pp. 183-187, etc.). That Hume would not have shied at the latter of these terms is evident from the immediately preceding section, "Of the reason of animals" (*Treatise*, I.iii.xvi; Selby-Bigge, pp. 176 ff.).

as Hume maintained, there is no "real connexion" which could legitimatize cross-reference of content or character from one moment to another. Hence, even though a given pulse of awareness may have *prima facie* the guise of a verbal assertion that some particular cross-reference to another moment is valid, or the vaguer shape of one of those quasi-transitional moments denoted by such words as "from," "toward," "before," "during," "after," "hence," "although," "if," there is no real inter-communication between one moment and another. At a given moment, therefore, there is no valid ground for either retrospective, predictive, or other outward-pointing affirmations. Not even the affirmation that there have been, are, or will be other momentary experiences can claim validity. All talk of a series or "succession" of moments, supposing it by some quirk to be verbally or psychologically possible, is empty of cognitive purport. And any profession, such as Hume's, to refer present "ideas" (images or concepts) to previous "impressions" (percepts or emotions) as their respective sources,[11] and to distinguish between ideas which are, and ideas which are not thus traceable to legitimate origins in impressions, is meaningless and illusory. At the most, a single momentary experience can be as it is: it can not legitimately claim to tell nor to know anything of other moments.

2) But further, no such momentary experience could apprehend or affirm, in the way of interpretative cognition, even its own existence or character. The comparison which, as we have seen, enters into such interpretative cognition is not simply a stark coexistence of data side by side, a simple *Erlebnis* which for an instant is, and then forever is not. Such coexistence of unseparated data within a moment Hume's theory might, indeed, make room for. But that is

[11] *Treatise*, I.i.i.; *Enquiry concerning the Human Understanding*, sec. II. This is, of course, the corner-stone of Hume's thought, which without it must collapse into a "solipsism of the present datum" (George Santayana, in *Essays in Critical Realism*, p. 177, 1920.)

not cognition, not even cognition of the present moment itself. Interpretative knowing, once more, is an event or process significantly more complex; and this Hume also tacitly implied when he talked about "the mind" or "the imagination" as "separating" and "uniting" impressions in habitual ways.[12] Such comparison must be, in brief, a selective noting of particular data and ignoring of others, a remarking of likenesses and differences among those data which are attended to, and a taking of certain of these as signifying something (things, events, or other data) not now immediately present. As we have seen, this reference to what is non-present is involved even in interpretative cognition of a datum as such; and therefore in the cognition of a moment of experience, comprising both data and the actual event of their *being given*, it is involved *a fortiori*. But such operations as those just mentioned require a percipient which must differ from a momentarily given datum, however complex, and also from the momentary event of its appearing. The percipient must be selectively attentive, active, operative, whereas data as such are attended to, selected, taken in this way or that. Moreover, unlike a momentary event, the percipient must endure through a plurality of moments, and be able at need to recapture symbolically this or that past moment, and to anticipate this one or that still to come.

The knower, then, cannot be found within the limits of any discrete momentary experience. Neither is it simply to be identified with one or more of the data of knowledge, though certain of these data may signify it symbolically, and perhaps partially characterize it.

But this is, or should be, an old story in our day. Hume was himself aware of the central difficulty, and of his failure

[12] For example, in *Treatise*, I.i.iii; I.iv.vi (Selby-Bigge, p. 260); *etc.*

to deal with it satisfactorily.[13] In our time, his version of radical empiricism has largely given place to another which professes, with some plausibility, to be more radically empirical; more scrupulously observant of and faithful to experience, which it finds to be not a succession of discrete instants, but an unbroken continuum. Within this continuum are to be found both mind and matter, both knower, knowing, and known. The distinctions among these are held to be arbitrary and relative, rather than natural and ultimate disjunctions. In this continuum, moreover, "the present" is not an indivisible instant, but an internally unified, moving interval: " 'the *specious* present,' " "a saddle-back, with a certain breadth of its own on which we sit perched," a wave in "the stream of thought, of consciousness, or of subjective life," or as James would have said later, of "pure experience."[14] Every such concrete moment "has movement from and towards *within* it."[15] Plainly Hume's discrete "indivisible moments" have no place in this newer empiricism.

Such concrete, internally unified, moving waves of "experience" include within themselves, we are told, both knower, knowing, and all that can be known. The existence of extra-experiential or trans-empirical realities of any sort cannot legitimately be affirmed.[16] And at a given moment,

[13] *Treatise*, Appendix to Book I (Selby-Bigge, pp. 633-636); a passage of rare candor and insight, which might well have led to a rewriting of large portions of the *Treatise* and the *Enquiry* which followed, and to a different place for their author in the history of philosophy.

[14] James, William, *Principles of Psychology*, I, p. 609, p. 239. Cf. his *Essays in Radical Empiricism* (1912), p. 93, etc.

[15] Dewey, John, *Experience and Nature*, p. 29.

[16] Dewey, John, *Essays in Experimental Logic* (1916), pp. 85 ff. James, *Essays in Radical Empiricism*, p. 42; *Pragmatism* (1907), p. 260. The views referred to are so familiar as to need no piling up of citations. Moreover, the ambiguity of the term *experience* in this version of radical empiricism has been commented upon by various critics—Montague, Lovejoy, most recently by W. T. Feldman, in *The Philosophy of John Dewey* (1934), pp. 14-24, and by Dr. E. T. Adams in an unpublished dissertation submitted before the appearance of Dr. Feldman's book—and need not be rediscussed here.

in a given place, the knower is to be sought within just that wave, that specious present which then and there is being experienced. Such a wave, it is said, "points" or flows in a certain manner, and thereby "denotes" (points to) concrete experienced and experienceable things and events both within and beyond its own limits. But everything thus "denoted" is itself of the flowing stuff of "experience," in all respects correlative to and conditioned by the "subject" or knower, which in turn arises in the midst of, and is continuous with, what it denotes. In this continuum, the subject is distinguished from its objects not by any "isolation of the ego," but by practical emergence, within (not out of) the experiential stream, of "uniquely individualized events" called minds, "in which objects undergo directed reconstitution."[17]

This view obviously has advantages over Hume's more atomistic account. It is true that experience has the look of a continuum, or rather of numerous continua each of appreciable duration, associated in various ways. It is true, moreover, that we seem to experience interconnections and mutual conditionings among the successive phases of such a continuum, and that some of these connections may fairly enough be called by such terms as "pointing to" or "denoting." But knowing is more than denoting, as Dewey's phrase "interpretation and classification" frankly recognizes.[18] A weather-vane denotes the direction of the wind; the flow of a brook denotes the slope of a tilted field; a photograph denotes its original; the direction of my eyes denotes the object of my gaze. But in the absence of some-

[17] Dewey, John, *Experience and Nature*, p. 224, p. 222, p. 220. Cf. his *The Quest for Certainty* (1929), pp. 231 ff. Mead, G. H., "The Definition of the Psychical," in *Decennial Publications, University of Chicago*, III (1903), pp. 77-112; *The Philosophy of the Present* (1932), pp. 3-5, pp. 85-89; *Mind, Self, and Society* (1934), Part III.
[18] See above, note 8. Cf. also Dewey: *Experience and Nature*, p. 18, p. 20: ". . . *being* and *having* things in ways other than knowing them, . . . exist." "But *knowing* involves classification." (Italics in the original.)

thing more than mere pointing, none of these would serve as an instance of knowledge. Even denoting with awareness, or being aware of (something), is no adequate account of interpretative knowing. How is *such* knowing to be accounted for within the limits of radical empiricism? Naturally, no serious inquirer will be put off this track by the impatient demurrers of the pragmatists themselves. The problem is not, as Dewey would suggest, whether we can know anything,[19] but how we can know reflectively or interpretatively. This is not a pseudo-problem.

It seems to me that for a radical empiricist, the analysis will differ according as his theory affirms knowledge at a given moment of things and events beyond the specious present centered in that moment, or contents itself with affirming knowledge only of what is presented in a single attention span or specious present.

1) As to the former alternative, analysis may proceed as follows. What is actually given at any moment is the experience included within a brief interval (at most a few seconds in duration)[20] which empirically has such-and-such qualitative and relational characters. Among these may be noticed a certain durational "flow" and perhaps a felt strain suggestive of something outside what is given—a before and an after, a beyond. On what condition, now, may these

[19] "But a problem of knowledge in general is, to speak brutally, nonsense. For knowledge is itself one of the things that we empirically *have*." ". . . what has gone by the name of theory of knowledge . . . has been a discussion of whether we can know at all." See *Experience and Nature*, p. 21, p. 19; and cf. *The Quest for Certainty*, pp. 193-194.

[20] Mead's conception of "functional presents" which "are always wider than the specious present" in "temporal spread" may be useful for psychological exposition or metaphysical speculation, but in epistemological analysis it is more apt to raise problems than to solve them. Likewise, his definition of "a present" as the duration of any unique emergent event, even one so protracted as the emergence of "a galaxy of galaxies," is full of ambiguities. See *The Philosophy of the Present*, p. 88, pp. 23-24. Neither concept can be stated within the limits of a rigorous empiricism.

present data legitimately be accepted as symbolizing, say, an event in the past? Only on condition that the "suggestive" data are now present to a percipient which has experienced and can recall events now past, as well as experience the data now present. But do we not find such a percipient in the continuing "stream of consciousness" (or of "pure experience") which constitutes the experienceable "self"? That is, of course, a happy phrase of James's, but in cold fact no such protracted "stream" beyond the brief dimensions of a specious present is ever immediately present all at once; and unless there be a percipient enduring, as no immediate experience endures, through many specious presents, able to compare and to synthesize data of past as well as of present experiences, one may not argue cogently from a single specious present (which is the most that is ever immediately presented) to an indefinitely protracted past. To note that within a specious present one can distinguish a direction of "flow," from before to after, is highly important but definitely not sufficient. The distinction of before and after is not equivalent to the distinction of past, present, and future.[21] So far as I can judge, one indispensable condition for the latter distinction's being experienced and known is that a knower has actually lived through the lapse of successive presents into the past.

Or take a different sort of instance. On what condition may the data in a given presentation be fairly regarded as signifying a causal agent, say the sun, situated at a distant locus in a public space-time order? On condition, first, that there has been experience of causation not merely as "the conformation of the present to the immediate past,"[22] but

[21] Whether or not one agree with J. M. E. M'Taggart, *The Nature of Existence*, II (1927), sections 306, 348, that the former distinction is in fact abstracted from the latter, on which it is strictly dependent. In any event, it seems clear that the latter cannot be derived simply from the former.

[22] Whitehead, A. N., *Symbolism*, p. 46. Even the "immediate past," if it be really *past*, is outside the specious present, and knowledge of it involves transcendent reference of present data, which are *not* past.

as operative through a considerable interval of time. But this again requires an enduring percipient. Secondly, there must have been experiences of exploration of space: discrimination, selection, and correlation among spatial data on many occasions. Again a task for an active and enduring observer. Finally, there must have been reports interpreted as signifying experiences had by *other observers*, whose experiences have not as such been matter of immediate apprehension by the present observer, yet without whom any reference to a public space loses its most obvious meaning. It is needless to dwell here on the large and basic place of social reference in the whole pragmatic theory.[23] Both the order of nature and the private life of the individual require it for their interpretation. But reference to experiences of other observers takes one definitively beyond the limits, not merely of what is now experienced, but of all that can be immediately experienced by oneself. By such reference, in short, the position of scrupulous radical empiricism is in principle abandoned. Pragmatists are not thoroughgoing empiricists.

2) A different problem would be presented by the position of a thinker willing to eschew all knowledge of past, remote contemporaneity, and future, and confine himself strictly to knowledge of what is immediately given, remaining within "a solipsism of the specious present."[24] Yet even so modest a position seems to me not to escape the burden of epistemological troubles. In principle, the sort of queries we have been raising seem to me apposite, with some shifts

[23] See, for example, *Experience and Nature*, Chs. v-vii; *The Quest for Certainty*, pp. 217 ff., pp. 270 ff.; *Mind, Self, and Society, passim*.

[24] Lovejoy: *The Revolt against Dualism*, 52. Santayana calls it "solipsism of the present moment" (*Scepticism and Animal Faith*, pp. 14-18, 1923), and declares that any other professed solipsism is "logically contemptible." Whether any thinker of note has publicly committed himself to such a view, I do not know; but in semi-formal discussion I have heard an able teacher of philosophy defend it as his own.

of emphasis. First, if one holding this view should urge its superiority to Hume's on the ground that it employs the more truly empirical concept of the specious present having continuous duration, rather than the unmanageable notion of discrete instants, it would be in place to inquire whether a specious present can be *known* as such, except from a point of view not wholly within it. As seen wholly from within, such a brief span would not, I think, announce itself as "specious." It is rather by comparison of one such interval with others that each is seen to have the truncated character of an arbitrarily isolated, extended segment. Since what is included within such an interval is, by definition, ostensibly all *present*, such recognition of its relativity as that implied by the term specious must derive from some other source. Further, if such an interval were merely lived (*erlebt*) as *what is*, and not compared with other such intervals which now are not, I question whether it could be known even as *present*, in implied contrast with past or future. One may, indeed, experience strain or urgency or trend within an unreflective moment of intuition; but one cannot, I think, recognize that from which, nor that to which, a present experience points—to wit, a past and a future—without comparison between what is present and what is existentially non-present. "Solipsism of the specious present," that is to say, is precluded from knowledge of itself or its presented content in the way of "interpretation and classification," and therewith from any reflective claim to superiority over other views. Such solipsism, in short, could only *be*, not know.

Let us glance, finally, at a more critical version of radical empiricism, which frankly affirms that knowledge necessarily involves *a priori* "construction or interpretation by *the mind*," and that "pure empiricism" is caught in a "vicious circle."[25] With very much in Professor Lewis's common-sense account of knowing I find myself in hearty agreement; and at the very point to which this paper addresses itself, there are statements in his book which seem at first to suggest that its author is not really a radical empiricist at all.[26] But his determination to avoid all traffic with *Dinge-an-sich*[27] leads him to declare roundly, in words, that talk of a mind "which is not to be found *in* experience" is philosophically inadmissible.[28] In defense of such exclusion of trans-empirical entities—things and minds alike—he argues, on the strength of Peirce's principle, that all one should mean by *thing* or *mind* is the sum total of its conceivably experienceable effects.[29]

This effort to stay within the bounds of radical empiricism, however, not only begs the question at the outset. It subjects the arguments also to severe strain at more than one point. 1) It requires that *experienceable* be taken to include not merely what is actually observed or observable, but whatever is conceivable, and whatever is even possibly or conjecturally intelligible.[30] Even so, it turns out that the effort to extend this elastic verbal net widely enough to include all reality reduces to "a willingness to bet on our capacity to triumph over *any* apparently chaotic character of experience and reduce it to some kind of intelligible order." It is, moreover, candidly admitted that an affirmation of such universal intelligibility of all things "is saved from being falsified" only "by the fact that it sets no time-

---

[25] Lewis, C. I., *Mind and the World-Order*, pp. 27-28, 44, etc., 1929. Italics in quoted passages mine.

[26] For example: "Whatever experience may bring, the mind will be there; whatever belongs to the mind is assured in advance" (p. 212). This sounds more like Kant than like Dewey.

[27] *Ibid.*, p. 64, p. 180.

[28] *Ibid.*, p. 415. Italics in the original.

[29] *Ibid.*, pp. 416-422. Cf Peirce, C. S., *Collected Papers*, V, p. 1, p. 258, (ed. Hartshorne and Weiss, 1934).

[30] Lewis, C. I., *Mind and the World-Order*, p. 418, pp. 224 ff., 1929.

limit on our efforts to understand, and hence no failure can be final."[31] In short, the dictum is an article of faith, not a philosophical conclusion.

2) Further, the difference implied by the distinction between knowing and being (*ratio cognoscendi* and *ratio essendi*) is continually cropping up with its reminder that knowing does not tell the whole story. What are given in experience—to wit, certain data or phenomena—serve as a "clue to" the presence and nature of an existing entity which is their "cause."[32] This is true both of things and of minds. The ontal roots of the latter are, in part, basic needs and modes of behavior directed to their satisfaction: "very fundamental tendencies to action."[33] That these deeper springs, indicated by the characteristic behavior of minds in observable thought processes, are in fact partly hidden, is at length frankly affirmed. "The mind—and particularly its purpose and activity—is, of course, ultimately mysterious, just as concentration upon the presentation of the starry heaven reveals it as something ultimately mysterious." Any theory is wrong which "ends by identifying cognition and creation, by affirming that there is no *ratio essendi* save the *ratio cognoscendi*, the content of knowledge or the mind."[34] Precisely. Professor Lewis has too stout a hold on things as they are to be as radical an empiricist as certain of his theme phrases would make him out to be.

Indeed, the "transcendentalism" which he denounces would appear to be just the view which this paper also has disclaimed as bizarre and unacceptable: the notion of mind as an entity wholly sundered from the concrete, observable processes of knowing. Whether any thinker of importance has held such a view, I do not know. At all events, the view defended here is not that one, but rather such a one as that

[31] *Ibid.*, p. 226.
[32] *Ibid.*, p. 425.
[33] *Ibid.*, p. 113, p. 92, etc.
[34] Lewis, C. I., *Mind and the World-Order*, p. 424, p. 426; cf. p. 421.

to which Lewis's own discussion of "Mind's Knowledge of Itself" finally comes round.

"Whether this mind is an immaterial agent, or a Democritean complexus of smooth, round atoms, is simply a further question with which we are not here concerned. . . . To characterize the mind as a whole is a metaphysical problem of the first magnitude. But on any metaphysical account which should be even conceivably correct, what we mean by mind must be just what is revealed in the totality of those phenomena which are *ascribed to* mind."[35]

Quite. But this is a different thing from saying what is said earlier, in familiar pragmatic terms, about "the fountain pen in my hand": to wit, that the pen wholly consists of a supposable sum total of experiences (largely the "experiences" not of actual but only of conceivable observers), in which all possible predictions about its behavior would be exemplified.

"These implicit predictions—too numerous and too complex to mention—are all of them about further possible experience. If experience could exhaust *all* such prediction, what I mean by "the fountain pen in my hand" would completely coincide with what this totality of experience would include."[36]

No. For even this totality of experience would not include the ontal cause, over against any and all observers, from which in part these numerous experiences would stem as effects.[37] No sum total of experiences by however many observers would ever include the whole of the pen *qua res et causa.* To say otherwise is to affirm "that there is no *ratio essendi* save the *ratio cognoscendi.*" In like manner, no sum of observations would ever include the whole of a mind, as real and active, subject and cause. An "ultimately

[35] *Ibid.,* 421. Italics in the orginal.
[36] *Ibid.,* 416. Italics in the original.
[37] *Ibid.,* Ch. 2, and p. 425: "The star is the cause of the light and the light is evidence of the star."

mysterious" mind is not, after all, to be found wholly "*in* experience," however widely (short of complete nullification) that term be stretched. But to accept this conclusion, to which Professor Lewis's more realistic insights might bring him if he were not too unwilling, is to pass the bounds of radical empiricism.

What lies beyond these bounds? "An immaterial agent, or a Democritean complexus of smooth, round atoms"? A substantial soul, or a sentient body, or a subject of some other sort? These are queries which cannot be examined here. But as radical empiricism grows more self-critical, they cannot much longer be called pseudo-problems and brushed aside.

If these considerations be well founded, they apply no less forcibly to religious experience and to what may be taken as knowledge of God than to knowing of any other sort. Radical religious empiricism may in theory take either of two main forms. It may assimilate the object of religious knowledge to the subject, and declare that God is merely a datum in human experience; or it may assimilate the subject to the object, and represent man as absorbed in God or as a "mode" of God's Being. The argument of this paper bears most directly upon the latter of these alternatives.

The former of them is the way of what Professor Macintosh has aptly called "subjective idealism in religion."[38] It disparages in principle not the independent reality of the subject, but that of the supposed Object of religious knowledge; and only in special cases, when the subject also is reduced to a moment in a general flux of "pure experience,"[39] does subjective idealism take a form which is open to criticism of the present type. One who regards it as mistaken

---

[38] King, W. P., ed., *Humanism, Another Battle Line*, p. 61, 1931. Cf. Macintosh, D. C., *The Pilgrimage of Faith*, pp. 155 ff., 1931.
[39] See above, note 17.

in its general and essential denial of the independent reality of God must bring to bear another sort of argument, chiefly metaphysical and analogical rather than epistemological and analytical in character.

But upon the other alternative, the tendency of extreme mysticism, Spinozism, absolute idealism, or various sorts of relativism, to affirm the existential identity of men with God, the present analysis has a direct and, I think, an important bearing. It presumes to offer cogent grounds for affirming as true the conviction of a recent writer that "the religious awareness has an incurable dualism in it"; and it keeps the way open for his further judgment that God and the human soul stand "over against one another in that tension of independent wills without which a personal relationship could not exist."[40] This is familiar traditional Christian doctrine, and I think sound doctrine. It needs reaffirming just now wherever Schleiermacher's "philosophy of identity"[41] has proved too seductive, and led to an undue softening of the contrast between men and God. It needs reaffirming also, however, against the ostensibly opposite tendency now appearing among his most vehement critics, to exalt God by attenuating man, and declaring that man's existence or essential being consists wholly in a relationship to God.[42]

[40] Farmer, H. H., *The World and God*, p. 86, 1935.

[41] Most strikingly formulated, perhaps, in his posthumously published lectures in philosophy, the *Dialektik* (ed. Halpern, 1903), pp. 214-224. This passage, with some similar though more rhapsodic passages from the *Reden*, is the *locus classicus* for such indictments as those of Karl Barth: *Die Theologie und die Kirche*, pp. 151-152, 1928, and Emil Brunner: *Die Mystik und das Wort* (2e Aufl., 1928), p. 56 ff. The whole question of the relation between Schleiermacher's thought and Schelling's, treated earlier by Süskind and Wehrung, has been most recently and closely examined in an unpublished dissertation by Dr. Richard B. Brandt.

[42] So Professor Brunner: *Gott und Mensch*, p. 83, p. 85, 1930: "Darum ist das menschliche Ich kein für sich bestehendes, keine Eigenschaft des Menschen, sondern ein Verhältnis zum göttlichen Du." "Das Wesen des Menschen als Menschen, so haben wir gesehen, ist identisch mit seiner Stellung zu Gott."

From the standpoint of traditional Christian doctrine, both these opposing emphases are one-sided. They begin, indeed, as avowed antagonists, but they both end by jeopardizing the real "otherness" of man. Interestingly enough, it is their respective accounts of religious knowledge and its implications which lead to their curiously similar denials of human independence. The "philosophy of identity" in its most frequent contemporary versions lays primary stress upon the ultimate unity of the All through Mind, Reason, or Spirit, and holds that man as rational and spiritual discerner of essentially spiritual Reality approves himself one therewith. At the other extreme the "dialectical theology," in its avowed renunciation of reason and stress on stark revelation, runs some risk of reducing to the vanishing point man's activity as recipient of revelation, and thereby of approaching, if it ventures into metaphysics at all, that reduction of man to a mode or a function of God which it began by decrying. The two sorts of doctrine differ in intent, but some of their implications are surprisingly alike.

The truth seems to be that if a gospel of salvation such as the Christian gospel is to have anything like its *prima facie* meaning, it must be held that each man stands over against God as a real other self.[43] Whether or not any such gospel or any such religious philosophy is in fact defensible, by and large, cannot be argued here. But so far as it goes, the result of the present inquiry accords better at this point with the traditional Christian doctrine than with any view, ancient or modern, which would nullify the real otherness of each man. Thus far, at least, epistemological analysis gives support to the moral and religious interests which are at stake in the affirmation that man is a substantial self, existentially other than God.

[43] How clear this seems to a thorough conservative may be judged from A. Schlatter: *Das christliche Dogma*, pp. 35-36, 1911.

IX

THE NEW SCIENTIFIC AND METAPHYSICAL BASIS FOR EPISTEMOLOGICAL THEORY

By

Filmer S. C. Northrop

Professor of Philosophy, Yale University

In one of his most profound dialogues, Plato says, "If I find any man who is able to see unity and plurality in nature, him I follow, and walk in his footsteps as if he were a god."[1] This is an exceedingly strong statement. It is equivalent to the contention that anyone who correctly solves the metaphysical problem of the one and the many possesses the clue to all other problems. It is also very empirical in its emphasis. Apparently, a merely hypothetical theoretical solution will not suffice. Unity and plurality must be combined as they are seen "in nature." In other words, a philosophy which provides an adequate solution of this metaphysical problem must have its basis in the natural sciences.

If Plato is correct, then very important events have occurred in contemporary science. Certain discoveries in biology,[2] physics and mathematics are necessitating an entirely new solution of the metaphysical problem of the one and the many. Evidences of irreducible unity and plurality have

---

[1] *Phaedros*, p. 266.
[2] Burr, H. S., and Northrop, F. S. C., "The Electro-dynamic Theory of Life," *Quar. Rev. of Biology*, Vol. 10, pp. 322-33.

been found in nature which necessitate a fundamental modification in the basic assumptions of modern scientific and philosophical thought. The consequences of this for the validation of knowledge in general and religious knowledge in particular merit attention.

The issue involved in this metaphysical problem of the one and the many is an exceedingly simple one. Stated in its most elementary form, the question is whether nature is one thing or many things. At first sight this may seem to be a very trivial matter and one quite easy to resolve. The history of scientific and philosophical thought, however, indicates that this is far from being the case.

Consider the more technical forms in which the problem exhibits itself. In mathematics it appears in the age-old question concerning the relative primacy of arithmetic and geometry; in physics, in the issue between atomic theories and field theories; in biology, in the issue between entities and organisation; in theology, in the conflict between theism and pantheism; and in economics and politics, in the debate concerning "rugged individualism" *versus* national and international planning. These examples suffice to indicate that the problem is difficult to resolve, and also of so far-reaching significance that a solution of it on the general metaphysical level might, as Plato hinted, provide the clue to the resolution of the most basic difficulties in practically every field of human experience.

The core of the difficulty which the problem presents appears the moment one attempts to pursue any possible answer to its logical consequences. Suppose, for example, that one accepts the monistic thesis that nature is one thing. Then atomicity becomes a mystery, any distinction between the human mind and the divine mind becomes difficult to understand, and the existence of ignorance and error becomes impossible to explain. If, on the other hand, one embraces the pluralistic alternative the result is little better. Then the existence of the continuous, relatively constant relatedness exhibited in space and time becomes difficult to account for without recourse to the artificial absolutes which the theory of relativity has rejected; any community of understanding between one mind and another becomes unintelligible, and the existence of any valid knowledge of anything other than one's private impressions is rendered a mystery.

Nevertheless, when we attempt to combine the two answers a contradiction seems to confront us, for how can nature be one thing and many things at the same time? It is quite true, as Professor M. R. Cohen has suggested,[3] that there is no insuperable logical difficulty here, since nature can be one thing in certain respects and many things in certain other respects without any contradiction. But this is hardly a resolution of the problem, unless one specifies both sets of factors and constructs a metaphysical system in which they are shown to fit together without formal contradiction or a conflict with empirical evidence. The traditional scientific and philosophical theories in which this has been attempted have ended in one or the other of the extremes with the respective difficulties indicated above. It appears that something is wrong with the traditional empirical assumptions from which the problem has been attacked.

This makes the present developments in science of considerable importance. It is to be noted that traditional modern science rested upon the thorough-going pluralistic answer to the metaphysical problem of the one and the many. Two examples suffice to indicate this. First, physics and chemistry were formulated in terms of an atomic theory. Second, mathematics reduced geometry to arithmetic. The first evidence of the inadequacy of these assumptions appeared in biology in the last half of the last century when the French physiologist, Claude Bernard, called attention to the fact that although the traditional pluralistic physico-chemical theory of living creatures gives an excellent ana-

[3] Cohen, M. R., *Reason And Nature*, New York: 1931.

lytical account of the constituents of biological systems, it fails to provide for their organic unity and their organic relationship to the rest of the universe. This internal relationship between the organic and the inorganic was emphasized later in the more explicit terms of the physical chemistry of Willard Gibbs by Professor L. J. Henderson.[4] General thermodynamic considerations, particularly those indicating the absolute dependence of living creatures upon energy from the solar system, re-emphasized this conclusion. Thus gradually it became evident that not merely the organism as exhibited in its local adjectival characteristics, but also the organism in its essential relations to the rest of nature, must be considered under the category of unity as well as under the category of plurality.

At the opening of our century much the same thing became evident in physics. It had been concealed before because all previous signs of unity or continuity in observed nature, such as its systematic spatial and temporal order or its continuous field manifestations, had been separated from the physical content and set up either in the background of nature as the unobservable, unverifiable absolutes called space, time and the ether, or in the background of the philosopher's mind as necessary forms of intuition in terms of which the mind must necessarily constitute its experience. As we now know, this was a mistake. The theory of relativity removed this artificial dichotomy between pluralistic matter and monistic synthetic structure. The monistic continuous structure of experience and nature is not a ghostly set of absolutes in the background of either nature or mind, but the very structure of the physical content of nature itself. But to discover this is to come face to face with the fact that physical nature is one as well as many.

As long as we confine ourselves to biological and physical considerations in treating this basic metaphysical question there is always the possibility of error. Our conclusion may

[4] Henderson, L. J., *The Order of Nature*, Cambridge: 1925.

be due merely to the incompleteness of our empirical information or to our failure to analyze our findings with sufficient thoroughness. In mathematics and especially in logic, however, this is not the case. For in the latter sciences we are concerned with the concepts in terms of which any clearly formulated theory concerning any subject-matter whatever must be expressed. The concepts of logic and mathematics hold not merely for this world but for any universe of discourse whatever. This is especially true if the type of consideration in question is one involving the logical foundations of mathematics.

It is precisely in connection with these most fundamental concepts of modern mathematics that the present shocking and perplexing difficulty in that science occurs. There are contradictions not merely in its most fundamental concepts and principles, but these contradictions are of such a general nature that they pass over into logic also. This means nothing less than that the most elementary assumptions underlying modern scientific, philosophical, and logical thought are inadequate.

The full account of the character of these assumptions is too large an undertaking to be attempted here. However, the following brief summary will suffice to provide what is relevant for our present purposes. The first rigorous, complete, deductive formulation of modern mathematics in purely logical terms was made by Russell and Whitehead in their monumental work *Principia Mathematica*. Without its "Theory of Types," which is now generally regarded as unsatisfactory,[5] contradictions appear in this work both in mathematics and logic. It has now become generally accepted that the attempt to escape these contradictions within the premises underlying modern mathematics is doomed to failure.[6] It becomes necessary, therefore, to determine what

[5] See Ramsey, F. P., *The Foundations of Mathematics*, pp. 11, 21-32, London: 1931.
[6] *Ibid.*, p. *xii.*

these fundamental assumptions underlying modern mathematics are, and to modify them in a way which will avoid the paradoxes.

An examination of the history of modern mathematics shows that these assumptions were first framed by Dedekind and, more particularly in a more generalized and logical form, by Georg Cantor. Fortunately Cantor leaves for us a published paper in which he specifies what his premises involve, not merely on the mathematical, but also on the metaphysical side.[7] This paper shows that modern mathematics rests upon the assumption of the actual infinite many. In other words, modern mathematics has attempted to account not merely for the discontinuity of matter but also for the unity of the number continuum and the spatial continuum in terms of the pluralistic answer to the metaphysical problem of the one and the many. Since the paradoxes of Mengenlehre demonstrate the failure of Cantor's pluralistic answer to this mathematical and metaphysical question, it appears that logical and mathematical as well as biological and physical considerations enforce a return to at least a partially monistic solution of our basic metaphysical problem.

The full force of the mathematical and logical basis for this conclusion must not be lost. When considerations involving the foundations of mathematics necessitate a certain conclusion, we reach a position which must hold for any logically or mathematically formulable universe whatever. Thus no appeal to the contention that our empirical knowledge in biology and physics is incomplete can enable us to escape the verdict that the modern attempt to conceive of nature in terms of thorough-going pluralism has failed. It appears that only by conceiving of any mathematical or logical system, and hence, of any scientific or philosophical theory whatever, as involving irreducible continu-

[7] Cantor, Georg, *Gesammelte Abhandlungen*, pp. 370-376. Berlin: 1932.

ity and unity can one escape the logical and mathematical paradoxes of Mengenlehre.

Already the mathematicians Brouwer and Weyl have drawn this conclusion, locating the irreducible unity and continuity in the intuitively given continuum of sense awareness.[8] Whether this particular basis for unity is the sole one need not concern us here. There are important reasons for believing that it is not. The point remains, however, that contemporary logic and mathematics join with biology and physics in enforcing the conclusion that this physical universe or any other conceivable possible universe involves *in part* a monistic solution to the metaphysical problem of the one and the many.

This is the novel and essentially anti-modern metaphysical conclusion established by the scientific work of our day. But immediately, if we are not to go hopelessly astray, we must place beside this factor another equally certain and important one: There is also irreducible plurality.

Never before were there verified scientific theories which require atomicity and purality to the extent of the scientific theories of the present moment. There is atomicity not merely of matter and electricity but also of energy. Moreover, down in the regions of the sub-atomic there are increasingly weighty suggestions that the continuous theory of space and time may fail. True as it is that irreducible unity exists, it is also even more overwhelmingly true that irreducible atomicity and plurality are also present.

Certainly were Plato alive today he would be following our mathematicians and logicians and physicists, as he followed those of his day, as if they were gods. But having followed them and having learned what they have discovered, how would he formulate the philosophy which is involved? Certainly not in terms of the scientific and philosophical ideas of the fourth century B.C., nor in terms of those of the eighteenth century A.D. The man who created

[8] See, Weyl, H., *The Open World*, Ch. III, New Haven: 1932.

a new philosophy for the new Greek science would insist on a twentieth century philosophy for the new twentieth century science. But how would this philosophy be formulated?

This is the basic question of our day. To work out an explicitly formulated solution of the metaphysical problem of the one and the many which will combine the present scientifically verified evidences of irreducible unity and irreducible plurality without contradiction, placing each where observation, experiment, and logical analysis of the foundations of mathematics reveal or require it to be *in nature* is the tremendously thrilling and important basic scientific and philosophical undertaking of our time.

The beginnings of one attempt to work out such an explicit solution of the problem have been indicated elsewhere,[9] with results sufficient at least to show that it is possible to construct a system which combines irreducible unity with irreducible plurality without contradiction. Here we shall assume that some such solution is possible and necessary, and concern ourselves with indicating in very rough form the consequences for the cultural sciences and the theory of knowledge.

This can be done most easily by approaching the matter from the historical standpoint. If one takes any major branch of human experience or any of the major cultural factors in Western Civilization and compares their characteristics in the Medieval and Modern World a very interesting fact appears. In politics, for example, the final locus of sovereignty in the Middle Ages is in the will of God as expressed in the Divine Right of Kings in the many kingdoms and as exhibited even more concretely in the one Holy Roman Empire, whereas in the Modern World its locus is in the wills

[9] Northrop, F. S. C., *Science and First Principles*, New York: 1931.

of the many individuals as expressed in democratic majorities and exhibited in the pluralism of nations. Similarly in religion, the Medieval World has its one authoritative Roman Church Catholic whereas the Modern World has its many Protestant and other denominations. Likewise in economics and sociology, there is in the Medieval Era the one unified commercial and social heirarchy of feudalism, as opposed to the free play of many economic forces and the liberty of the many "economic men" of modern industrialism.

So one could go through every major phase of thought and culture. Medieval educational institutions have their systematized course of study with its definite sequence, beginning in logic and the scientific and philosophical works of Aristotle, and culminating in the theology of a Saint Thomas[10]; modern education has its many separate subjects of study, each tending to be taught by itself and prone to regard itself as self-sufficient. Thus in matters political, economic, social, religious or educational the ultimate appeal of reason in the Medieval World is to the systematic theoretical formulation of all the materials of knowledge considered in their unity, just as the ultimate appeal of practical conduct is to the one will of God as represented in His one authoritative church and His divinely appointed political representatives; whereas in the Modern Era the ultimate appeal of reason is to the facts of the independent fields of knowledge considered in their manyness, in and for themselves, just as the ultimate source of appeal in practical affairs is to the many consciences or opinions of the many individual men. Clearly one epoch is dominated by the monistic, the other by the pluralistic solution of the metaphysical problem of the one and the many.

This is not to deny that there were important men in each period who held the opposite view, or that even the

---

[10] Compayré, Gabriel, *Abelard and The Origin and Early History of Universities*, Part III, New York: 1893.

generally accepted outlook of each period had the other pole of the problem of the one and the many represented in it to some degree. The fact remains, however, that these general differences between the Modern and the pre-Modern World do exist, and center in different answers to our basic metaphysical question.

Our thinking about the past and the present will be clarified if we consider these two epochs of Western Culture in terms of the explicit theoretical presuppositions which underlie them. In the case of the Pre-Modern World, these presuppositions are to be found in the metaphysics of Plato and Aristotle; in the case of the Modern World, in the physics of Galilei and Newton and its consequences as formulated in the dualistic metaphysics of Descartes and Locke.

The primary point to note with reference to the metaphysical systems of Plato and Aristotle is that, notwithstanding their fundamentally different conceptions of the nature of ideas and the way they are related to experience, both provide intellectual foundations for unity. In the case of Plato, this rational basis for unity is to be found in the Idea of the Good which merges with the frenzy principle of the Boundless to constitute the perfectly rational frenzy of God; in the case of Aristotle it is located in the Unmoved Mover also identified with the Divine source of creation. If we would understand the theory which underlies the cultural institutions, political, economic and religious, of the Middle Ages we must understand these two metaphysical systems and realize that they represented the universe as constituted in its determinate character by a single, perfectly rational principle of unity. If, in addition, we would appreciate why this conception carried conviction not merely with the masses but also with the informed intellectuals of the time, we must go back, behind the philosophical systems of Plato and Aristotle, to the mathematical, biological and astronomical science which gave them their authority.[11]

This is an undertaking yet to be adequately treated, and one quite beyond the scope of this paper. However, two crucial points are to be noted. First, mathematics, which was the dominant Greek science, reached its culminating point with the demonstration of the primacy of the concept of ratio over the concept of number which came in the general theory of proportions of Eudoxos given in the Fifth Book of Euclid's *Elements*. With this demonstration the earlier Pythagorean, and later Democritean, attempts to reduce geometry to arithmetic failed, and the primacy of the one over the many was established. Secondly, astronomy, which was second in importance to mathematics, had shown, first with Eudoxos and later with Callippos and Hipparchos, that the universe is a changeless eternal system of perfect geometrical forms related into a single unity by the ratio of their distances. Thus, not merely Greek mathematics, when it pursued its ideas to their foundation in the concept of ratio, but also Greek astronomy, when it revealed supposedly perfect, eternal, incorruptible ratio and unity to be the stuff of which the universe as a whole is constituted, gave authority to the intellectual foundations for unity which the metaphysical systems of Plato and Aristotle formulated.

It is not an accident that the Greek word for ratio in the key definition of equal proportions in the Fifth Book of Euclid's *Elements* is the same Greek word λόγος which is the term for the Divine in the first sentence of the Fourth Gospel. Nor is it a careless use of words which leads the Latin writers of the Middle Ages to use the mathematical word "ratio" as the root of the word "rational." When the Greek or medieval educated man regarded his universe as grounded in rational unity he was doing little more than

[11] See, "The Mathematical Background and Content of Great Philosophy, *Philosophical Essays for Alfred North Whitehead*, pp. 1-41, New York: Longmans, Green and Co., 1936.

uttering what seemed to him an established conclusion of the science of his time. Such is the basis of the authority which the principle of unity had in the intellectual outlook and cultural institutions of the pre-modern World.

There is one other source for the confidence which the medieval man had in his knowledge, a source bound up explicitly with his monistic solution of the metaphysical problem of the one and the many. An appreciation of this additional factor will not merely help us to understand our predecessors in the Middle Ages, but it must also make us somewhat sceptical, because of the contemporary scientific developments mentioned previously, of the modern man's equal confidence in his own thorough-going scepticism. The crucial point of the matter was noted by Plato when he indicated the connection between the metaphysical problem of the one and the many and the theory of knowledge.

Put very briefly, the relationship is this: If pluralism represents the unqualified and complete solution of the problem of the one and the many, then knowledge of anything other than oneself is a mystery, and scepticism and sophistry are inevitable. This is the case because thorough-going pluralism entails external relations between the knowing subject and anything he presumes to know, thereby providing no basis whatever for any connection or agreement between the knower's ideas and the objects to which they purport to refer. If, on the other hand, thorough-going monism is valid then the knower is internally related to what he may know, his ideas transcend him, and a basis for knowing something more than his own private impressions is provided. To be sure, in the latter case, one must wonder why there should be more than one mind in nature and how ignorance and error are possible, but in any event the truth remains that if monism is to some extent valid then certain characteristics at least of the known provide categories which apply to more than the knower himself. Hence, since the thinkers of the Middle Ages had reason to accept a metaphysics which provided for the validity of the principle of unity, they had specific epistemological grounds for believing in their knowledge.

Why then did the Medieval World disappear? Why did the metaphysical systems of Plato and Aristotle, with their intellectual foundations for unity, lose their authority? Undoubtedly there are many reasons. There is one, however, which is quite simple and all-sufficient. In the sixteenth and seventeenth centuries science removed the grounds which gave the philosophical systems of Plato and Aristotle their authority. When Galilei revealed many masses in motion to be primary, and when Newton showed not merely that the geometrical orbits of the heavenly bodies can be derived from them, but also that these geometrical forms must alter and even disappear with the decomposition of the molar masses, the entire supposedly eternal incorruptible rational unity of the heavens came crashing down. Nature, instead of being conceived as a rational unity in eternal repose, was revealed as a material many in motion. A little later Georg Cantor, in placing the calculus of Newton and Leibniz upon rigorous foundations, found himself forced to introduce the notion of the actual infinite many. Therewith the one continuum of the real numbers and of space was reduced to a theory of aggregates, the concept of number again took priority over the concept of ratio, the arithmetization of geometry was achieved, and the final Greek and medieval theory of mathematics was repudiated. Thus both modern physics and modern mathematics inaugurated an entirely new intellectual outlook by resolving the metaphysical problem of the one and the many in terms of the primacy and all-sufficiency of the principle of plurality.

This new pluralistic physics had no more than appeared before Galilei, Descartes and Locke proceeded to formulate its philosophical consequences. Galilei himself drew the distinction between the primary qualities in terms of which the objects of physics are conceived, and the secondary qualities which we directly perceive. The fact that the secondary qualities were not attributes of the material substances of physical nature made the addition of Descartes's and Locke's thinking or mental substances necessary. Thus the metaphysical pluralism of the new physics gave rise to an additional metaphysical and epistemological dualism. It was not long before Hume drew the inevitable sceptical consequences which Plato had predicted for such a pluralistic solution of the metaphysical problem of the one and the many. To understand Plato's insight into the theory of knowledge or, more specifically, to recognize the epistemological consequences of the pluralistic answer to the metaphysical problem of the one and the many is to realize that there is no escape from the present relativity and scepticism concerning fundamental matters within the intellectual outlook of the Modern World.

The philosophy of Kant provides no exception to this rule. In this philosophy there are two factors: the notion of the creative ego as a simple substance, and the transcendental theory of ideas. These factors are incompatible. If the creative ego is primary and an individual simple metaphysical substance, then all ideas are creations of its own activity and the transcendental theory of ideas is invalid. But upon this basis Kant's knower stands in the same relation of otherness to anything, other than itself, which it purports to know, as does Descartes's or Locke's or Berkeley's mental substance; in which case, Hume's analysis holds. This emphasis in Kant, falling back on the practical norm, leads straight into the relativism and scepticism of contemporary pragmatism. Kant only escapes from solipsism by emphasizing the transcendental theory of ideas, but this emphasis is incompatible with the notion of the individual creative ego conceived as a simple substance, and leads directly into the absolute monism of Hegel, as history shows. The result is not a solution of the fundamental epistemological problem of modern philosophy, but a mere retreat from the fundamental difficulty which it presents.

In any event these reasons why are irrelevant. The fact is that scepticism is upon us. The outcome of the modern solution of the problem of the one and the many in terms of thorough-going pluralism is precisely what Plato predicted and Hume formulated. Situated as the modern man is, with only his own private thinking substance, characterized by qualities fundamentally different from the primary qualities which characterize that which is before him to be known, how can we except him to be anything else but a thorough-going relativist and sceptic? Being but one of a metaphysical many, he is so completely isolated from any possible object of knowledge, that no ground exists for regarding his own ideas as referring to anything beyond his private impressions and opinions.

His epistemological position is made no better by the humanist's or Protestant's pluralism of souls, for the crux of the difficulty is not *what* the many metaphysical substances are, but the fact that they are *many*.

What must be realized is that the sophistry and scepticism which characterize the contemporary attitude toward secular and religious knowledge are a necessary result of the pluralistic answer to the metaphysical problem of the one and the many upon which the Modern World rests. Within this traditional standpoint there is no answer to the epistemological problem raised by sixteenth century physics and formulated by Descartes and Locke, except the sceptic's answer. The final word in modern philosophy was written by David Hume. Moreover anyone in the sixteenth century who had learned what Plato has to teach on this matter, or who had thought through the relation between thorough-going metaphysical pluralism and epistemology would not have needed to wait until Hume to know what the outcome would be.

This makes it evident that there can be no possibility of

authoritative philosophically-validated knowledge, either religious or secular, which will integrate consistently with our positive scientific information, unless natural science itself modifies its traditional thorough-going pluralistic solution of the metaphysical problem of the one and the many, and popular humanistic philosophy and Protestant theology reject their personalistic pluralism.

As we have indicated, this is precisely what contemporary science is doing. Moreover, it appears that the change does not involve a complete reaction to the monistic extreme, but requires the supplementation of the traditional atomic pluralism with an irreducible element of monism. When the metaphysics for this new physics is explicitly and systematically formulated, it should be possible to designate those concepts which, because they refer to irreducible continuous factors, transcend all local private impressions. Thereby the limits of scepticism may be defined, and some knowledge of the whole of nature and experience may be obtained and philosophically validated, without rendering the obvious fact of human error and ignorance a mystery.

This means that the modern epistemological problem, so fairly and systematically investigated in Professor D. C. Macintosh's classic work, *The Theory of Knowledge*, is not to be solved within the moderns' premises, and can be resolved only by rejecting the fundamental dualistic and pluralistic metaphysical premises from which, consciously or unconsciously, all modern epistemological discussion, even when it turned monistic, has proceeded. In other words, the solution of the fundamental epistemology problem of modern philosophy is not to be found in the selection of one or the other of the rival dualistic, idealistic or realistic premises concerning which modern philosophers have differed, but in the rejection of the common premises defining their problem in the first place, upon which all modern philosophers, dualists, idealists and realists alike, have agreed. This rejection amounts to an abandonment of modern philosophy similar to, and as far reaching in its significance for western thought as, the abandonment of medieval philosophy which came in the seventeenth century with Descartes.

What the effects of this will be for religious knowledge in particular will depend upon the specific character of the principle of unity which the breakdown of thorough-going pluralism in physics and mathematics entails. This can be determined only by an analysis of the fundamental concepts of these sciences, and is a problem in the philosophy of science taking one beyond the limits of this paper. However, the mere fact that thorough-going plurality has failed in science, and that some irreducible unity must be accepted, is sufficient to place an important restriction upon the devastating effects of thorough-going scepticism for religion. Although this is not a sufficient condition for the validation of religious knowledge, it is a necessary one.

To the contemporary sceptics—the disciples of Hume and the consistent disciples of Descartes—all this will seem absurd, just as the conclusions of Galilei seemed absurd to the traditional philosophers of his day. It is to be noted, however, that no paper has ever expressed any more unreserved recognition of the finality of Hume's conclusions, assuming the premises of modern philosophy, than has this one. But no philosophical premises are self-evident. A theory is no better than the empirical factors upon which it rests. These, in Hume's case, are to be found in the peculiar relation to its object of knowledge, in which the physics of Galilei and Newton, with its distinction between primary and secondary qualities, placed the knowing subject. But if the strength of these scientific assumptions measures the strength of Hume's position, their limitations likewise measure the weakness of that position.

It is precisely these limitations which contemporary science has demonstrated. The *thorough-going* principle of plurality has failed in physics on empirical grounds and in mathematics on logical grounds. A solution of the metaphysical problem of the one and the many is required which consistently combines irreducible unity with irreducible plurality. Science has discovered "unity and plurality *in nature*" and the mind of man must "follow as if led by a god."

X

A PSYCHOLOGICAL APPROACH TO REALITY[1]

By

HUGH HARTSHORNE

Research Associate in Religion, Yale University

IT IS impossible to move empirically out of the cross-section of immediately present reality. Psychology, like all scientific effort, stretches beyond the immediately present only by piling one speculation on another. At best, it can give plausible accounts of the remote in time and space and of the mechanisms by which the near and remote together constitute systems of behavior. Such systems are never observed in their entirety, even when they are purely imaginary, much less when they are attributed to external events, for attention is always focalized, and therefore partial. Small unities, to be sure, are observed, such as a circle inscribed in a square, or the thought of bodies falling. These in turn may be caught in symbols and so be connected in thought with other like symbols to form a more complex pattern. But such a pattern is a construct, increasingly removed from its original parts. It is a specious unity, but a precious one, apparently. At all events, the struggle to comprehend, to think things together, goes on unabated, even though the thinkers are not aware that these unities are based on

[1] By arrangement of the publishers this essay appeared in *Social Science*, Volume XI, Number 4, October, 1936.

unproved assumptions—including the assumption of the possibility of proof.

Having said so much, it would seem hardly worth while to continue. To do so, indeed, might be taken as highly presumptuous, and defensible only on the ground that the first paragraph constitutes an alibi for ignorance. It will be obvious enough that some such alibi is needed, but my temerity is based on the feeling that theories of reality and of knowledge of reality usually lack a genetic account of themselves, and also give too little attention to the processes by which a newborn organism gets to be a knower or even a philosopher. A psychological approach to the comprehension of reality should be genetic. It must inevitably be speculative.

Philosophers, all being adults, begin their investigations of the nature of reality *after* "reality" has become stereotyped in accordance with a cultural pattern. Agreed that there is no way to escape this cultural patterning. But something would be gained if it could be observed at work on the child, or if the growing organism could report its experiences from even the foetal stage. It may be that our sundry dichotomies or pluralities would prove to be artifacts of language and that progress toward unity would come through recovery of naïveté.

Take, for example, the bifurcations of reality or of experience into matter and mind, fact and value, self and environment, self and society, experience and nature, things and persons. Adults tend to attribute to one term of such dichotomies a degree or type of reality not attributed to the other. Thus some take facts to be the reality rather than values. Others give to values the superior status. To some, selves are the only reals. To others, selves are figments of the imagination. The only reality society possesses is found in the nervous systems of individuals. Or, *per contra*, the only reality individual selves possess is in their incorporation in a social entity which sustains them. Nature, likewise, remains in an ambiguous position, for it seems uncertain whether it exists only as it is experienced or whether the experiencer exists only within nature. And as for the natural and the supernatural, how should any such dualism have arisen, and to what specific objects, or relationships, or values do these two words point?

Somehow or other, contrasted ideas about reality have been developed, presumably in response to contrasted experiences. But it is not clear whether these contrasted experiences were, genetically, experiences of any reality other than the already classified reals which had been sifted through the screen of culture, particularly the screen of language. Apparently, philosophy must look to anthropology as well as to genetic psychology for suggestions as to man's flair for paradox: the desire for synthesis *versus* the desire for analysis; security *versus* adventure; pursuit *versus* quarry; change *versus* stability; the many *versus* the one; differentiation *versus* integration. Certain it is that if we could know how points of view arise regarding the nature of reality we could appraise them more intelligently, and discover in ourselves the force of this or that "logical" argument or conviction. The systems of thought which merely reflect adult stereotypes would lose their sense of finality. The *process* of reality-seeking might be more clearly revealed, and the doors be opened to fresh excursions into the unknown.

In other words, it is the contention of this paper that human problems need to be reformulated. Religion, science, practical management of life, are all cursed by problems which have been so conceived as to develop highly specialized, differentiated pursuits, leading into one *cul-de-sac* after another, and nowhere opening up paths into a future of unlimited creative effort. Not only do religion, science, and art (in a broad sense) each tend to break up into orgiastic cults, but religion as a whole goes one way, science another, and art another, with little or no effort to combine forces in a common attack on man's chief job on this planet.

The complex picture of specialized interests, each with its appropriate set of antithetical dualisms, may be simplified, for present purposes, into three major structures of experience: the time-space structure, the value-will structure, and the self-society structure. With reference to each of these structures, there has been no end of thinking and a vast deal of experiment. They constitute the typical adult and, therefore, philosophical, trichotomy: natural and social science, with psychology floating somewhere in between. It is our problem to consider how these three may be reunited with fruitful results for speculative research and the practical conduct of life. In the pursuit of this inquiry it will be necessary to cover familiar territory. Our difficulties arise from the necessity of putting together in one comprehensive view a variety of facts which we are accustomed to deal with separately. The very specific character of attention, already referred to, makes unification almost impossible. Nevertheless we shall essay the task in which all the king's horses and men are alleged to have failed—doubtless with a similar result.

Time and space as characteristics of reality are, of course, hypothetical. But as hypotheses they are well-grounded because of the structure of organic life, which makes the apprehension of time and space possible and which presumably reflects a significant characteristic of the conditions of life in that this structure "fits" and has been not only conserved but enormously elaborated. The capacity to link passing events in such a way as to distinguish here-now from not-here-now, which protoplasm seems to have acquired, is the original germ out of which have developed not only time and space but also value and the self. Granted the capacity thus to link events, and the rest follows as the day follows the night. The distinction was biologically conserved because it worked, *i.e.*, because the structure which could make it could sustain itself longer than one which could not.

But this is only to say that things happening in the organism created a condition of disequilibrium between it and the environment, the resolution of which, instead of destroying the organism, sustained it, thus affording a structural link between the here-now and the not-here-now. The fact of sustaining is the fact of value, and the resulting continuity of structure is at the same time the primordial basis of the "mine." But the building of protoplasmic structures took place *en masse*, setting the stage for all sorts of competitive and cooperative relations among organic structures, opening the way to the ultimate distinction between the not-mine as merely not-yet-appropriated and the not-mine as "yours," and still later the combination of yours and mine in "ours." One might say, then, that reference to the origins of the three typical structuralizations of reality as a world of time-space facts, a world of values, and a world of selves suggests their fundamental identity as the organic way of apprehending and utilizing the conditions capable of sustaining life and satisfying its developing demands.

If one should attempt to illustrate inorganic happenings one might use a series of dots thus:

. . . .

Only the dots appear one at a time and as each appears the one preceding drops out. Under these conditions there could be no apprehension of time or space or value or selfhood. Only as the successive dots or events are linked in series could the structure be said to react to or apprehend time or space. This might be diagrammed in this way:

. . . . [. | .] . . . . . .

That is, a sheer cross-section of passing events affords no basis for the setting of these events in a framework of time or space, or for the organization of the structure with reference to not-here-now. This expansion of cross-section, seemingly characteristic of primitive organisms,[2] increases enormously as more complex organisms emerge. With the beginning of language with its peculiar capacity to serve as a symbolic substitute for actual situations, the expanded section is potentially extended as far as meaning may be given to words.

The utility of this extension, particularly when it is symbolic, depends upon its correspondence with events, and this type of organic response would be selected for survival only under conditions which promoted such objectivity. This objectivity is secured by increasing the number of experiences of any one organism and the number of organisms undergoing any one type of experience. In this way a singular point of view is acquired by the organism and this, in turn, is supplemented by the experiences of other organisms so as to round out the picture of reality which is included in the expanded set of linked events. Such a composite picture, however, could grow only through the cooperation of organisms, and this in turn gives survival value to communication, and to language as the vehicle of communication. Whatever is real, therefore, comes to be whatever is socially sustained as real because of its functional relation to the satisfaction of developing needs of communicating organisms. Fact, value, and society continue, thus, their functional unity through stages of accelerating interrelationships. But it is the perversity of language that what God joined together in this functional unity, man has tended to set asunder, calling the time-space structure "nature," to be investigated by natural science, largely ignoring the value structure, and forgetting that both are abstracted reflections of changing culture patterns. The reinstatement in man's thinking of the essential unity of his approach to reality would, it is claimed, give him far greater hope of control

[2] This does not imply that some other structure than what we know as organic might not make possible the same type of time-space transcendence.

over both the social process and his interpretation of its cosmic meaning.

Complete elaboration of this notion is impossible in a brief paper, but several incidents in man's career will serve to illustrate the point of view and will lead to its more adequate formulation.

Let us note, first, the relation of the growth of language to ritual and the value structure. How or why words came into being—*i.e.*, how or why vocal signs and signals came to be dissociated from the activities of which they were originally a part—may never be known. The automatic grunts and growls of an animal are, at first, signals only to his opponent or victim.[3] The skillful fighter (through the process of conditioning) "reads" his opponent's intention in his movements, and thus these movements become signs, or conditioned stimuli. Sounds are likewise signs of what is to come next, and are responded to in such a way as to make their continued use of value to the life-system in which they appear. But such sounds are not words. They are not used intentionally by the one who makes the sounds *in order* to convey a signal or meaning. Reference to still more primitive modes of response will suggest how this later usage may have come about.

It is necessary to associate the here-now *versus* there-then disconnection with some practical need to account for its emergence and development. This practical need is, clearly enough, the discrimination between what is usable and what is destructive or unusable. The one is accepted, the other rejected. As time goes on, one is approached, and the other is avoided. And still later, the approaching response is either for appropriation or destruction. Out of such simple beginnings have come our own complex loves, hates, fears, angers,

[3] See Mead's analysis in *Mind, Self and Society* and his further proposal of the function of "grunts" in revealing to the individual that utters them the discriminated rôles of the several individuals involved, and thus leading on to the sense of selfhood.

disgusts. But they signify, in each case, an attempt to translate a signal of some kind. They are a response not merely to a present fact but to a possible fact. "Beware, watch out," marks the line between what we call organic and inorganic behavior. What possibilities are there in this situation? What signs of advantage or danger? Only past experience, conserved in the structure of the protoplasm, could suggest an answer. Thus the past came to be used as a bridge into the future, and "meaning" came into existence as the answer to the question, "What does this portend?"

Variations in portent, and the growing capacity to respond with discrimination to these variations, and with types of behavior appropriate to the possibilities, naturally came into being together.

One type of portent, for example, signified chase; another, flight; another, aggression; and for these elaborate responses elaborate machinery came into use—too elaborate, indeed, save for emergencies, and requiring that a distinction be made between situations portending something and situations portending nothing, or roughly, between live things and dead things. So a dog becomes accustomed to respond to a bone as a dead thing, but if it be suddenly moved by a string, his whole attitude toward it changes. At once he is alert to what this may portend. "What next?" These emotional responses would be stimulated far more frequently by other organisms than by physical objects, leading to recognition of other organisms as different from physical objects. These organisms, however, are not just existing. They are pursuing satisfactions of cravings. Their actions are directed or organized with reference to their own changing conditions. They are building up a structure which reflects the time-space world. Thus each organism is in constant contact with other organisms behaving in the same way, and its most vivid experiences, ominous or potentially satisfying, are inevitably associated with these other organisms.

A part of this experience of organisms is vocalization—

grunts, growls, screeches, roars, etc. With whatever takes place in contact with such organisms, the sound is associated, and therefore becomes a signal, which, like an incipient motion, brings forward into the present as an immediate stimulus a situation that has not yet appeared. Response to time-space is thus intimately tied up with response to organisms, since it is organisms that are most portentous, but whatever is portentous elicits exactly the same type of emotional response—the mechanisms of alertness and readiness to run or fight are brought into play in response to storms and earthquakes, or even whispering winds and murmuring brooks or rolling stones. Nature has a face, the expression of which must be read, just as the gestures of an approaching animal must be read if life is to be safe.

So far, however, with regard to both organisms and physical objects, impending developments are to be thought of as portents, not as intents. The translation of portents into intents marks a long step ahead in evolution and opens up the distinction between the impersonal and personal, nature and the self, science and religion. How this transition took place is concealed in the dim past. Nevertheless, the distinction was made and probably occasioned the development of human selfhood, with all its powers of mental control. The seeds of this development are undoubtedly in the experience of obstructed pursuit of desire, but more particularly in obstructions which arise from competition with other organisms seeking the same objectives. To win a mate, or a meal, it is necessary to defeat a rival first, and having won it, it is necessary to defend it against those who want it—whose actions portend aggression. It is not a far step from this conflict of wants to a conflict of wills and to the distinction between my will and thy will, and the accompanying translation of portent into intent.

But before this step can take place it would seem that signals must become communications. And this is where ritual

seems to supply a needed link, for in ritual signals first become symbols and are used apart from their associated activities. A certain grunt has come to be associated with a
certain activity, such as the kill. A group of hunters all come
to use the same grunt. Later on, when they have slept out
their repletion, one of them happens, by accident, to make
the characteristic grunt of the kill. Granted the powers of
association of which even primitive brains are capable, the
grunt may start going another pursuit, and granted still
higher powers of association, it may start only visions of a
pursuit, with no clear distinction between any one of a
thousand previous experiences and one which is only in
prospect. One has only to assume the survival value of such
symbolic use of signals to account for their development
into means of communication. It remains only for one man
at some time to discover that when he grunts in a certain
way he can control not only his own images but also the
images and actions of others. He has at hand a new tool of
social intercourse—a word, which gives him power, and
which comes to mean, therefore, not only its object, but also
the means by which the object is obtained.

From this point, one can easily read the steps to more
elaborate reviews of what has happened on the hunt or
chase, as the word-signals are repeated which call out images
of what took place; to rehearsals of an impending event,
such as a foray on a neighboring village.

Of such materials were the primitive rituals composed.
Their function was to bring past and future experience into
mind, and so to keep alive the feelings of satisfaction which
otherwise would occur only at the moment of their realization. Furthermore, in anticipating the hunt or battle, and
working up emotional enthusiasm in anticipation of what
was coming, these ritualistic observances served to enhance
the sense of value and at the same time to focus attention
on the objective sought.

By all these means, the cross-section of the here and now

is expanded in time and space in such a way as to fill the time-space framework with a value structure.

The animal capacity for distinction in an embryonic fashion, between the mine and the thine, between my will and thy will, was provided, through language, with a vastly enlarged arena in which, by checking the varied accounts of what had taken place as these were offered by different individuals, the individual imagination was disciplined to the social pattern of consent. The world of fact was the socially accepted world. The world of value was the same world. Selfhood was the individual apprehension of this socially approved world of fact and value.

The evolution of these three worlds from this point constitutes our next problem.

This evolution depends, on the one hand, on the capacity of organisms to assimilate the past and future to the present —that is to respond to immediate situations in terms of their potential values; and on the other, on the fact that organisms exist in such relation to each other that, with the aid of language, this process of value-realization takes place in part jointly and in part in mutual competition of wills. Culture thus embodies the ways by which the potentially real becomes the experienced real. Language, as noted, enormously expands the field of the potentially real in terms of tradition and foresight, which are the forerunners of experiment and natural law, but language provides not only the community of experience which constitutes the life of the group but also the imaginative experience of the individuals composing the group. As this imaginative experience is evolved it is also individualized as my *versus* thy experience, with a large measure of overlapping, representing our experience. Expansion in the world of experience, both as consciously apprehended and as unconsciously participated in through the folk-ways, will depend on the adequacy and stability of the environment in terms of physical resources and group competition. In periods of changing conditions variations in behavior would be at a premium, and these variations would be incorporated, if successful, into the culture. Thus also, man would become conscious of his wants, and of the possibilities of imagined situations to supply them, and thus also, would the process of value-seeking associate itself with the process of world building, self building and society building.

The question "What is reality?" could only be asked if the here-now had already been transcended. It could only be asked by an organism able to respond effectively to the not-here-now, and able, therefore, to distinguish what is from what was or what might be. Prediction, law, idealization, hypothecation, value-seeking are processes which grow out of this faculty of the organism to deal with events in series rather than separately. In so far as this sense of dealing with successive events can be trusted, it enables us to draw a picture of what happens—of what the processes of reality are—and to use as evidence of the validity of our impressions the fact that this time-space-transcending activity has been not only conserved biologically, but increased in range and power. But this time-space-transcending power is itself a biological fact, *i.e.*, it is a function of life processes the basis of which is continuity of protoplasm through changing conditions and events and the capacity of protoplasm to retain and utilize reaction patterns which resist annihilation. The period of time during which this biological process of pattern-forming has been going on is a period of significant proportions in terms of the total history of the planet, so long a history, indeed, that one wonders at the sense of astronomical inferiority that seems to possess so many modern cynics. They forget that the patterns of response embedded in their own natures reflect not only conditions but processes, and afford in themselves a clue to the nature of the reality exhibited in these processes.

But this is by way of parenthesis. The question "What is reality?" could be asked only by a self-conscious questioner —*i.e.*, by a member of a social group—and it could only be answered by the cooperation of other members of this group and the members of successive generations—among whom the contributions of preceding generations are conserved in culture. Only history can answer.

The dependence of answers as to what reality is on the biological and cultural patterns of behavior in response to environmental demands, explains the variations in these answers. The four sets of variables are the individual organisms each with its own heritage and experience, the particular culture in which these individuals operate, the environmental demands to which both the culture and the individuals within it are sensitive, and the varying processes by which individuals assimilate and react to given cultural patterns as they grow from childhood to old age. The discovery of trends in these processes of biological adjustment should throw some light on the reality that sustains them.

It is needful to recall that the reality to which organisms are adjusting and into which they are fitting themselves is inclusive of these same organisms. They are within the total, not outside it. The reality is within them, then, in the double sense that the organic-social structure reflects reality, or builds a picture of it, or provides a point of vantage from which it may be viewed, and that whatever it is that is thus reflected is built into the structure of the organism and its culture patterns. These are aspects of reality, continuous with it and embodying the results of a sufficiently long process to justify being incorporated, even by the physicist, in any theory of the total. It is perhaps this feeling which has led so many physicists to appendix their abstract views of the nature of the world with comments on what their pointer readings omit—*viz.*, the cultural fact of man's personality. Our specialized approaches, valuable as they have been for running down specific data, leave the total almost as incomprehensible as before, and provide no practical techniques for controlling processes which in their nature include factors omitted from the analysis.

Our contemporary efforts to overcome this deficiency in method take the form of attempted syntheses of specialized techniques and specialized bits of knowledge. This movement appears in philosophy and education as well as in science. It fails for the reason that the basic facts to be dealt with are not separable parts of a mechanical whole, but aspects of a process which is in its own nature dynamic and organic. It fails just as the effort to put body and mind together after first separating them fails. When the essence of a fact is togetherness or relatedness or organic structure, can this fact be observed or understood merely by piecing together some other facts? Knowing is a part of the known and the known of the knowing. The attempt to deal with the known apart from the knowing leads to the logical amplification of knowledges, which in turn are thought of as knowledges of independent realities. Then comes the task of trying to unite these realities in some one reality.

Such unity as may be achieved, however, will remain a unity of thought so long as it deals only with thought elements. That is, we cannot expect to think together what is, by hypothesis, separated in fact. The unity thus achieved is specious in the sense that it is not a unity of the here-now; it is an imagined, not an achieved unity, a logical, not an organic unity. The unity of the here-now must be *grown*. That is, the unity of reality is not just a sum of its parts but an essential character, comparable not so much to the logical completeness of a system of thought or the esthetic completeness of a work of art as to the dynamic unity of an organism. It is ever present, but ever changing. It can be described only in terms of functioning relationships, *i.e.*, of relationships which are valuable because they are instrumental to some objective which is itself, therefore, an integral part of the unity. Reality thus achieves progressive unification in terms of emerging ends. The here-now is a resultant not only of the accumulated actualizations of the past but also of the anticipated possibilities attributed to it, provided these anticipated possibilities are so dealt with as to function as determinants of change. Many dreams fail to come true because they are not articulated with the here-now.

It is thus suggested that unity is not just a something thought of but something actual, that it is dynamic in the sense that it enters into a creative process as a factor in the actualization of values. It is not a finality but a functional relationship.

The biological factor in the achievement of progressive unity has been pointed to several times—the capacity to utilize past experience and to rearrange and appraise the past in terms of possibilities of value and of the space-time conditions of value-realization. This process of value-realization is by no means steady, however. For the very biological structure that makes it possible also tends to hold the value-fixing process in equilibrium, because of the fact that organisms live in groups and, with the aid of language, build cultures which provide for each new generation relatively fixed forms of value-realization. Reality is for human beings chiefly whatever society predetermines it to be. But the determination is not absolute for the reason that each individual varies more or less from others in capacity and experience and so tends to break away from the cultural stereotype. When such variant tendencies are purely individual, they are usually abortive. The individual is eliminated. But when several individuals create among themselves a minority culture at variance with the total culture, there is greater chance for change in the total pattern. The same thing happens where large cultures compete and intermingle as in the case of war and trade.

The content of the growing culture may be thought of as originally concerned with the satisfaction of biological necessities but as passing beyond these immediate necessities by slow degrees into esthetic and philosophic pursuits of a more abstract or a more theoretical nature. Culture tended to split up into the practical management of affairs and a group of specialized activities such as philosophy, art, and later science, the practical activities including politics, the economic life, and family life. Religion, or the original totality of culture, out of which these separate interests arose, continued to overspread them all, but as these interests developed their separate cultures, religion was left with less and less of the here-now and more and more of the has been, the might be, and a hypothetical supernatural world of ideas and values existing somewhere else than in the world known through ordinary activities of life. To each of these increasingly organized pursuits, reality was what it dealt with. The scientist, *e.g.*, tended to abstract from experience its space-time features and deal with these by themselves. He has been the most successful, on the whole, in building a picture of reality. But the religionist has at times been powerful enough to oppose to this world a world of values either removed from space-time or existing in some other space-time framework than that of the scientist.

None of these cultural forms, however, could have been built up and organized without a type of mutual interchange of reflective experience which has by no means been universal; which has, indeed, been only partially practiced at any time. The social structure which grew up with the transformation of primates into men so disciplined its growing members that free interchange of reflective experience was all but impossible. In consequence there was little of what a modern would recognize as selfhood. Even today, the average modern is so embedded in his culture, so stereotyped in his action, that, although his vision is enormously expanded both backwards and forwards beyond that of primitive man, he is still operating at a level far below his capacity. His culture creates him, but it also chokes him. He is unable to utilize his biological mechanism in such a way as to react creatively to his environment. The relationships into which he grows and which determine the kind of self he is, antecede him. These relationships have doubt-less been of biological significance. Groups characterized by a certain pattern of relationships survived. Most of them are comparable to the pecking order often found among animals. Chicken A picks on chicken B; chicken B picks on chicken C, but not on chicken A, etc. In human society, however, each individual occupies not just one rôle, but several in succession and sometimes several at the same time. In one he is pecked on and in another he pecks. Hence there is present a factor of instability which now and then results in an upset in the system. This very fact that each one carries his culture pattern in his own nervous mechanism constitutes a threat to any alternative pattern—a sort of drive toward a relationship of dominance to all other humans. In the long run this would tend toward some form of social organization which would be a draw between all human beings—a recognition of the rights of all. Whenever this is achieved, each member is able to contribute his maximum to the life of the group.

Social evolution toward equality of privilege is aided by group conflict, all insiders being held superior to all out-siders and as relatively equal to each other. They hang to-gether, as in a patriarchal society, the brothers presumably in a pecking order to each other—a condition of rivalry. In turn this condition of rivalry becomes rivalry between minor groups, and out of this situation develops the parlia-mentary system of government, with its majority rule and majority definition of right. This in turn gives rise to the demand of minorities for the restraint of majorities, and hence to constitutions. Even here, however, many are dis-franchised, without rights and privileges, slaves, not persons.

Only here and there have particular groups emerged tem-porarily out of this type of relationship to one in which each has full opportunity to function adequately as a human being or person.

Now it is this adequacy of personal functioning which

seems to offer substance to the psychological approach to reality. It is through functioning that reality is known, and the character of the reality known is in turn a function of the process by which it is known. The complete schema of functioning is based on the biological structure of organisms in relation, which allows for the expansion of the here-now in such a way as to permit response in terms of projected values. That is, to permit the realization of the possibilities of value. This takes place, however, only when organisms are in such relations with each other as will permit and stimulate the accumulation of a culture which can be used for the guidance and control of experimental dealings with the environment. Such culture patterns have been character-istic chiefly of the special groups working in natural science, or on problems of space-time relations, and it is these groups that have advanced furthest their special bodies of knowl-edge and their special techniques for the control of physical processes and events.

As suggested earlier, the specialized interests tend to reach a dead end, however, just because of their abstraction from the total process of experience. We cannot get on with the total problem of human evolution until we work out the values of creative personal relationships in terms of our entire approach to reality, that is, in terms of the natural human task of value-realization. This may not require the breaking down of existing specializations in science, art, etc., but it will involve a return to the basic problems which antecede all specialization, and the building up of new tech-niques which reinforce the total process of creative living. These techniques will not be techniques of science, or reli-gion, or politics, or art, or industry, but rather of complete, that is of meaningful, masterful social functioning through creative group experience. Since the induction of children into such experience is entirely practicable, it opens the gateway to a totally new concept and use of culture as the road not out of but into reality.

A DEFINITION OF RELIGIOUS LIBERALISM

By

DANIEL S. ROBINSON

Professor of Philosophy, Indiana University

TODAY religious liberalism is faced with a veritable crisis, or rather, with both an internal and an external crisis. The main purpose of this essay is to lay bare the nature of the internal crisis by analyzing the conflicting interpretations that are now being made as to the essence of religious liberalism. But before beginning that task a brief statement about the external crisis may help to connect this discussion with the main interest of this volume.

Before the World War there was reasonably close cooperation and a spirit of good-will among liberal theologians of the three relatively independent cultural areas in which religious liberalism is centered—Germany and the Scandinavian countries, England, and the United States. The early days of the war set the liberal theologians of Germany at enmity with those of England, and the injury done then has never really been healed. Moreover, the terrible economic and political consequences which have worked themselves out in the creation of the National Socialist régime in Germany have been well nigh disastrous to religious liberalism in that suffering land. The only hope lies in the possibility of rebuilding the cooperation among liberal religious leaders of all Protestant countries, which was practically destroyed by the World War and its aftermath of severe economic depression.

One proof that this is a real possibility is to be found in the close friendship which has continued for a period of more than a quarter of a century between Professor Macintosh, now generally and justly recognized as one of the leading liberal theologians among English-speaking peoples, and Professor George Wobbermin, whose leadership among German liberal theologians has just been demonstrated by his appointment to the professorship of systematic theology in the University of Berlin, a position first held by Schleiermacher. This friendship began when Professor Wobbermin gave the Nathaniel William Taylor Lectures at the Yale Divinity School in 1909. It was entirely due to the advice of Professor Macintosh that I went to the University of Breslau to study under Professor Wobbermin in 1912, and it was wholly due to the former's influence that my translation of the latter's important little book entitled *Christian Belief in God* was published by the Yale University Press in 1918, while the World War was still furiously raging. And it was due to Professor Wobbermin that Professor Macintosh's Bross Prize essay, *The Reasonableness of Christianity*, was translated into German. Thus these two great liberal theologians have kept their hands clasped in Christian fellowship through all of these years of bitterness and strife. May this not be symbolical of the deep unity of all genuinely religious liberalism? Will it not ultimately prove to be God's providential guidance to a full restoration of good will among religious liberals of all cultures and of all sects?

I owe to Professors Macintosh and Wobbermin most of the insight into the essence of religious liberalism that I have attained, and perhaps the best contribution that I can make to this volume of essays, written in honor of Professor Macintosh's distinguished service as Professor of Systematic

Theology in the Yale Divinity School, is to give an analysis of the internal crisis of present-day religious liberalism.

A difficulty in defining religious liberalism arises from a peculiar paradox which characterizes all of the higher experiences of men. In pursuit of the cultural values of science, art, and religion man frequently finds himself forced by the practical exigencies of modern life to narrow the range of his inquiries to some one type of value. For each type claims the whole energies of a person to such an extent as to exclude him from any very active pursuit of the values belonging to the other forms of human experience. In developing his capacities to appreciate, to conserve, and to enhance one kind of value he must let his interest in the others remain relatively dormant. Thus most persons gradually turn away from the specific values of those fields of human experience to which they are unable to devote sufficient energy to develop a genuine appreciation. We are all acquainted with artists who are indifferent to the values of science and of religion, with scientists who are blind to the values of art and of religion, and with pious religionists who completely ignore the findings of science, and who even try to purify their religion by eliminating art in every form from their houses and services of worship. By such narrowness many human beings deprive themselves of cultural values that are of incalculable significance in the development and enrichment of human personality. Since religious experience shares with the other cultural experiences this paradoxical tendency to become narrow and genuinely illiberal, that is to say, this tendency to withdraw within itself and to claim for itself the exclusive possession of all value, the essence of religious liberalism is hard to locate and to define.

Nevertheless it is just by centering our attention upon this tendency in religious experience that we may find one good clue to the essential nature of religious liberalism. For in the attempt to overcome it the religious consciousness itself produces various spurious forms of religious liberalism. There is a deep-seated urge within religious experience, interpreted either as a social or as an individual phenomenon, to rise above the narrowness that results from ignoring the other cultural values. Now I believe that the working out of this urge produces certain spurious forms of religious liberalism, and drives many religious persons into one or another of these spurious forms. Let us, then, examine some of these views that claim to be the essence of religious liberalism in the hope that an understanding of them may yield an insight into what that essence really is.

The best approach to an understanding of these spurious forms is to set them in sharp contrast to a genuinely illiberal form of religious experience, since they arise normally and inevitably as protests of growing minds to naïve, uncritical and traditional dogmatism. On the analogy of the so-called "economic man" of the classical economists, let us summarize this illiberal form of religious experience by explaining the concept of the "religious man" as popularly conceived. No doubt every dogmatic form of religion has its own idea of what would constitute an ideal religious person, but it is neither possible nor necessary here to formulate a separate description for each existing sect. Perhaps the conception can be made definite and concrete by answering the question: what is the popular conception of the religious man for orthodox Protestantism?

According to this conception, being a religious person means devoting one's energies exclusively to the love of God, by practicing such forms of private worship as reading the Scriptures, praying, meditating on one's sins, thinking of death, and preparing to die. In his study of the Scriptures the religious man must take everything literally, regardless of how much it conflicts with what scientists have learned about the universe since the biblical literature came into existence. The so-called modern use of the Bible is excluded by the principle, "We must silently adore mysterious truths, and not explore." In particular the application of the critical methods of studying the Scriptures, comprised under the general name of Biblical criticism, is rank heresy. The religious man must live by faith, but he should not attempt to analyze the act of believing. This has to be taken in the highly emotional sense of a loving trust in the absolute veracity of each saying contained in the Scriptures. Since every word of Scripture is held to be directly inspired by God himself, to disbelieve or to question any Biblical saying is rank heresy. The religious man is required to prove his inner piety by regular outward acts of public worship, and to strengthen it by uniting with other likeminded persons in the winning of converts, and in the religious nurturing of the young. Thus he is supposed to be a person who isolates and insulates himself from the wider social environment, in which all secular life is necessarily spent. His religious activities are intended to give him the kind of training and discipline that will prepare him for heaven rather than for this life.

This popular conception of the religious man is widespread. Nevertheless it is pernicious, not because it is entirely false, for it does contain a germ of truth, but because it represents the crystallization of a quite immature stage of religious experience. Since such religion definitely restricts growth, anyone who remains at this level of religious development is genuinely illiberal.

Suppose that a youth, brought up in a community where this conception of the religious man prevails, normally becomes a religious person within such an environment, as thousands upon thousands have actually done. So long as he remains within that narrow circle of believers his religion may be fairly satisfying even though it is illiberal, for he may never discover for himself how illiberal it is. But suppose that this youth leaves this narrow religious environment, and establishes contacts with highly cultured persons who do not at all sympathize with such an illiberal conception of the religious man. To make the supposition as concrete as possible, let us assume that he enters a university where he is exposed to all varieties of cultural values, and that he there becomes devoted to the pursuit of knowledge in some science such as zoölogy. He may then experience the great satisfaction that comes from actually discovering for oneself a new truth. He will become familiar with the marvellous facts which constitute the evidence for biological evolution. Inevitably there will result some kind of conflict between the narrow illiberal conception of the religious man and this new type of value. How will this conflict be resolved? That will depend upon whether the youth in question is fortunate enough to obtain help from a genuinely religious liberal, who can show him that the love of God is entirely compatible with the disinterested pursuit of truth. If he is thus fortunate, or if he can work this out for himself, he will grow naturally into a real religious liberal. He will retain his piety and devotion to God, but he will reject all creeds and dogmas which he finds to be in conflict with his recognition and acceptance of such other cultural values as he discovers for himself.

However, when a religious youth is unable to effect this solution of his personal difficulty by rising to a higher form of religious experience *his naïve religious experience may turn into its opposite*. If he finds that his religion excludes other values he may reject all religious beliefs in much the same way that he rejects his belief in Santa Claus. Thereafter God will be to him a purely imaginery being, such as children and grandmothers believe to be real, but which no intelligent person can take seriously. This experience of rejecting religion may even take the form which psychologists designate *a counter-conversion*. In the strictest sense this means a pronounced and emotionally violent rejection of religion, culminating in a profound conviction that religious experiences, which religionists accept as a valid basis for a knowledge of God, are wholly meaningless.

Today there are thousands upon thousands of this kind of lost souls in our land. They have never learned how to rise to a higher level of religious experience than that of uneducated naïve people such as they shared in their childhood. They wander pathetically and helplessly in the no-man's land of the soul. They know not how to re-affiliate with the narrow illiberal group in which they originally had a genuine satisfaction of their religious needs, because their education has opened their eyes to the existence of other cultural values more meaningful to them than the sentimental type of religious value that was stressed in that illiberal group. But neither do they know how to be their own priest and achieve for themselves a higher level of religious experience, in which these other cultural values are brought into a synthesis with the love of God.

Now it is such lost souls who have created the spurious forms of religious liberalism. Consequently the source of these spurious forms is the religious consciousness itself, which these lost souls, consciously or unconsciously, keep suppressed. It forces those who have repressed it to give it some kind of recognition. And the kind of recognition it wrests from them determines the type of spurious religious liberalism which results. Hence these spurious forms may be regarded as various substitutes for a genuine religious liberalism, made by those who have rejected both the dross and the gold in the naïve religious experience of their youth. And this brings us back to the question which was raised above: What are some of the chief types of spurious religious liberalism?

Perhaps the most natural substitute for a naïve form of religion that a sophisticated person can make is the identification of religion with the creation, enhancement, conservation, and just distribution of all cultural and economic values within the social order as a whole to which the religious person belongs. But the social order as a whole may be, and often is, interpreted to include the whole of humanity instead of some specific cultural group. When one discovers the values which all educated people recognize as real and important in human life, such as knowledge in all of its forms; art in architecture, in the plastic arts, in music, and in literature; and economic values as represented by the entire wealth of a technological society, including the numerous artifacts that are shaped by the skill and are designed by the mind of man, he naturally comes to a realization of the dependence of human beings upon some share in these values. In fact it must be conceded that these values are in their entirety essential to the very existence of any civilized society. Often the intellectual appreciation of this fact assumes an emotional and almost a mystical character, so that some intellectuals actually conceive of the totality of these cultural and economic values as being infused with a vital unifying principle. They then hold that each person's regard for the welfare of this whole living tissue of values is not only essential to a proper maintenance of a healthy society, but is the real essence of religion. Sinners are those who seek to possess these values for their own exclusive use. Saints are those who exert all of their creative energies in the effort to add new treasures to the storehouse of human values. Godliness consists in the active endeavor to enhance and to conserve the treasury of cultural values, and to make all of these values available to every member of society. Thus to be religious merely means to do one's work in the social order with unselfish devotion to the welfare of the group, and it is wrong to seek for one's own use and possession what are essentially communal goods, no matter how much such a person may profess to be religious. Now, according to those who hold this view, the people who believe in substituting the active endeavor to conserve, enhance, and to add to socially recognized values are the real religious liberals, and all others are religious reactionaries, fanatics, or sentimentalists.

There are two reasons why this must be judged a spurious form of religious liberalism. In the first place, it assumes that there are no specifically religious values in worship. And that means a denial of the existence of God in the sense in which the historic religions of the Western world have always used that term. This kind of religious liberalism recognizes no value in the mystic's experience of a conscious communion with a spiritual being on whom all nature and all creaturely life depend. It substitutes for this genuine religious relationship the pursuit of a collection of purely relative values, which admittedly have no existence apart from the earthly social order. Now since this kind of religious liberalism is necessarily essentially atheistic, it breaks completely with the historic forms of religion in the Western world, all of which are definitely theistic. Second, this is a spurious form of religious liberalism because it subordinates religion to the other aspects of culture. The values of science, art, and economics are elevated to a higher position in culture than religious values. For these secular values are thought to enter into the constitution of a civilized society as intrinsic elements in its being, whereas religious values are made wholly subservient and instrumental to the other activities that are going on in the social order. For even though religious behavior might have been essential in the earlier stages of the evolution of society, the implication is that a degree of human enlightenment can be reached where people can entirely dispense with it. In any case the religious man is most religious, according to this view, when he is strenuously devoting his energies to purely secular activities. Surely so paradoxical a conception of the nature of religion demands such a complete reversal of the testimony of religious experience itself that it cannot possibly be true. Every person who allows the religious consciousness within him to speak at all will hear its still small voice proclaim that it apprehends a value so unique and so original that it cannot be described in the same terms as are used to describe secular values. We must reject every form of religious liberalism as spurious which degrades religious values by making them purely instrumental. Religious experience protests against the subordination of its specific goods to the relative and transitory goods of earthly creaturely life. It holds that human beings will remain lost in wandering mazes until they find their rest in God. Any form of religious liberalism which rejects this testimony of every genuine religious experience must be regarded as a spurious form.

However, this does not mean that it is valueless. Modern men must admit that the conception of salvation needs to be extended beyond the individual. The discovery that every human being is essentially social by nature cannot be disregarded. Then, too, there are social and institutionalized evils, there are the sins of society, and a modern man cannot be considered genuinely religious who blinds his eyes to the existence of such impersonal evils and sins. The naïve conception of the religious man treats godliness and saintliness as wholly personal characteristics, which a man may have, regardless of the part he may have in and the attitude he may take towards these social evils, but this is not possible for a genuine religious liberal.[1] The social gospel, the social program of changing the institutions through which human beings seek to enrich their personalities, certainly has to be included as an essential part of religious liberalism. As a matter of fact it is a special atheistic social philosophy, rather than the social program for the improvement of institutions, which has to be rejected as a spurious form.

There are a number of special variants of this first spurious form of religious liberalism, which it will suffice merely to enumerate. They are obtained by identifying religious

[1] See the excellent formulation of this opinion in Carl Sandburg's poem: *To a Contemporary Bunkshooter*.

liberalism with the conservation of some one type of value, rather than with the conservation of all values. Usually the type of value selected will itself be held to be more central or more important or more necessary to human welfare than other types. Thus some thinkers would identify religious liberalism with a distinct kind of metaphysics, such as pragmatism, vitalism, fictionalism, emergent evolutionism, or what-not. The religious liberal is one who accepts the philosophy in question and who re-interprets religious beliefs in terms of it. Others identify religious liberalism with some other branch of philosophy than metaphysics, for example, with aesthetics or with ethics. Those who are so positivistic and agnostic as to be entirely out of sympathy with all philosophies are convinced that some special brand of psychology offers the key to all of the mysteries of the universe. They identify religious liberalism with the application of the theories of that brand of psychology to a restatement of religious beliefs. In all of these types of thought religious liberalism becomes merely an application of the principles of some special body of philosophical or psychological doctrine to the interpretation of the facts of religious experience and the dogmas of orthodox theology.

Such spurious forms of religious liberalism are open to the same objections that have already been made to the general type of which they are variants. But they are also open to the criticism that they are obviously onesidedly intellectualistic and extreme interpretations. Whoever subordinates religion to, or identifies it with, some special aspect of culture is perforce more illiberal than one who equates it with the conservation of all socially recognized values.

A second general spurious form of religious liberalism is the identification of it with some sect, in the sense of an organized group of religious people, who represent a definite and sharp break with the main line of development of religion. Especially important here are the numerous esoteric sects, among which theosophy, anthroposophy, and

Christian Science are especially prominent today. To their own adherents such sects constitute the very essence of genuine religious liberalism, and many educated people, who have ceased to believe in orthodox forms of Christianity, are turning to such groups to find satisfaction for their religious needs. That such esoteric sects are in fact illiberal is proven by their extremely dogmatic doctrines, each set of which is a completely closed system of thought, comprehensible only to those who are indoctrinated with the precepts of that sect.

Professor Wobbermin has made the illuminating suggestion that theosophy and anthroposophy are the counterparts among modern civilized peoples of mythology among the ancients, and that Christian Science is the modern counterpart of magic.[2] The tendency for religious experience to divert itself into the creation of all kinds of concrete religious beings is attested by the widespread belief in angels and demons, which characterizes popular Christianity, Judaism, Mohammedanism, Zoroastrianism, Buddhism, and Hinduism. In modern highly educated people this tendency expresses itself in the acceptance of fantastic uncritical conceptions of the spiritual world as being composed of various levels each with its own peculiar character that is revealed only to the initiates. Theosophy and anthroposophy are the exploitation of this tendency, and many of the lost souls who have left orthodox religious groups have sought a home in these two modern esoteric sects. Similarly in all religions the attempt has been made to exploit the divine power or powers by some special manipulative device, and Christian Science is a modern form of that tendency. As Professor Wobbermin has rightly pointed out, there are genuine religious motives in such esoteric sects, but these are violently submerged by the main tendency.

[2] See Wobbermin, George, *The Nature of Religion*, translated from the German by Theophil Menzel and D. S. Robinson, New York: Thomas Y. Crowell Co., 1933.

Such sects can never make good their claim to be the genuine form of religious liberalism, since their pretense that they possess the only religious truth is highly illiberal and sharply contradictory to this claim.

The genuine religious liberal knows that no sect possesses the hidden secret of religious knowledge and power, because he knows that this is not and never has been a secret. Modern men must abandon the belief that there is a special key possessed by some person or sect that will unlock the door behind which religious knowledge and power are hidden. Hence we can lay down the generalization that every identification of religious liberalism with some special esoteric sect, and its particular set of doctrines, is a spurious form of religious liberalism. It follows that no religious person can pass from naïve religious experience of an illiberal type to a genuinely liberal religious experience by affiliating with any esoteric sect. To attempt this is to jump from the frying pan into the fire. The illiberal orthodox sects contain more genuine religious experience than do these esoteric sects. In view of the fact that so many educated people are today turning to such sects for satisfaction of their religious needs, it is especially important that their illiberal character be emphasized. They claim a liberality they do not possess. Every inquiring religiously-minded person needs to be forewarned of this incontrovertible fact.

Exoteric religious sects which claim to be the special guardians and institutional embodiments of religious liberalism, for example, the Unitarian and the Universalist churches, are on a different basis from the esoteric sects. Instead of being obscurantist groups they are genuinely liberal in their general attitude and teaching. Nevertheless they have no right to claim exclusive possession of liberal religious ideas, and too many of their leaders and adherents err by adopting an extreme humanism or intellectualism of the type that we have already rejected under our discussion of the first general spurious form of religious liberalism.

The religious person who develops beyond the naïve sectarian point of view within his own religious community is not likely to find a solution of the conflict between his more liberal views and those of his religious community by joining one of these so-called liberal sects. Undoubtedly they have made important contributions to religious liberalism, but in making these contributions they have had to over-emphasize and exaggerate the importance of certain liberal doctrines, and in so doing they have broken with the main line of evolution of the religious consciousness as a social and cultural phenomenon within western culture. Hence these liberal sects today are peripheral and tangential movements. Genuine religious liberalism includes them, but within it they remain relatively insignificant and unimportant. The next century of religious history in the West should, and undoubtedly will see the gradual fusion of separatist liberal movements, and the creation of a united church within which all liberals can feel at home. This can only be accomplished by liberals working within their own groups with a view to making every group liberal enough to cooperate with others in efforts to blot out all schisms so deep that they set religious groups at enmity with each other. And this brings us to the genuine type of religious liberalism.

What conclusions and generalizations have resulted from this examination of the spurious forms of religious liberalism which now need to be utilized in a definition of the genuine form? Three principles have emerged and each is of central importance.

(1) Genuine religious liberalism is continuous with the main line of development of historic religion within our western culture, and any type of liberal religious thought which violently breaks this continuity and claims to be the true religious liberalism is a spurious form. This means that genuine religious liberalism rises above the naïve form of orthodox piety without ceasing to be religion, without sub-

stituting the pursuit of purely secular goods for the worship of God, and without severing its connection with some actual religious community, however imperfect that community is and is known by the liberal to be.

(2) Genuine religious liberalism claims no special occult method either of knowing or of controlling the religious object, God, other than the normal religious experience that is mediated to the inquiring mind by some actual religious community.

(3) Genuine religious liberalism incorporates within itself the social program of gradually modifying the whole body of institutions which constitute Western culture until they are thoroughly purged of their evils, without going to the extreme of identifying religion with the progressive activities that are going on in the world today. In other words, it includes the social gospel, but it excludes dogmatic Marxian social materialistic philosophy.

What, now, should be added to these basic principles to complete the definition? First of all, genuine religious liberalism is the best name for a certain attitude or spirit possessed by those who are truly liberal in their religion. This attitude is not one of mere tolerance, since a person can be tolerant towards views the falsity of which he is firmly convinced. For example, a Protestant may be tolerant towards the Roman Catholic dogma of the immaculate conception of the Virgin Mary or that of the infallibility of the Pope's *ex cathedra* pronouncements, or a Catholic may be tolerant towards the Protestant dogma of verbal inspiration of the Scriptures or that embodied in so-called typology, although each is firmly convinced that the dogma in question is entirely fallacious. Tolerance is an attitude towards doctrines and dogmas, viewed separately or in systems, and hence it is a purely intellectual attitude, even though it may be advocated with emotional fervor and heat. Liberalism, on the other hand, is a sympathetic appreciation of the inner value of the experience of a person or group different from that of the liberal or his group, based upon the recognition of the kinship between the two different forms of experience. It contains an intellectual element, but it is a profound response of one's whole being to the presence of intrinsic value. For example, a Protestant is a liberal if he can sympathetically appreciate the value a devout Catholic gets from witnessing the priest's celebration of the mass, and a Catholic is a liberal if he can sympathetically appreciate the significance of a faithful Protestant's devout reading of the Scriptures as he keeps the morning watch. Ernst Troeltsch's attitude towards Catholic worship was not merely tolerant, but liberal, and Baron von Hügel's attitude towards Troeltsch's interpretation of Christian history was not merely tolerant, but genuinely liberal. To generalize this again, genuine religious liberalism, as an individual possession, is the sweet spirit whereby one religious person is able to recognize the intrinsic value of the piety of another religious person, even when that other worshipper is a member of a totally different religion. It is the spirit the possession of which creates the Church Invisible, made up of all devout persons of all sects and of all religions, that church membership in which Savanorola, in his famous reply to the Papal Bull of Excommunication which was read to him before the fagots that were to burn him to death were lighted, rightly denied to be within the control of any earthly ecclesiastical potentate. Ultimately it is the profound inner experience that all men are united by a common bond of obligation to love and to worship God, which no other obligation can obliterate, annul, or disregard.

However, genuine religious liberalism is more than an individual possession, as this reference to the Church Invisible suggests. It is the Blessed Community of all devout persons who, through the ages and still today, possess the liberal spirit. But it is more than that. It includes all of the effects which they, individually and through their cooperation, have wrought in the religious institutions of the Western world. Religious liberalism today is constituted by the actual present liberal structure of organized religion in the Western world as compared with its earlier illiberal status. Differently expressed, it is the totality of all existing religious institutions, as these have been made over by the growing religious experience of Western civilized men and women. It includes all organizations working for unity among religionists, and all organizations that are trying to deepen the spiritual life within each sect, and to bring that sect into closer accord with modern knowledge.

In this sense, genuine religious liberalism is the active principle of growth that is pushing the historic religion of the Western World steadily forward toward the realization of the high purpose of God for mankind. And what is that purpose? It is a complete actualization of the religious ideal. It is such a transformation of human society as will make it a city of God, and such a remaking of every natural self as will make him or her a child of God. It is the absolute rule of God in all human affairs. For the consummation of this high purpose every true religious liberal, be he Gentile or Jew, Catholic or Protestant, works and prays within his own religious community. But as he works and prays he remains conscious of his unity and solidarity with all others who are doing likewise in a Blessed Community that is the real essence of the New Jerusalem so pictorially described in the Book of Revelation.

THE PUBLICATIONS OF
DOUGLAS CLYDE MACINTOSH*

BOOKS AND PARTS OF BOOKS

The Reaction Against Metaphysics in Theology, 86 pp., Chicago: Published by the Author, 1911.
Ph.D. Dissertation, University of Chicago, 1909.
The Problem of Knowledge, 503 pp., New York: Macmillan 1915; London: Allen and Unwin, 1916.
God in a World at War, 60 pp., London: Allen and Unwin, 1918.
Theology as an Empirical Science, 270 pp., New York: Macmillan, 1919, 1927; London: Allen and Unwin, 1920.
"Preface" to *Christianity in its Modern Expression*, by G. B. Foster, edited by D. C. Macintosh, New York: Macmillan, 1921.
"Theology in a Scientific Age" in *Education for Christian Service*, by Members of the Faculty of the Divinity School of Yale University . . . pp. 133-162, New Haven: Yale University Press, 1922.
The Reasonableness of Christianity, 293 pp., New York: Scribner, 1925, 1926; Edinburgh: Clark, 1926. Translation, *Vernunftgemässes Christentum*, mit Einführung von Professor D. K. Bornhausen . . . Übersetzung von O. H. Fleischer, 166 pp., Gotha: Klotz, 1928.
A selection from the first ten chapters was made for the Nathaniel W. Taylor Lectures, delivered at Yale University in April, 1925. The Bross Prize, 1925.

* A complete list from which these publications were selected is on file in the Library of Yale University Divinity School, New Haven, Connecticut.

"What God Is" in *My Idea of God; A Symposium of Faith*, edited by J. F. Newton, pp. 135-158, Boston: Little, Brown, 1926.

Also published as "The Meaning of God in Modern Religion," *Journal of Religion*, Vol. VI, pp. 457-471, September, 1926.

"Contemporary Humanism" in *Humanism, Another Battle Line*, edited by W. P. King, pp. 39-72, Nashville: Cokesbury, 1931.

The Pilgrimage of Faith in the World of Modern Thought, Stephanos Nirmalendu Ghosh Lectures, 299 pp., Calcutta, India: University of Calcutta, 1931; New York: Longmans, Green, 1931.

"Preface" and "Experimental Realism in Religion" in *Religious Realism*, edited by D. C. Macintosh, pp. v-vi, pp. 303-409, New York: Macmillan, 1931.

"Toward a New Untraditional Orthodoxy" in *Contemporary American Theology; Theological Autobiographies*, edited by Vergilius Ferm, Vol. I, pp. 275-319, New York: Round Table Press, 1932.

Is There a God? A Conversation, by H. N. Wieman, D. C. Macintosh, and M. C. Otto, with an Introduction by C. C. Morrison, 328 pp., Chicago: Willett, Clark, 1932. Republished with slight modifications from the *Christian Century* (Chicago), Vol. XLIX, 1932.

"Some Reflections on the Progress and Decline of Religion in New England," in *The Process of Religion; Essays in Honor of Dean Shailer Mathews*, edited by M. H. Krumbine, pp. 93-119, New York: Macmillan, 1933.

"Introduction," to *The Nature of Religion*, by G. Wobbermin, translated by T. Menzel and D. S. Robinson, New York: Crowell, 1933.

"Foreword," to *Polity and Practice in Baptist Churches*, by W. R. McNutt, Philadelphia: Judson Press, 1935.

"Romanticism or Realism, Which?" in *American Philosophies of Religion*, by H. N. Wieman and B. E. Meland, pp. 325-332, Chicago: Willett, Clark, 1936.

ARTICLES AND REVIEWS

University Studies, *McMaster University Monthly* (Toronto), Vol. XII, pp. 153-157, pp. 210-215, January, February, 1903.

William Rainey Harper: An Appreciation, *McMaster University Monthly* (Toronto), Vol. XV, pp. 241-248, March, 1906.

The Significance of Gnosticism in the Development of Christian Theology, With Special Reference to the "Pistis Sophia," *Review and Expositor* (Louisville, Kentucky), Vol. IV, pp. 405-422, July, 1907.

The New Theology, *Review and Expositor*, Vol. IV, pp. 600-617, October, 1917.

The Function of History in Theology, *American Journal of Theology* (Chicago), Vol. XI, pp. 647-652, October, 1907.

Some Philosophical Discussions of Religious Problems, *American Journal of Theology*, Vol. XII, pp. 162-167, January, 1908.

Review of *The Freedom of Authority; Essays in Apologetics*, by J. M. Sterrett, New York: Macmillan, 1905; *Pragmatism: a New Name for Some Old Ways of Thinking*, by William James, New York: Longmans, Green, 1907; *The Religious Conception of the World: An Essay in Constructive Philosophy*, by A. K. Rogers, New York: Macmillan, 1907.

The Baptist Perspective, *Western Outlook* (Brandon, Manitoba), Vol. II, p. 5, March, 1909.

Recent Expositions of the Philosophy of Religion, *American Journal of Theology*, Vol. XIII, pp. 630-633, October, 1909.

Review of *Modern Thought and the Crisis in Belief*, by R. M. Wenley, New York: Macmillan, 1909; *The Philosophy of Revelation*, by H. Bavinck, New York: Longmans, Green, 1909; *Science and Immortality*, by Sir Oliver Lodge, New York: Moffat, 1908.

Can Pragmatism Furnish a Philosophical Basis for Theology? *Harvard Theological Review* (Cambridge), Vol. III, pp. 125-135, January, 1910.

Paper read before the Baptist Congress at New York, November 9, 1909.

Some Fundamental Problems of Modern Theology, *American Journal of Theology*, Vol. XIV, pp. 136-141, January, 1910.

Review of *Le Discernment du Miracle*, by P. Saintyves, Paris: Nourry, 1909; *Essais sur la Connaisance*, by G. Fonsegrive, Paris: Gabalda, 1909; *System Theologischer Erkenntnislehre*, by K. Dunkmann, Leipzig: Deichert, 1919.

Idealism as a Practical Creed, *American Journal of Theology*, Vol. XIV, pp. 320-321, April, 1910.

Review of *Idealism as a Practical Creed*, by H. Jones, New York: Macmillan, 1909.

The Efficient Church and Current Philosophy, *Yale Divinity Quarterly*, Vol. VII, pp. 1-15, July, 1910.

The Pragmatic Element in the Teaching of Paul, *American Journal of Theology*, Vol. XIV, pp. 361-381, July, 1910.

Personal Idealism, Pragmatism, and the New Realism, *American Journal of Theology*, Vol. XIV, pp. 650-656, October, 1910.

Review of *Philosophy and Religion*, by H. Rashdall, New York: Scribner, 1910; *The Principles of Pragmatism: A Philosophical Interpretation of Experience*, by H. Heath Bawden, Boston: Houghton, Mifflin, 1910; *Essays Philosophical and Psychological in Honor of William James*, by His Colleagues at Columbia University, New York: Longmans, Green, 1908.

Review of *The Problem of Human Life as Viewed by the Great Thinkers from Plato to the Present Time*, by Rudolf Eucken, translated by W. S. Hough and W. R. Boyce Gibson, New York: Scribner, 1910; *Yale Divinity Quarterly*, Vol. VII, pp. 63-64, November, 1910.

Pragmatism and Mysticism, *American Journal of Theology*, Vol. XV, pp. 142-146, January, 1911.

Review of *The Influence of Darwin upon Philosophy*,

and Other Essays in Contemporary Thought, by John
Dewey, New York: Holt, 1910; *Faith and Its Psychology*,
William R. Inge, New York: Scribner, 1910.

Review of *The Meaning and Value of Human Life*, by R.
Eucken, London: Black, 1910; *Christianity and the
New Idealism: A Study in the Religious Philosophy of
To-Day*, by R. Eucken, New York: Harper, 1909;
Yale Divinity Quarterly, Vol. VIII, pp. 16-18, May,
1911.

The Conservative and the Radical Method in Theology and
Preaching, *Homiletic Review*, Vol. LXI, pp. 359-363,
May, 1911.

Is Belief in the Historicity of Jesus Indispensable to Christian Faith? *American Journal of Theology*, Vol. XV,
pp. 362-372, July, 1911; Vol. XVI, pp. 106-110, January, 1912.

The Idea of a Modern Orthodoxy, *Harvard Theological
Review*, Vol. IV, pp. 477-488, October, 1911.

What Hinders the Union of Baptists and the Disciples of
Christ? *Proceedings*, Baptist Congress, 1911, pp. 88-97,
Chicago: University of Chicago Press, 1912.

Representational Pragmatism, *Mind*, N. S., Vol. XXI, pp.
167-181, April, 1912.

Bergson and Religion, *Biblical World*, N. S., Vol. XLI, pp.
34-40, January, 1913.

The Religion of the Future, *Faith and Doubt*, Vol. I, pp.
94-101, March, 1913. Republished from *The Western
Outlook*, Vol. I, pp. 4-5, November, 1908.

Contemporary Philosophy and the Problem of Religion,
American Journal of Theology, Vol. XVII, pp. 307-
316, April, 1913.

Review of *The Positive Evolution of Religion: Its Moral
and Social Reaction*, by F. Harrison, New York: Putnam,
1913; *The New Realism: Co-operative Studies in Phi-
losophy*, by E. B. Holt, W. T. Marvin, W. P. Montague,
R. B. Perry, W. B. Pitkin, and E. G. Spaulding, New
York: Macmillan, 1912; *The Problem of Religion*, by
E. C. Wilm, Boston: Pilgrim, 1912; *The Interpretation of
Religious Experience*, 2 v., by John Watson, Glasgow:

MacLehose, 1912; *An Interpretation of Rudolf Eucken's Philosophy*, by W. T. Jones, New York: Putnam, 1912.

Is "Realistic Epistemological Monism Inadmissible"? *Journal of Philosophy, Psychology, and Scientific Method*, Vol. X, pp. 701-710, December, 1913.

What Is the Christian Religion? *Harvard Theological Review*, Vol. VII, pp. 16-46, January, 1914.

Hocking's Philosophy of Religion: An Empirical Development of Absolutism, *Philosophical Review*, Vol. XXIII, pp. 27-47, January, 1914.

The Religious Philosophy of W. E. Hocking, *Yale Divinity Quarterly*, Vol. X, pp. 73-80, January, 1914.

Review of *The Meaning of God in Human Experience*, by W. E. Hocking, New Haven: Yale University Press, 1912.

The New Christianity and World-Conversion, *American Journal of Theology*, Vol. XVIII, pp. 337-354, pp. 553-570, July, October, 1914.

Haering's Dogmatics, *American Journal of Theology*, Vol. XIX, pp. 304-308, April, 1915.

Review of *The Christian Faith: A System of Dogmatics*, by Theo. Haering, translated from the Second (1912) German edition by John Dickie and G. Ferries, 2 v., New York: Hodder and Stoughton, 1913.

Professor Ten Broeke's Introduction to Theology, *McMaster University Monthly*, Vol. XXIV, pp. 232-236, April, 1915.

Review of *Constructive Basis for Theology*, by J. Ten Broeke, New York: Macmillan, 1914.

Christianity as Religion Made Moral, *Biblical World*, N. S., Vol. XLV, pp. 195-201, April, 1915.

A Sketch of the Philosophy of Religion, With Illustrations of Critical Monism, *Mind*, N. S., Vol. XXVIII, pp. 129-161, April, 1919.

Substantially the same as The Appendix to *Theology As an Empirical Science*, 1919.

Troeltsch's Theory of Religious Knowledge, *American Journal of Theology*, Vol. XXIII, pp. 274-289, July, 1919.

Why I Believe in Immortality, *Biblical World*, N. S., Vol. LIV, pp. 570-573, November, 1920.

A Neo-Realist's Conception of God, *Journal of Religion* (Chicago), Vol. II, pp. 92-97, January, 1922.

Review of *Space, Time and Deity*, by S. Alexander, 2 v., London: Macmillan, 1920.

A Defense of Christian Theism, *Journal of Religion*, Vol. III, pp. 214-215, March, 1923.

Review of *Studies in Christian Philosophy*, by W. R. Matthews, London: Macmillan, 1921.

The Idea of God, *Journal of Religion*, Vol. III, pp. 652-655, November, 1923.

Review of *The Idea of God*, by C. A. Beckwith, New York: Macmillan, 1922.

Books That Help Faith, *Christian Century* (Chicago), Vol. XLI, pp. 1370-1371, October 23, 1924.

Religious Values and the Existence of God, *Journal of Religion*, Vol. VI, pp. 315-320, May, 1926.

Review of *Religious Values*, by E. S. Brightman, New York: Abingdon, 1925.

The Baptists and Church Union, *Crozer Quarterly* (Chester, Pa.), Vol. III, pp. 259-278, July, 1926.

Paper read before the American Theological Society (Eastern Branch) at New York, April 10, 1926.

Review of *Mind and Its Place in Nature*, by D. Drake, New York: Macmillan, 1925; *Journal of Philosophy*, Vol. XXIV, pp. 129-136, March, 1927.

Review of *A Theory of Direct Realism and the Relations of Realism to Idealism*, by J. E. Turner, New York: Macmillan, 1925; *Personality and Reality; A Proof of the Real Existence of a Supreme Self in the Universe*, by J. E. Turner, New York: Macmillan, 1926; *Journal of Philosophy*, Vol. XXIV, pp. 157-159, March, 1927.

Professor Coe and an Empirical Theology, *Methodist Quarterly Review* (Nashville), Vol. LXXVI, pp. 202-218, April, 1927.

Canon Streeter's Theory of Reality, *Journal of Religion*, Vol. VIII, pp. 147-151, January, 1928.

Review of *Reality: A New Correlation of Science and Religion*, by B. H. Streeter, New York: Macmillan, 1926.

The Next Step in Epistemological Dialectic, *Journal of Philosophy*, Vol. XXVI, pp. 225-233, April, 1929.

Paper read, with some omissions, before the American Philosophical Association (Eastern Division), at the University of Pennsylvania, December 28, 1928.

Religious Knowledge and Reasonable Faith, *Colgate-Rochester Divinity School Bulletin* (Rochester, New York), Vol. II, pp. 160-174, November, 1929.

Review of *Individuality and Social Restraint*, by G. R. Wells, New York: Appleton, 1929; *Bulletin of the Hartford Seminary Foundation* (Hartford, Connecticut), Vol. XVI, pp. 122-124, May-June, 1930.

Christianity According to Paul, *Christian Century Pulpit* (Chicago), Vol. I, pp. 14-17, October, 1930.

What Is Worship? *Religious Education* (Chicago), Vol. XXV, pp. 944-946, December, 1930.

Is Christianity Essentially Irrational? *Crozer Quarterly*, Vol. VIII, pp. 16-29, January, 1931.

Humanism Viewed and Reviewed, *New Humanist*, Vol. IV, pp. 16-19, July-August, 1931.

Review of *Humanism in Religion Examined*, by Robert J. Hutcheson, Chicago: Published by the Meadville Theological School, 1931.

Disarmament, *Yale Daily News* (New Haven, Connecticut), Vol. LV, p. 1, November 23, 1931.

War, *Unity* (Chicago), Vol. CVIII, p. 341, February, 1932.

Conscience and War, *Religion in Life* (New York), Vol. I, pp. 163-168, July, 1932.

Also published in *The Bulletin, Crozer Theological Seminary* (Chester, Pennsylvania), Vol. XXIV, pp. 133-140, July, 1932.

What Has Professor Brightman Done to Personalism? *Religion in Life*, Vol. I, pp. 304-307, Spring, 1932.

A Postscript to the Conversation, *Christian Century*, Vol. XLIX, p. 1276, October 19, 1932.

Mr. Wieman and Mr. Macintosh "Converse" With Mr.

Dewey, *Christian Century*, Vol. L, pp. 300-302, March 1, 1933.

A Communication: Mr. Macintosh Restates His Position, *Christian Century*, Vol. L, pp. 531-533, April 19, 1933.

What Is Vital in Religion? *Adult Student* (Nashville, Tennessee), Vol. XXVIII, pp. 387-388, September, 1935.